ENERGY AND ENVIRONMENT

The Policy Challenge

Energy Policy Studies
Volume 6

Edited by

John Byrne
Daniel Rich

Transaction Publishers
New Brunswick (U.S.A.) and London (U.K.)

HO
9502
A2
E5417
1992

Copyright © 1992 by Transaction Publishers, New Brunswick, New Jersey 08903.

Library of Congress Catalog Number: 92-14716
ISBN: 1-56000-573-4
ISSN: 0882-3537
Printed in the United States of America

Library of Congress Cataloging-in-Publication Data

Energy and environment: the policy challenge/edited by John Byrne, Daniel Rich.
   p.   cm. —(Energy policy studies: v. 6)
   Includes bibliographical references.
   ISBN 1-56000-573-4 (paper)
   1. Energy policy. 2. Environmental policy. 3. Renewable energy sources—Government policy. 4. Energy development—Environmental aspects. I. Byrne, John, 1949- . II. Rich, Daniel. III. Series.
HD9502.A2E5417   1992
363.7'056—dc20   92-14716
                                                CIP

ENERGY AND ENVIRONMENT

ENERGY POLICY STUDIES Series

Technology and Energy Choice, Volume 1,
John Byrne and Daniel Rich

Energy and Cities, Volume 2,
John Byrne and Daniel Rich

Politics of Energy Research, Volume 3,
John Byrne and Daniel Rich

Planning for Changing Energy Conditions, Volume 4,
John Byrne and Daniel Rich

Energy, Land, and Public Policy, Volume 5,
J. Barry Cullingworth

Energy and Environment, Volume 6,
John Byrne and Daniel Rich

To the memory of our friend
Bill N. Baron
who understood the challenge

Contents

Part IV: The Policy Challenge

List of Tables

List of Figures

ACKNOWLEDGEMENT

The editors wish to thank Patricia Grimes for preparing the manuscript with extraordinary skill, good humor and patience. We are grateful as well to Anita Hoover for her considerable effort on behalf of the manuscript. And sincere thanks are due to Professor Barry Cullingworth for his critical reading of our chapter and for his editorial assistance throughout this project.

Introduction

John Byrne and
Daniel Rich

> [T]he sulphurous atmosphere...the starvation of the
> senses, the remoteness from nature and animal activ-
> ity — here are the enemies. The living organism de-
> mands a life-sustaining environment.
>
> Now it is not a river valley, but the whole planet, that
> must be brought under human control: not an un-
> manageable flood of water, but even more alarming
> and malign explosions of energy that might disrupt
> the entire ecological system on which man's own life
> and welfare depends. The prime need of our age is to
> contrive channels for excessive energies and impetuous
> vitalities that have departed from organic norms and
> limits...It is time to come back to earth and confront
> life in all its organic fecundity, diversity, and creativ-
> ity, instead of taking refuge in the under-dimensioned
> world of Post-historic Man.
>
>   Lewis Mumford (1934: 248; and 1961: 571)

For over a half century, Lewis Mumford reprobated Western
technological culture for having lost all semblance of balance between social and natural life. While commending the West for

1

breaking free in the 16th century of the rigidities of medievalism and inspiring revolutions in science, letters and industry, he condemned its four-century failure to exercise environmental responsibility for the impacts of mechanism and material production. Whether in knowledge, politics, economics or physical energy, the equation of more with better prevailed — "numbers begot numbers" (1938: 160). The ideal of *the good life* had been replaced with that of *the goods life* propelling the drive for what Mumford called "quantification without qualification" (1934: 104):

> Happiness was [defined as] the true end of man, and it consisted in achieving the greatest good for the greatest number... The quantity of happiness, and ultimately the perfection of human institutions, could be reckoned roughly by the amount of goods a society was capable of producing: expanding wants: expanding markets: or expanding body of consumers. The machine made this possible and guaranteed its success. To cry enough or to call a limit was treason. Happiness and expanding production were one.

Mumford drew attention to the energy-technology nexus that underpinned and provided the motive power of industrialism, and in this nexus he located industrial society's tendency toward environmental disregard and degradation (1934: 168):

> [T]he environment...like most of human existence, was treated as an abstraction. Air and sunlight, because of their deplorable lack of value in exchange, had no reality at all.

The prospect of global climate change, the thinning of stratospheric ozone and the acidification of snow, rain and even large bodies of water, were not specifically predicted by Mumford, but their link to the spread of industrial development and energy use surely would not have surprised him. While the precise magnitudes and dynamics of these global phenomena remain the subject of much debate, a growing body of scientific research agrees that these problems are acute and that industrial energy practices are a significant contributor (see, e.g., COSEPUP, 1991; National Research Council, 1989; Watson et al., 1988; MacKenzie and El-Ashry, 1988).

Current global environmental problems have largely been caused by the industrialized countries (including Eastern Europe and what was formerly the Soviet Union). Together they account for nearly two-thirds of the "greenhouse gas" buildup,[1] and over 55 percent of the sulfur and nitrogen oxide pollution (the principal precursors of acid deposition and lower atmosphere ozone pollution), and they are almost entirely responsible for the "ozone holes" in the upper atmosphere (OECD/IEA, 1991; World Resources Institute, 1990). Within the industrialized tier, the United States is far and away the largest national contributor to this pollution stream. Its annual carbon dioxide, sulfur and nitrogen oxide emissions represent 20 percent of the world total; its chlorofluorocarbon (CFC) releases amount to one-fourth of worldwide emissions (World Resources Institute, 1990; OECD/IEA, 1991). On a per capita basis, the United States burns twice as much carbon and emits 2.5 times the volume of greenhouse gases of other industrial societies. Transportation in the least energy-intensive large American city (New York) consumes 2.6 times as much energy per person as the typical large European city (Newman and Kenworthy, 1989).

Many analysts believe international action should be taken to implement the principles of sustainability enunciated by the World

---

[1]The principal greenhouse gases include carbon dioxide (CO_2), nitrous oxide (N_2O), methane (CH_4), ozone (O_3), and chlorofluorocarbons (CFCs). CFCs are released by refrigeration systems and solvents. The most important human activity contributing to the buildup of all other greenhouse gases is fossil fuel combustion. Increased concentrations of these chemicals in the upper atmosphere are thought to lead to the absorption of radiative heat in the same way that glass traps heat in a greenhouse, causing surface temperature to rise.

Commission on Environment and Development (WCED) in 1987. This would mean a dramatic change in the fuel mix and technology base of the world energy system generally and, especially, the systems of the industrialized countries. Specifically, it would require a shift toward energy conservation and energy efficiency in the design and operation of industrial processes, as well as rapid development and deployment of renewable energy technologies. Fossil fuel use (particularly, coal and oil) would have to decrease considerably, and significant changes in the utility and transportation sectors (the most energy- and pollution-intensive parts of the industrial energy system) would be needed. Electric utility managers would be called upon to meet energy demand through investments in "demand-side management" (DSM) alternatives that would significantly reduce power requirements. Transportation planners and engineers would be expected to improve fuel efficiency and design route networks and transport systems that have much lower energy consumption than present ones.

Yet, energy and economic policies of industrial countries have either ignored or only modestly addressed global environmental problems. In the United States, for example, most recent policy proposals, if implemented, would actually lead to an *increase* in greenhouse pollution by the U.S. (MacKenzie, 1991). So called "green" policy options have been rejected in several countries because of their purportedly negative impacts on inflation and economic growth. Instead, national policies for electricity and transportation tend to offer more of the same. In the U.S., federal policy has sought to weaken existing auto fleet fuel efficiency standards and to encourage a switch to methanol and ethanol fuels which may have larger global-warming impacts than gasoline or diesel. Rather than promoting DSM strategies, the U.S., Japan, France and others propose to turn again to nuclear power as the solution to national electricity needs.

The industrialized countries have generally substituted social complacency for responsible action, despite overwhelming evidence of the instability of the world energy system and the growing costs of protecting this system in the face of environmental self-contradiction. Throughout the 1980s, it was fashionable to re-gard the oil price shocks of the previous decade as freak storms that eventually would be weathered, permitting the resumption of an era of energy abundance. This view gained credibility among government leaders of the industrial nations as oil prices dropped and world markets exhibited excess capacity. Yet, only a few years earlier these freak storms had resulted in an estimated $1.2 trillion economic loss among the industrial nations (Yergin, 1982: 5).

The industrial view of energy and economic stability was hardly descriptive of the Latin American, African and Asian (excluding Japan) experience in the 1980s. The supposedly good news about the 'economic adjustment' of the industrial economies to the en-ergy crises of the 1970s contained a sobering message for the Third World. Many of these countries saw decades of economic progress (modest to begin with) reversed as energy-induced debt ballooned and per capita income fell. One gauge of the cost to the Third World of energy stability for the industrial world has been the tripling of trade deficits between rich and poor nations. It was the good news of economic adjustment in the industrial world which reduced demand for Third World goods and brought on staggering debts and shrinking trade opportunities (Yergin, 1982).

Now, Third World countries must cope with the cumulative effects of 200 years of uneven development and exploitation *and* they must face the most severe consequences of the globalization of pollution. Despite the fact that the Third World has neither shared the benefits of industrialism nor been responsible for its environmental toll, these countries will surely be hardest hit. With highly fragile material and technological infrastructures, the poor nations pay an especially heavy price for the complacency of the industrial tier.

It has been 20 years since the Stockholm Conference on the Human Environment when the world community began its search for an international strategy to address mounting environmen-tal problems. While progress has been made in that time in the form of policies to limit air and water pollution and to regulate

toxic and hazardous waste disposal, the *silent springs* of industrial
pollution and waste continue to present significant environmental
and health dangers. Industrial leaders have shown little interest
in addressing their countries' contributions to such transbound-
ary problems as acid rain, upper atmosphere ozone depletion and
surface warming. Now the politics of global economic competition
obstructs effective international initiatives to reconstruct energy,
environmental and development policies. A stalemate could doom
global action for the rest of the century and leave the nations most
vulnerable to environmental crisis — the developing countries of
the Third World — with little hope for sustainable development.
We have far to go in meeting the challenge posed by Lewis Mumford of realizing the human potential *within* organic norms and
limits.

*   *   *   *   *   *   *

This volume of *Energy Policy Studies* examines our linked
problems of energy, environment and economic development from
several vantage points. An overview of the science and policy
issues opens the discussion and sets out the interdisciplinary dimensions of the problem. Two historical analyses follow that ex-
pose the industrial assumptions about energy and the environment
which took root in Europe and North America and subsequently
spread worldwide. Contemporary issues surrounding the two most
energy- and environment-intensive sectors of industrial development — transportation and electricity generation — are taken
up next. Three papers analyze in depth the environmental and
energy impacts of these sectors and offer detailed programs for
reorienting our transportation and electric power systems. In the
final section, the international policy challenge that confronts the
world community is examined. Two papers argue for a break with
the existing industrial paradigm and the adoption of a sustainable
development orientation in which priority is given to fulfilling the
needs of developing countries while averting global environmental
degradation. While the authors are hopeful about the capacity of
the world community to act upon our linked problems, they are
cautious in their optimism.

James MacKenzie's chapter provides an overview of the energy and environmental challenges that will be faced well into the 21st century. He argues that the world is experiencing a third major transition in its energy sources. This transition will not be driven by a shortage of fossil fuels, but rather by the need to respond to the threat of global climate change resulting from the burning of fossil fuels; by growing air pollution in the form of smog and acid rain; and by continued economic insecurity created by reliance on oil as a primary energy source. MacKenzie examines each of these challenges in detail and concludes that in the coming decade we must begin a transition away from reliance on fossil fuels. He analyzes the advantages and disadvantages of the only two non-fossil supply options available — renewable energy technologies and nuclear fission — and, recognizing the neither offers a fix, concludes that it would not be prudent to count on nuclear energy to save us from the global threats posed by our existing energy system. Instead, he argues that actions must be taken now that support improvements in energy efficiency and accelerated reliance on renewable energy sources and the storage technologies to support their widespread use. In addition, international cooperation and agreements are needed that promote the long-term goal of reducing global emissions with special responsibility falling on the industrial nations, especially the United States, who are the largest sources of energy-related carbon dioxide gases and who have the resources to develop the alternative energy sources needed for the third energy transition.

The current debate in the United States that pits economic progress against environmental protection has its political and social roots in the 19th and early 20th century. While examining these historical antecedents of the current controversy, **Martin Melosi** also demonstrates that the terms of the modern debate have not advanced much beyond those of the 19th century despite the ominous prospects of global warming. He shows that the issue of economic growth versus environmental protection was not successfully addressed, much less resolved over the last century, leaving for the 20th century a legacy that sustains this fundamental dilemma. Melosi's analysis suggests that political solutions of environmental problems caused by energy-intensive economic growth are unlikely until the functionality of environmental degradation to the existing process of industrial development is challenged. Many remedies to environmental problems currently under consideration are piecemeal proposals reflecting the continued lack of an integrated policy approach to the nexus of energy, environment and economic growth. Melosi's analysis underscores the importance of recognizing the historical context of industrial experience in order to effectively address the environmental problems of our time.

Dolores Greenberg's analysis of the illusion of progress links current environmental controversies to the history of industrial development in Europe. She demonstrates how a single-source fossil-fuel mentality, long equated with progress, has clouded assessment of the industrializing process. Examining the uneven transition to fossil fuels, she highlights the importance of the diverse mix of wood, water, and muscle power to the dynamics of development in England as well as in Western, Central, and Eastern Europe. Greenberg demonstrates that the entrenched bias against renewable energy — as primitive and noncommercial — is insupportable, as is the common energy stage theory that wood was replaced by water, then by coal, and then by oil. Reevaluating assumptions about modern energy transitions, she dates the significant adoption of coal in the 1880s and, contrary to the usual emphasis on the shift to oil, she documents that coal remained the preeminent "commercial" fuel of Europe into the 1950s, with the major swing to oil, even in Western Europe, delayed until as late as the 1960s. The fallacy of the illusion of progress is the equation of carbon use with social improvement. Greenberg's analysis of European experience suggests that renewables and industrialization are not incompatible; rather, the conventional interpretations of industrial experience contain a deep-set bias that obstructs reasonable assessment of the possible role of renewables in industrial development.

Dean Abrahamson presents the case for a shift to renewable energy supply options to respond to the social challenges of climate change. Abrahamson argues that conservation is important in meeting the challenge of climate change, but observes that whatever the level of energy consumption, we must make new and different choices in relationship to energy supply. Because fossil fuels are the largest single source of greenhouse gas emissions, and because there is no practical means of burning these fuels without further adverse effects on global climate, the replacement of fossil by non-fossil primary energy sources is a necessary requirement for meeting the environmental challenge of industrial development. In this regard, Abrahamson considers the advantages and disadvantages of nuclear power and solar power as primary energy sources for the future. He concludes that the threats posed by nuclear power should preclude a reliance upon it as a means of addressing the problem of climate change. Technologies for the utilization of solar power, Abrahamson argues, are available now at competitive prices. Moreover, reliance on solar power engenders none of the hazards that are characteristic of a nuclear economy. Yet, Abrahamson points out that recognizing the advantages of reliance on solar energy is not sufficient. Comprehensive policy action is needed to bring about a solar-based primary energy supply system. Thus far, he concludes, our scientific understanding of what must be done exceeds our political commitment to change what we do.

A major obstacle to meeting contemporary environmental and energy challenges is the failure of market systems to incorporate environmental and other social costs in energy prices or energy decision-making. As Olav Hohmeyer points out, decisions about the use of competing energy options generally are based upon the relative costs at which the energy service can be delivered. Because social costs are not included in market prices, energy decisions often result in economic gain at the expense of environmental degradation. Documenting the existence of significant social costs associated with energy consumption, Hohmeyer presents the results of a recent extension of his earlier analysis of the total costs to society created by the choice of different technology for electricity generation. His analysis compares the total social costs of reliance on fossil and nuclear fuels with reliance on renewable energy sources represented by wind and photovoltaic electricity. Hohmeyer demonstrates the existence of important cost elements not reflected in market prices of conventional electricity generation that, when adequately taken into account, favor societal investment in wind and photovoltaic technologies. The differences documented in the current analysis are even greater than those in Hohmeyer's earlier study, leading him to conclude that the failure to incorporate these cost elements puts renewables at an even greater disadvantage than has been assumed until now. The type of analysis conducted by Hohmeyer is fundamental to realistically considering the environmental consequences of energy choice.

Marc Ledbetter and **Marc Ross** focus on the linkage between energy use and environmental impacts in the transportation sector, which is a significant source of emissions contributing to air pollution and global warming, especially in the United States and other industrialized countries. Focusing on light vehicles, automobiles and light trucks, Ledbetter and Ross argue that earlier fuel economy improvements in the U.S. have stalled. They demonstrate that fuel prices alone will not be a sufficient incentive to improve fuel economy to levels that are cost-effective from a societal perspective. In particular, they point out that the market price of vehicle fuels does not reflect environmental and other social costs necessitating the use of public policies to induce changes in consumer behavior and investments that are justified on grounds on societal benefit. Ledbetter and Ross consider a wide array of policy options that may improve energy efficiency and reduce greenhouse gas emissions, while providing adequate transportation access for people and maintaining or improving safety and environmental quality. In addition to policies that result in fuel economy improvements, they propose initiatives to slow the growth in vehicle miles of travel and advocate transportation alternatives to low-occupancy light vehicles.

Mohan Munasinghe addresses the difficult dilemma facing developing countries of reconciling development goals — which will require increased use of energy and raw materials — with responsible stewardship of the environment. He argues that, in view of the severe financial constraints that developing countries already face, the response of these countries to the need for environmental preservation cannot extend beyond measures that are consistent with near-term economic development goals. In particular, the energy policy response of developing countries in the coming decade will be limited to conventional technologies in efficiency improvement, conservation and resource development. Munasinghe proposes that the developed countries can and should show leadership by providing the financial resources that the developing world needs today for investment in environmentally-sensitive energy development, and by undertaking research and development of the technologies that are needed to harmonize economic goals with environmental stewardship. He regards the problem of balancing development and environmental goals as the central policy challenge of the late 20th and early 21st centuries. Munasinghe advocates international initiatives, including the Global Environmental Facility and the Ozone Fund, to facilitate participation of developing countries in addressing the linked issues of energy, environment, and development at the global level.

In the concluding chapter, **John Byrne** and **Daniel Rich** propose that our most serious policy challenge is to recognize the systemic nature of our interconnected global development, energy, and environmental problems. They argue that these systemic problems arise from the persistence and dominance of a worldwide energy and development orientation that, with few exceptions, values economic growth and power over all else. This development orientation, termed the politics of commodification, is based on the assumption of a separation between the natural order and the social order. The assumption of dual realities, one natural and one social, rationalizes environmental degradation as the necessary price of progress. Byrne and Rich argue that we need to abandon the politics of commodification and pursue a reconstruction of energy, environment and development relations. At the core of this reconstruction is the need to create political and economic institutions that embody the value of sustainable social development. Byrne and Rich examine the policy and institutional requirements necessary to foster a transition to sustainability, and they evaluate the sources of resistance to this transition. The authors emphasize that our current economic, political and technology systems are transformable, however impervious to change they may appear from our present vantage point in history, and support international commitments to address the systemic problems of commodification.

References

COSEPUP (Committee on Science, Engineering, and Public Policy). 1991. *Policy Implications of Greenhouse Warming.* Prepared for the U.S. National Academy of Science. Washington, DC: National Academy Press.

MacKenzie, James J. 1991. "Toward a Sustainable Energy Future: The Critical Role of Rational Energy Pricing." *WRI Issues and Ideas.* Washington, DC: World Resources Institute.

MacKenzie, James J. and Mohamed T. El-Ashry. 1988. *Ill Winds: Airborne Pollution's Toll on Trees and Crops.* Washington, DC: World Resources Institute.

Mumford, Lewis. 1961. *The City in History.* New York, NY: Harcourt Brace.

_____. 1938. *The Culture of Cities.* New York, NY: Harcourt Brace.

_____. 1934. *Technics and Civilization.* New York, NY: Harcourt Brace Jovanovich.

National Research Council. 1989. *Ozone Depletion, Greenhouse Gases and Climatic Change.* Washington, DC: National Academy Press.

Newman, Peter and Jeffrey Kenworthy. 1989. *Cities and Automobile Dependence.* Brookfield, VT: Gower Publishing.

OECD/IEA. 1991. *Greenhouse Gas Emissions: The Energy Dimension.* Paris: OECD Publications Services.

World Commission on Environment and Development (WCED). 1987. *Our Common Future*. New York, NY: Oxford University Press.

Watson, R. T. and the Ozone Trends Panel, M. J. Prather and the Ad Hoc Theory Panel, and M. J. Kurylo and the NASA Panel for Data Evaluation. 1988. *Present State of Knowledge of the Upper Atmosphere 1988: An Assessment Report*. NASA Reference Publication 1208. Washington, DC: U.S. Government Printing Office.

World Resources Institute. 1990. "Atmosphere and Climate" section. *World Resources 1990-91*. New York, NY: Oxford University Press.

Yergin, David. 1982. "Crisis and Adjustment: An Overview." In D. Yergin and M. Hillenbrand (eds.), *Global Insecurity*. New York: Penguin Books.

PART I

Overview

Chapter 1

Energy and Environment in the 21st Century:
The Challenge of Change

James J. MacKenzie

As the world nears the end of the twentieth century, it finds itself facing the third major transition among energy sources. This transition will not be driven by an underlying shortage of carbon fuels: the world has huge coal resources which in principle could be converted into synthetic oil and natural gas. Rather, the transition will occur in response to three serious problems intimately connected to the use of energy: climate change — in large measure the result of burning fossil fuels; air pollution in the form of smog and acid rain; and growing reliance on the part of many nations on insecure sources of oil, jeopardizing their national and economic security. These three problems are linked together by the burning of fossil fuels and together they point to the urgent need to develop new energy sources (MacKenzie, 1989).

In this chapter we begin by sketching out the historical role that energy has played in the development of human affairs. From the discovery of fire, to the development of agriculture, the harnessing of animal power, the invention of the steam engine, and the splitting of the atom, energy use has allowed humankind to adapt to — indeed, to triumph over — the natural environment and to prosper over the millennia.

The transition from renewable energy sources to fossil fuels, a change which began in the mid 19th century, shifted human development onto a non-sustainable development path. The large-scale burning of fossil fuels now threatens human welfare and security as well the natural environment. Protecting the earth's climate will require a major, relatively rapid shift from fossil to non-fossil energy sources. The technological and institutional implications of this transition are discussed, as are the relative roles of the industrialized and developing countries.

Energy in Human Affairs:
A Historical Overview

Energy has played a crucial role in the evolution of the human species (Cook, 1971; Foley, 1987; Harrison, 1968). By harnessing various forms of energy, humankind has survived ice ages, accommodated to hostile weather, and industrialized. In a cruel reversal it now appears that — unless drastic changes are soon made in the forms of energy and it uses — uncontrolled energy use may lead to far-reaching, possibly irreversible, changes in the earth and its climate and to the widespread jeopardy of many forms of life itself (Gribbin, 1990).

Over the millennia, humankind has moved from dependence on renewable resources — wood, the winds, water power, and human and animal power — to our present dependence on depletable resources, mostly fossil fuels. While the burning of fossil fuels has enabled mankind to remake the surface of the earth, it has also brought with it its own seeds of decline. Over human time frames, fossil fuels must be considered non-renewable. As a result, we are living — unsustainably — on our capital, not our income. For its long-term survival, mankind must once again move to renewable energy sources. How quickly must such a transition occur? How would the new world differ from that of the 20th century? And how would the technologies differ? These are some of the issues we address in this introductory chapter.

Transitions over the Millennia

According to present understanding, land-based life began some 300-400 million years ago (Foley, 1987; Parker, 1986). What we call modern man began his evolution in Africa some 5 to 8 million years ago. These first humans were probably vegetarians and their food consumption constituted their entire energy consumption, some 2000-3000 kilocalories per day. Primitive people had no access to fire or domestic animals.

It is estimated that only about 40 million people could live on earth as gatherers, less than 1 percent of the earth's present level. The first tools, chipped stones, were probably used to cut up dead animals some 2 million years ago. The use of tools reflects an important step in evolution: it allowed early people to expand their diet and to use materials for shelter and other purposes. However, energy use was probably not much greater than with gatherers.

Homo erectus was the first user of fire, some 100,000-400,000 years ago (Foley, 1987). Fire and the development of clothing allowed people to live in colder climates and to cook meat. They developed elaborate tools including the hand axe. The energy use of these early people was probably double that of vegetarians.

These early humans had to cope with major changes in the earth's climate. About 1.5 million years ago the first full-scale glaciation occurred with huge ice sheets covering much of the earth. These patterns of ice ages have continued with a periodicity of some 80,000 to 100,000 years. The last ice age was at its maximum some 18,000 years ago, and ended some 10,000 years ago. The present interglacial is some 10,000 years old and presumably is approaching its end.

The first fully modern human, homo sapiens, developed around 40,000 years ago. This species spread over the entire globe partly as the result of the ice age which dropped oceans levels hundreds of feet allowing the migration among continents. In addition to

using fire these people had stone lamps using animal fat as the
fuel.

Advent of Agriculture

Food is humankind's most indispensable energy form. Of the
2 million years or so that man has been on earth, he was a gath-
erer for the first 1,990,000. Agriculture is only some 10,000 years
old. On average, the development of agriculture allowed about
five times as many people to live on the same area than if gatherers were there. Agriculture allowed the domestication of animals through the growing of grain to feed them and produced the
surpluses of food that made possible the evolution of the great
civilizations of antiquity.

Animals have been used in agriculture and as means of transportation for thousands of years. Wind was used to power ship
and grain mills, and to pump water. The domestication of animals allowed milk and meat to be obtained from grass that was
otherwise indigestible for humans. Animals were used to lift water, plow the land, and haul loads; they also served as sources of
hides for clothing and other purposes. Energy consumption per
person in a primitive agricultural setting was probably six times
the minimum 2,000 kilocalories per day.

The progression in per capita energy use can be seen in Figure 1.1. Food still accounts for a small fraction of human energy
needs. Yet many people today still live at the level of the gathering
or primitive agricultural stage and about 2 billion rely on wood to
meet most of their energy needs. Wood is the most widely used
fuel worldwide and in many developing countries, people meet
90 percent of their energy needs with wood and other forms of
biomass (Foley, 1987).

The Industrial Revolution: The Transition to Fossil Fuels

Until about the middle of the 19th century, the world was
powered almost totally by renewable resources: wood for heat and
smelting; and water wheels, wind mills, sailing ships, and animal

Figure 1.1

Evolution of Human Energy Use (Daily Per Capita Energy Consumption)

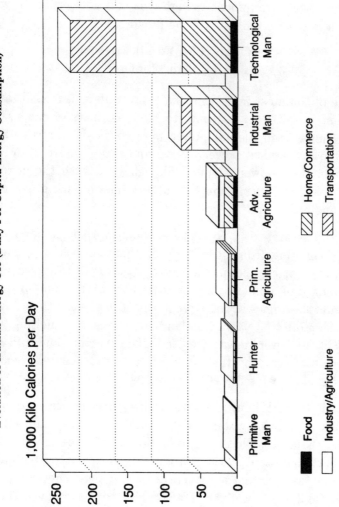

Source: Cook, 1971

Why we need this policy

power for mechanical energy. Over the past century two major transitions among energy sources have occurred (Landsberg and Schurr, 1968; Schurr et al., 1960). The first was from wood to coal beginning in the middle of the 19th century. The second, to oil and gas, began in the early part of the 20th century. A third transition is now imminent though it is still not certain to which energy sources humankind will be moving.

Coal: The Fossil Fuel
of the 19th Century

One of the most important limitations of ancient civilizations was their inability to concentrate large amounts of energy on a task. Human and animal power were the main sources of concentrated mechanical power. Wind and water wheels were quite limited in their power output. This changed with the introduction of coal for smelting and the subsequent widespread use of the steam engine.

Coal was first used to replace wood as a source for heating and for smelting iron. In England, charcoal used for smelting iron, lead, tin, and copper led to a widespread improvement in the standard of living but at the cost of the destruction of forests. The wood shortage was so severe in the 16th century that England had to ship ore to Ireland, Scotland, and Wales for smelting where forests in turn, were devastated to make charcoal. The entire iron industry was saved by the substitution of coke (made from coal) for charcoal — a fossil fuel for a biofuel.

Until the middle of the 18th century, mechanical energy was available only from water wheels, wind machines, and animals. All this changed with the introduction in 1776 of the steam engine, itself facilitated by the introduction of coke into iron making. Steam engines allowed a concentration of energy never available before. Coal, iron, and the steam engine together paved the way for the industrial revolution.

The widespread use of fossil fuels in the United States began in the mid 1800s when 90 percent of our heat energy was still obtained from wood (Landsberg and Schurr, 1968; Schurr et al.; 1960). Though in 1850 about five times as much work was obtained from wind and water wheels as from steam engines, only twenty years later the amounts were about equal. By 1900 about 75 percent of the country's heating needs were met by coal. In the latter part of the 19th century, coal became the energy source for U.S. industry, iron and steel making, and transportation. Wood, the energy source for households, was growing scarcer and coal was cheaper and more convenient than wood.

From the middle of the 19th century until about 1910, coal use grew at over 6 percent per year, accounting for all the growth in energy supply. By 1910, coal production was 60 times as great as in 1850 and it supplied 80 percent of total fuel needs. Steam boats and locomotives converted from wood to coal. In the latter part of the 19th century, sailing ships were largely replaced by iron ships powered by steam.

The relative contribution of coal in the United States declined from a peak of about 75 percent of total energy supply in 1910 to about 17 percent in 1973, back to about 23 percent in 1989. During the past 80 years, coal lost many of its important markets. Locomotives and ships converted from steam to diesels; buildings switched to natural gas and oil; and industry converted from steam engines and pulleys to electric motors.

In 1989 about 86 percent of domestic coal consumption was accounted for in electric power production. The rest was used by industry and to make coke. The decline in coal was precipitated by the convenience, cleanliness, and efficiency of new competing technologies.

Coal is both the most abundant fossil fuel worldwide and the most environmentally damaging. From its mining to its consumption, coal takes a heavy toll on the land, water, and air. In addition to mining impacts, it is a major source of sulfur dioxide, nitrogen oxides, particulates, and, perhaps, the most serious pollutant, carbon dioxide.

Oil and Natural Gas:
The Fuels of the 20th Century

The switch from wood to coal in the mid-19th century represented the first major transition in energy sources. The second
transition, to oil and natural gas, began at about the turn of the
century and has just been completed.

In the United States, the first successful oil well was completed
in 1859 in Titusville, Pennsylvania. The goal of the Pennsylvania
Rock Oil Company was to find enough oil to begin meeting the
illuminating and lubrication needs of the country. Within ten
years of the first well, oil production had reached four million
barrels per year. Within 20 years it reached 26 million barrels per
year; and by 1900, 63 million barrels.

Kerosene, used in lamps, comprised 85 percent of refinery output in the 1870s. There was a genuine reluctance at the turn
of the century to use oil as a heating fuel because of the abundance of coal and wood, the high price of refined oil, and the lack
of suitable burning equipment. These obstacles were eventually
overcome and by 1910 about one-half of total oil production was
being burned as a heating fuel by railroads, manufacturers, the
navy, and the electric utilities.

During the nineteenth century, gasoline was regarded as a
waste product of oil refining. The first internal combustion engine
using gasoline was made in 1876 and by the 1890s the basic motor
car had been developed. The convenience and efficiency of the
internal combustion engine soon led to its dominance over steam
and electric systems. In 1900 there were 8000 registered motor
vehicles in the United States. By 1921 there were 10 million, and
by 1925, 20 million. Gasoline production went from 11 percent of
refinery output in 1909, to 25 percent in 1918, to 42 percent in
1930. Today oil is the nation's single largest source of energy with
almost two out of three barrels consumed in transportation.

Domestic oil production in the United States is declining
sharply (see Figure 1.2). With demand growing, oil imports have

increased and in 1989 were approaching half of domestic supply. The Persian Gulf war with Iraq demonstrated the economic and security risks of relying on the Middle East for significant amounts of petroleum. Reducing long-term security and economic risks will require becoming more energy efficient and developing alternative energy sources. Nowhere is the urgency greater than in transportation.

Figure 1.2
Trends In U.S. Oil Production

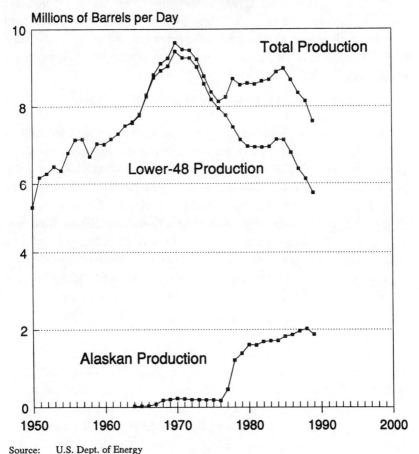

Source: U.S. Dept. of Energy

Natural gas, like gasoline, was first considered a useless waste product and was normally flared at the well or vented directly into the atmosphere. Until the late 19th century, transporting it was difficult due to the crude pipeline technology. The first high-pressure pipeline in 1891 transported gas from northern Indiana to Chicago. It was not until the late 1920s that seamless, high-pressure, large-diameter pipes and underground pipe-laying equipment became available, enabling the gas industry to expand rapidly. Other factors favoring increased gas use include low price, no on-site storage needed, and gas-burning equipment that is virtually maintenance free. Over the decades the markets for natural gas have slowly changed. Residential and commercial customers increased their use from about 20 percent in 1930 to 44 percent in 1989. Industry (40 percent) and power production (16 percent) consume the remaining gas.

Factors Driving the Third Transition

The transition from fossil fuels, which now account for nearly 90 percent of global energy supply, to non-fossil energy sources will be fundamentally different from previous ones. Factors such as physical scarcity, convenience, and relative fuel prices will be of secondary importance to the driving forces of global climate change, air quality, and international oil security. These latter issues are of vital importance to all nations both industrialized and developing, whether they are large consumers of commercial energy or not. In the following sections we summarize these threats as they exist today and their implications for global energy use.

Global Climate Change

The release of vast amounts of gases into the atmosphere is threatening an unprecedented global warming (IPCC, 1990). The buildup of greenhouse gases threatens to commit the world, as early as 2030, to a global temperature rise of as much as 9 F, a temperature change that was sufficient thousands of years ago to carry the earth from the coldest depth of the Ice Age into the warmest period ever known (Abrahamson, 1989; Gribbin, 1990).

Greenhouse warming occurs when a blanket of atmospheric gases allows sunlight to penetrate to the earth, but partially traps the earth's radiated infrared heat. Some greenhouse warming is both totally natural and necessary. Without it the earth would be about 60 F colder and life as we know it would not be possible. Over the past century, however, human activities have led to the buildup of carbon dioxide and other gases in the atmosphere, including ozone, chlorofluorocarbons (or CFCs), methane, and nitrous oxide that threaten to intensify this natural warming.

Presently, carbon dioxide, principally from the burning of fossil fuels, accounts for about half of the added, annual global warming commitment. At current growth rates, these gases are collectively committing the globe, each decade, to a 0.4 to 0.9 F eventual temperature increase. The resulting warming is expected to persist for centuries. While no nation can solve the greenhouse problem alone, the United States contributes more to the problem than any other, and so has a special responsibility to take a leadership role in dealing with it (WRI, 1990).

The global atmospheric concentration of carbon dioxide has increased about 25 percent since pre-industrial times, paralleling the burning of fossil fuels and the cutting down of forests worldwide. In the United States, electric utilities are the single largest source of carbon dioxide releases, accounting for about a third of all emissions. Transportation activities run a close second at 31 percent.

Between 1973 and 1988, global carbon dioxide emissions increased by more than 25 percent, while emissions from the United States increased by about 3 percent (ORNL, 1990). By offsetting increased U.S. coal burning, the use of nuclear power played an important role in reducing the growth rate in carbon dioxide emissions from U.S. electric power plants. In spite of this, emissions from U.S. power plants and transportation have increased substantially while those from industry and residential and commercial buildings have declined. With increasing electrification worldwide and the growing number of vehicles on the roads, emissions from these two sectors are expected to continue growing (MacKenzie, 1989).

In terms of their warming potential, not all fossil fuels were created equal. For each unit of useful energy, oil releases about 40 percent more carbon dioxide than natural gas, and coal about 75 percent more. Synthetic fuels derived from coal or oil shales would release even more carbon dioxide than coal because the conversion processes require so much energy. Hence, all things being equal, the substitution of natural gas for other fossil fuels would help reduce future greenhouse warming while the replacement of oil with synthetic fluids would substantially exacerbate it.

Petroleum accounts for about 45 percent of both global and U.S. fossil fuel supply and about the same percentage of fuel-related carbon dioxide emissions. Natural gas and coal each account for about 27 percent of U.S. fossil fuel supply. Worldwide, gas accounts for 24 percent of fossil fuel supply while coal contributes about 32 percent. Coal, used mostly for electricity generation and industrial purposes in the United States, accounts for about a third of U.S. carbon dioxide emissions. Natural gas contributes the rest.

With the continued buildup of these greenhouse gases, what will be the likely effects of global warming? The oceans, which act as huge heat sinks, have delayed by perhaps a few decades the warming already committed to from past emissions, estimated at 2 to 5 F. While uncertainties persist as to the timing and regional impacts, there is little disagreement that global warming will occur. By the year 2050, Washington, D.C., which now averages 36 days a year over 90 F, could have 87 such days. Chicago could go from 16 such days to 56 (Hansen, 1988).

A reduction in precipitation and soil moisture is expected in the mid-continental United States. Precipitation patterns will change, though exactly how is still uncertain. Some areas will receive less rain, affecting rivers and water supply. Ecosystems, both plants and animals, will be forced to migrate northward to keep up with changing climate conditions. Those unable to do so because of the rapid rate of climate change or because of inhibiting structures, roads, or developments, may decline or disappear altogether (EPA, 1989).

Sea levels could rise an estimated one to three feet by the end of the next century due to thermal expansion of the oceans and the melting of glacial ice. A three-foot rise could have devastating effects on coastal developments and river delta communities around the world. Many parts of the Gulf Coast and Florida will be more often inundated from a combination of higher ocean levels and more frequent and more intense tropical storms. Protecting coastal cities against a three-foot sea rise could cost hundreds of billions of dollars. Many rich coastal ecosystems, fisheries, and arable land around the globe will also be lost.

The summer of 1988 witnessed record temperatures across the country, a drought in the Mid-West, record levels of smog in cities, devastating fires in the West, and the worst tropical storm ever documented in the Western hemisphere. Though not proving that the greenhouse effect has arrived, these events are indicative of what we can expect from global warming.

Air Pollution

Air pollution is another major international problem linked directly to the burning of fossil fuels. In the summer of 1988, 76 U.S. cities exceeded EPA's health standard for ozone by at least 25 percent. In 1988, about 112 million Americans were living in areas that exceeded the ozone standard. Twenty-nine million live where the carbon monoxide limit was violated. Los Angeles exceeds these EPA limits for two out of every three days of the year, more than any other American city.

These air contaminants seriously affect asthmatics and others who suffer from respiratory ailments (ALA, 1989). Healthy lungs are damaged. Pollutants, particularly ozone, irritate the eyes and are believed to weaken the human immune system.

The principal precursors to this urban pollution are carbon monoxide, nitrogen oxides, and organic compounds. The sun's heat causes these chemicals to react with each other to create ground-level ozone, the principal component in urban smog. The primary source of these precursors is transportation, accounting for 70 percent of all carbon monoxide emissions, and 41 percent of the nitrogen oxides. The warmer it gets, the more these reactions are driven, the more ozone is created. In cities where the air stagnates, high smog levels can persist for days. Ozone also inflicts damage outside the urban arena, impairing the productivity of crops across the country. Beans, cotton, winter wheat, and peanuts are particularly vulnerable. U.S. losses in crop productivity attributable to ozone are estimated at up to five billion dollars per year (MacKenzie and El-Ashry, 1989).

Acid deposition and ozone, resulting from vehicle and power plant emissions, are also implicated in damage to trees, especially at mountainous sites in the eastern United States (MacKenzie and El-Ashry, 1989; Tomlinson, 1990). The average acidity of cloud moisture along the U.S. Appalachian Mountain chain is 10 times greater than cloud acidity at nearby lower elevations. The peak cloud acidity at several of these mountains reaches 2,000 times the acidity of unpolluted rainwater. In forests, ozone and acid deposition accelerate the leaching of nutrients from plant foliage. Acid deposition also leaches essential nutrients from forest soils, threatening long-term ecological changes. The cumulative effect of the acidity and ozone is to leave trees and plants more susceptible to natural stresses such as pests, disease, severe cold, and drought. Buildings and other structures are also vulnerable to the ravages of acid deposition.

The sources of air pollution are largely the same as the sources of greenhouse gases (MacKenzie, 1989). Fossil fuel power plants are the largest source of sulfur dioxide, accounting for two thirds of emissions. Power plants also account for 29 percent of the nitrogen oxide emissions, another major precursor to acid precipitation. Transportation, however, is the largest source of nitrogen oxides, accounting for 41 percent of all emissions in the United States.

In response to U.S. clean air legislation, many utilities built tall stacks to eject the pollutants further up into the air. However, this approach to meeting local ambient air quality standards led to serious longer-range acid rain problems, as the pollutants eventually oxidize to sulfuric and nitric acid: acid rain.

Oil Security

World oil consumption accounts for almost half of global carbon dioxide emissions and much of its air pollution. Heavy reliance on oil, primarily for transportation, also threatens the national and economic security of many importing nations. In the United States the problem can only grow more serious. The U.S. consumes 25 percent of the world's total oil, but has only 3.4 percent of world proven reserves. Despite a massive drilling effort in the 1970s and early 1980s, U.S. oil production in the lower 48 states continued to decline. As a result, the United States has become increasingly dependent on imported oil, almost 50 percent of supply in 1990.

Much of the oil that will be imported by the industrialized countries in the future will come from oil-rich, but politically unstable Persian Gulf nations. About two thirds of proven oil reserves are located in the Middle East. Moreover, the OPEC producers are slowly but steadily regaining market share: in the five years between 1985 and 1990 OPEC's share of global oil production rose from 31 percent to 40 percent. Unless the United States and other industrialized countries take major steps to reduce their consumption of oil, especially in transportation — where there are no ready alternatives — they will become increasingly vulnerable both economically, and politically.

End-Use Efficiency: The Bridge to a Sustainable Energy Future

Clearly, climate change, air pollution, and reliance on foreign sources of oil all have serious implications for energy decision making, and because they are closely linked, all must be considered together in the formulation of international energy policy. Of the

three, however, global warming will have by far the most pro-
found impacts: the Intergovernmental Panel on Climate Change
has estimated that it will take a reduction of at least 60 percent in
carbon dioxide emissions to stabilize atmospheric concentrations.

The policy responses to these linked problems can be divided
into near-term options and long-term options. In the near term
there are few measures more effective in reducing emissions than
improving international energy efficiency. The technologies exist
that would significantly cut energy use in almost every application
ranging from cooking and space conditioning to lighting and refrigeration (Lovins and Lovins, 1990; Williams, 1990). In buildings,
tighter energy-performance codes and demand side management
program (DSM) by utilities to improve the performance of existing structures would go a long way to reduce energy consumption.
Such programs are gaining in popularity in the United States and
have been proposed for developing countries as well (Reddy and
Goldemberg, 1990). There are still vast untapped opportunities
for efficiency improvements in homes, commercial buildings and
factories. Indeed, in the United States the Congress in 1987 took
an important step in this area by passing legislation establishing
national efficiency standards for major new appliances starting in
the early 1990s. As highly efficient refrigerators, air conditioners,
and lights are gradually introduced, the results will be fewer emissions from power plants, and less risk of climate warming and air
pollution. The greatest challenge to improving energy efficiency
worldwide is not technological but institutional: it is identifying
creative incentives to encourage more widespread use of these efficient appliances.

Shifting to highly fuel efficient vehicles will curtail carbon dioxide emissions, mitigating the greenhouse impact and reducing dependence on oil imports. Vehicles attaining over 50 miles per
gallon are now in dealer showrooms. In the United States, state
and federal governments can encourage the use of these highly efficient vehicles through increased fuel taxes and by adopting variable sales taxes or variable annual registration fees that increase
for fuel-inefficient vehicles. In the long term, though, if growth

in vehicle use continues along recent trends, improvements in vehicle fuel efficiency will — by themselves — prove incapable of holding down carbon dioxide emissions (MacKenzie and Walsh, 1990). Ultimately, therefore, emissionless vehicles — such as electric or hydrogen cars powered by non-fossil energy sources — will be needed.

Reducing the number of vehicles on our roads and highways is another element of an effective strategy to curb oil consumption and carbon dioxide emissions. Long-term investments in public transit will be required and will lead to reduced global warming, less air pollution, and fewer oil imports. At the same time it is essential to toughen inspection and maintenance programs for existing vehicles. Recent evidence suggests that a few older vehicles in fact are responsible for a large percentage of urban pollution.

The Role of Alternative Fuels

The possible role of so-called "alternative fuels" in dealing with our energy and climate problems deserves very careful consideration (CCE, 1990; MacKenzie, 1990; OTA, 1990). The fuels most commonly cited as possible substitutes for oil are ethanol, methanol, compressed natural gas, electricity, and hydrogen.

In the United States ethanol — grain alcohol — is a domestically produced fuel and so, in principle, could help with the problems of energy security and balance of trade. However, because of the large amounts of corn that would be required (it now takes four percent of the U.S. corn crop to displace one-half of one percent of U.S. gasoline), it is unlikely to ever play an important energy role in our transportation future. Moreover, making ethanol from corn takes almost as much energy as the ethanol contains; hence, it offers little if any global warming benefit. Nor is there much clean-air benefit. Ethanol is a very expensive option and one that will be subject to major disruption if — as expected — global warming takes a toll on U.S. agriculture in the coming years.

Methanol — wood alcohol — also has few advantages over gasoline. Compared with advanced gasoline-powered vehicles, methanol cars would provide no global warming and only small, uncertain clean-air benefits. Some air pollution benefit could arise, however, from methanol use in heavy-duty vehicles. Since the methanol would be imported, though, the switch from oil would provide no balance-of-trade benefit. If it were imported from friendly countries, it could provide some security advantage. Ultimately, because methanol is still made from fossil fuels and by nature a source of carbon dioxide, it should be considered only as a transitional fuel. It therefore makes little sense to substitute methanol for gasoline or diesel fuel in a major way.

Like methanol, compressed natural gas offers some security and clean-air advantages (especially in heavy-duty vehicles) but, if imported, little relief to our balance of trade. Its global warming benefits are only marginal. From a long-term perspective dominated by concern over climate change, it too can play only a transitional role. Heavy-duty urban vehicles and centrally housed automobile fleets are the logical, most cost-effective candidates for a limited natural-gas initiative.

Electric vehicles are probably the most attractive option for the next decade or two when they could serve primarily as commuting vehicles. They offer distinct climate, air pollution, and security benefits. They would mesh easily with the non-fossil energy sources likely to be in widespread use in the next century (renewable energy sources and, perhaps, nuclear power). Although they are expensive today, increased research on better storage methods is expected to bring down prices in the coming years.

Hydrogen vehicles are a promising longer-term alternative. If research can lower hydrogen's costs, improve storage, and lead to a practicable fuel cell, hydrogen vehicles will be very attractive indeed. Their introduction would cut oil imports and the emission of greenhouse and air-polluting gases. Wide-scale deployment could require a substantial refurbishing of the nation's natural-gas pipeline network, however. As in the case of electric vehicles, hydrogen vehicles would also be compatible with the energy sources of the 21st century.

In sum, while CNG and methanol — both fossil fuels — may have some useful temporary role in urban bus and truck fleets, a major shift to either should be avoided, primarily because of the threat of global warming and the need to reduce carbon dioxide emissions. Instead, international policies should logically begin now to promote a transition to the non-fossil transportation fuels of the next century: electricity and hydrogen.

The Third Transition:
Energy Planning in the Long Term

For the various reasons outlined above, the world must begin over the coming decades a long-term shift away from fossil fuels. At the moment there are only two alternatives: the renewable energy technologies and nuclear fission.

The Potential Role of Nuclear Power

Nuclear energy is the only practicable non-solar source of energy that is likely to provide large amounts of power in the twenty first century. In 1989, the more than 100 U.S. nuclear power plants in operation generated 19 percent of the nation's electricity. Worldwide there were more than 400 reactors in operation in 1988, accounting for about 5 percent of global energy supply. Another 100 were under construction. The largely favorable experiences in Japan and Western Europe suggest that nuclear power could provide significant amounts of electricity at reasonable costs with no air pollution or carbon dioxide emissions. Today, though, the U.S. industry is at a dead end, largely the result of years of poor management by both industry and government and, worldwide, there has been a slowdown in the placement of new orders over the past few years.

An international study conducted at MIT compared the performance of nuclear power plants in the United States with those of other industrial countries (Hansen, 1989). The study concluded that U.S. reactors, both pressurized and boiling water reactors, perform substantially worse than those in Switzerland, West Germany, France, Japan, or Sweden. The researchers found that good day-to-day management was the common ingredient to high performance among nuclear plants. The problems manifested by equipment breakdown were ultimately traceable to poor management and failures to learn from past mistakes and to communicate with other nuclear operators who are doing far better.

Over the past twenty years U.S. public confidence in nuclear power has badly eroded. As a result of unresolved safety problems, cost overruns, regulatory delays, poor operating experiences, and the Three Mile Island accident in 1979, neither U.S. utilities nor the financial community seems likely to undertake any further construction of nuclear plants with current designs.

With the growing recognition that global climate change will force major reductions in carbon dioxide emissions, interest in the United States in nuclear energy — at least on the part of the federal government and the nuclear industry — has begun to rekindle. Research is underway to develop new nuclear designs that would pose fewer overall risks. These new reactors would be smaller, modular, standardized, and more reliant than existing plants on passive design features for safe operation. Whether such plants will be deployed in large numbers will depend on the successful resolution of many issues, but they are unlikely to make a significant impact over the next 20 years.

At least in the United States, the management and operation of existing plants must significantly improve. Another serious nuclear accident in the United States would surely finish the industry altogether. In some circumstances improved operation may require transferring existing operating licenses to more competent utilities or to new corporations whose sole task would be to operate plants efficiently and safely.

Existing unresolved safety problems (such as thermal shock and the steam-generator tube failure in pressurized water reactors, station blackout, and failure of reactors to shut down automatically) must also be convincingly solved.

The design of new reactors must be simplified and incorporate more passive shut-down safety features. To achieve the benefits of standardization, no more than a few new power plant designs should be considered. The design of new plants should be complete and free of any unresolved safety issues before being considered for licensing. (In the past, U.S. nuclear power plant designs were sometimes no more than 12 to 20 percent complete when approved for construction by the Nuclear Regulatory Commission.) The quality of nuclear plant construction must also be improved. This may require new kinds of performance requirements for constructors.

There must also be tangible progress in solving the problems of storing radioactive wastes. The task of managing and disposing of nuclear wastes has been with us since the beginning of the nuclear age more than fifty years ago. It also has received comparatively little serious attention because most wastes were military in origin and because the problem was not considered to be of high priority. The history of wastes has been one of poor planning, inadequate management, and accidental releases of radioactive materials into the environment. It is not surprising that the public and potential host states have developed such a healthy skepticism of the federal government's ability to dispose of wastes in a responsible, safe manner.

The lessons of past mistakes in waste management are clear. To be successful the process of locating a repository — or other fuel cycle facilities — must be open and unrushed and must actively involve all the relevant players: state and local governments, citizen groups, academics, and anyone else with an interest. The federal government cannot override local concerns and objections. It must respond in an objective and responsible manner so as to instill public confidence. This is the biggest single obstacle to the solution of the waste problem.

Even if all of these requirements were met, the potential contribution of nuclear energy to solving the global energy-climate problem would be limited for several reasons. First, it is unlikely that any significant number of safer new reactors could be designed, approved, constructed, operated, and "debugged" in less than twenty years. This means that they would be unable to make a significant contribution to meeting the world's energy needs during the next twenty to forty years. Moreover, because of their inherent cost and complexity, nuclear plants are unlikely to be deployed in poor, developing countries. Such facilities demand a high level of sophisticated and expensive support to be safely constructed and operated, a condition unlikely to obtain in most of the developing world. And lastly, unless the world suddenly embraces peaceful solutions to its age-old ethnic and boundary problems, the prospect of nations using nuclear materials to clandestinely build atomic weapons will grow with nuclear plant deployment. For all of these reasons it would seem prudent not to count on nuclear power to rescue the world from the global threats posed by our existing energy system.

Solar and Hydrogen Options
for a Sustainable Energy Future

In the case of the solar technologies, by the nature of the diffuse resource upon which they depend, large collection areas will be required. Solar technologies do not use fuels but they are by no means cost free. Their use, therefore, will make most sense in an energy-frugal society.

We have seen that in the 19th century, the world was powered by renewable resources. Wind was used to power ships, pump water, and grind grain. Water wheels supplied the energy for manufacturing. Wood was the energy source for heat and, later, the energy source for the crude steam engines of the day. And animals provided the power for agriculture and much of transportation.

If the United States and other industrialized countries were to move back to renewable resources, the technologies would have to be far different from those of the past. The steam engines of the last century converted at best a few percent of the energy in wood into useful work. And trees capture less than 1 percent of the sunlight falling on them. Fireplaces are notoriously inefficient and in some cases lead to a net loss of energy by sucking cold air in from the outside. Nor is it clear that present forestry practices are sustainable over the long haul because of soil erosion and nutrient depletion.

The sun is the source of almost all of the energy on the earth. The exceptions are nuclear energy in the form of fission or fusion, and geothermal energy, basically the result of radioactive decay within the earth. In the United States, the land area of the lower-48 states intercepts about 47,000 quadrillion Btus of direct sunlight per year, about 600 times total U.S. primary energy use. Is it possible to capture any significant fraction of this sunlight? Is there any realistic prospect of efficiently harnessing solar energy to meet global energy needs? This latter question has been addressed for the United States — the world's largest energy consumer — and the answer is a clear yes. Consider just the use of photovoltaic cells. At a solar collection efficiency of 15 percent, readily achievable using present photovoltaic cells, it would take significantly less than 1 percent of the land area of the lower-48 states to meet all of its energy needs. This should be compared with the 20 percent of U.S. lands devoted to croplands, or the 31 percent to pastures. Moreover, many of the solar cells could be placed on the walls and roofs of existing structures, reducing the area of needed land. This seems hardly an unduly large commitment of land, considering the benefits.

Solar energy can also be captured indirectly. Sunlight is absorbed and dissipated in many ways as it passes through the earth's atmosphere to the surface. Some of it strikes lakes or the oceans and evaporates water. This results in precipitation and the energy of falling water can be captured via hydroelectric dams. More sunlight falls on the tropics than on the polar regions. This difference powers the earth's weather machine and leads to winds. Winds have long been used to power ships and turn the blades of windmills. Some sunlight strikes plants and is stored through photosynthesis. From this we obtain food and wood. Photosynthesis is very inefficient in capturing solar energy, and agriculture and forestry — as we now practice them — both have major environmental impacts in the form of soil erosion, nutrient depletion, and pesticide runoff.

For purposes of review, solar technologies can be broadly cataloged into one of three categories: electric technologies, including solar thermal power plants, solar ponds, wind turbines, photovoltaic cells, and hydroelectric dams; low-temperature thermal collectors that provide heat for domestic hot water, space heating, and industry (e.g. supplying hot water for car washes); and biofuels such as wood, urban and forestry wastes, and alcohol fuels.

Renewable energy sources already provide a significant amount of energy (Flavin et al., 1989; UCS, 1990). In the United States they account for about 9 percent of total energy supply, worth about $18 billion per year. The two big sources, worldwide, are biofuels and hydroelectric dams. (Whether these resources — "renewable" in the short term — are "sustainable" over the long haul is another matter.)

Currently, biofuels, mostly wood, supply about 3.5 quads of energy, about 4 percent of U.S. energy supply. Over six million homes burn wood as their principal heating fuel, over 7 percent of all homes. Industry, though, is the largest wood consumer. The paper and pulp industry burns wood scraps to provide heat and electricity to run its operations. Wood and other biofuels are also used to generate a small amount of electricity by utilities. All told, there are about 5000 MW of biomass fueled generating capacity in the United States.

There seems to be much enthusiasm for wood burning, but in the author's view the burning of biomass is, at best, an enterprise of uncertain value. Some energy analysts are proposing vast energy plantations of fast-growing trees to provide liquid or gaseous fuels to power gas turbines or supply fuels for transportation. And some propose using grains or other energy crops to provide ethanol as a transportation fuel. All are harnessing biofuels the environmental impacts of which are significant: wind and water erosion of soils, accelerated water runoff, air pollution, nutrient loss, and the disruption of wildlife.

The first U.S. hydroelectric dam was built at Niagara Falls in 1878. Hydrodams in 1987 accounted for about 71,000 megawatts of capacity, the equivalent of 71 large power plants. These dams normally provide 10 to 14 percent of U.S. electricity, or about 3 percent of total energy supply, depending on year-to-year rainfall patterns. Canada obtains about 30 percent of its total energy supply from hydrodams. Norway, about 70 percent. Worldwide, in 1988, hydroelectric dams accounted for about 7 percent of total world commercial energy supply.

The Federal Energy Regulatory Commission, which has jurisdiction over the licensing of these facilities, estimates that the hydro capacity of the United States could be doubled to a total of some 147,000 MW. This does not take into account, though, the many rivers that are protected for recreational purposes. A fifty percent expansion is more likely possible. But uncertainties about possible changes in precipitation patterns must be taken into account in future hydro development.

Less of a problem would be posed by small hydro dams, less than 30 MW. DOE estimates that there could be 10,000 MW of small hydro obtainable from existing small dams. The environmental impacts of small hydro are considerably less than those of big dams. Large dams have drowned out some of the most beautiful stretches of American rivers and have flooded agricultural lands, forests, and areas of historical and geological values. Dams disrupt the normal flooding and transfer of nutrients to agricultural lands downstream and to river deltas. Instead, nutrients and sediment accumulate in the reservoirs and eventually fill them up. For these reasons, large dams cannot be considered sustainable sources of energy over the long term.

A very successful form of solar electric power plant has been developed and built and is operated by Luz, International, a company founded in 1979 and located in Los Angeles. A series of 30- and 80-megawatt Solar Energy Generating Systems (SEGS) have been built in California's Mojave desert to help meet utilities' peaking needs. More plants are in the planning stages and a total of 600 megawatts are expected to be in service by 1994. Early units were small in size because of federal regulatory restrictions. Larger units are producing electricity at costs comparable to new fossil fueled power plants.

Wind machines are one of the most attractive and economical renewable sources of electricity. Wind technology is improving constantly and machines can be installed quickly, a single turbine in a day, an entire wind farm or wind plant in a year. There are now about 17,000 machines in operation in the United States, most of them in California. In California, wind machines with a capacity of over 1400 MW generated over 2.5 billion kWh in 1990, about the annual residential needs of a city of the size of San Francisco, or more than 1 percent of California's present total electrical use. In Denmark there are about 2000 wind machines operating and they meet 1 percent of Denmark's needs. Because of dropping oil prices and withdrawal of state and federal tax credits the installation of wind machines has slowed recently though it is expected to pick up soon.

There are enough good windy sites in California to meet about 20 percent of existing electricity demand. Advanced wind machines could supply energy to the United States in amounts far in excess of the nation's total present energy demand. The best sites are in the Great Plains and include North and South Dakota, Kansas, and Montana. Twelve states in the central portion of the United States could produce more than three times the nation's 1987 electrical energy consumption (Elliott et al., 1990).

The cost of electricity from wind machines has been dropping with improved designs and increased reliability. According to the Department of Energy, wind machines in the 1990s will generate power at 5-7 cents per kWh at good sites, which is lower than either nuclear or coal. Similar economics hold in Denmark where wind machines are generating power at 5 to 8 cents per kWh.

Photovoltaic cells are in many ways the most attractive solar energy source. They have no moving parts, can be quickly installed in large or small modules, and can be used anywhere there is sunlight. Solar cells need little maintenance, have little environmental impact beyond those of dedicating space to their use, and offer the long-term prospect for mass production and application in most parts of the world.

Great strides have been taken over the past few years in decreasing the costs of photovoltaic cells, increasing efficiency, and extending lifetimes. Lifetimes have been extended to 20 years, efficiencies have been improved from 9.8 percent to about 12 percent, and costs have dropped from $1140 per square meter to $480. Many new materials are being tested to reduce costs and automate manufacturing. Nonetheless, electricity costs are still high — about $.25 to $.30 per kWh — and widespread deployment will have to await significant further reductions.

There are other solar technologies that can provide significant amounts of energy. Solar domestic hot water heating is one. In these systems, so-called flat plate collectors are used to heat water, air, or some other fluid and the heat is transferred to a hot water tank. Hot water heaters make more sense economically than do residential central heating systems which may be needed for only a few months of the year. Tens of thousands of domestic hot water systems were installed in the United States in the late 1970s and early 1980s, largely in response to federal and state tax credits. Many were untried systems and unfortunately were not reliable. As a result the entire industry suffered. With the expiration of the 40 percent federal tax credit the solar thermal industry for hot water and active space heating essentially disappeared. Solar hot water systems could play an important role in the nation's energy future if gas and electric utilities were to take the lead in their installation. Utilities have the capital and could quickly develop the expertise to install, lease, and service solar collectors. Their doing so would eliminate essentially all of the economic and institutional barriers to widespread use of these environmentally attractive energy systems.

Solar ponds are shallow natural or man-made lakes in which there is dense salt water at the bottom. Sunlight penetrates the fresh water on top and heats the bottom layer which is denser. The bottom water can reach almost boiling and can be used to generate electricity with a low-temperature turbine or supply hot water for industrial applications. Israel started research on solar ponds in 1958 and experiments world wide showed that such ponds work. A solar pond in Ohio (1/2 acre) has been heating a municipal swimming pool since 1978. A pond in Texas has supplied electric power (100 kW), hot water, and fresh water. In 1979, Israel built a 1 1/2 acre pond that generated 200 kW of power. Israelis have also built a 62 acre pond near the Dead Sea that produced up to 5 MW at peak periods. The use of ponds is being pursued in many countries including Mexico, Australia, India, Italy, Argentina, Japan, and Portugal.

The Need for Energy Storage

Renewable energy sources are intermittent and therefore require energy storage technology for wide-spread use. Even if nuclear energy were to be widely deployed, energy storage technologies would be needed to support transportation, now almost totally reliant on oil. In all circumstances, therefore, the economies of the future will depend heavily on energy storage technologies.

Energy storage can take many forms. Pumped hydro, compressed air, batteries, and hydrogen are all candidates for wide-spread use in the next century. Hydrogen, a leading candidates as an "energy carrier" of the twenty first century, does not occur, by itself, in significant amounts in nature. Presently it is made from natural gas and is used in large amounts in the petroleum industry, in refineries, in making ammonia, and as a fuel in spacecraft. In many ways hydrogen is ideal as a fuel. It contains no carbon and so its burning results in neither carbon monoxide nor hydrocarbons. If it were produced from water using non-fossil energy sources it would not contribute to global warming.

Hydrogen can be obtained through the electrolysis of water at efficiencies of about 80 percent. To displace all of the oil used in the United States using photovoltaic cells and electrolysis would require an area of 24,000 square miles, a square 155 miles on a side (Ogden and Williams, 1989: 44).

Hydrogen can be stored as a cryogenic liquid (-422 degrees F), as a compressed gas, or in special storage tanks. If the gas is stored as a liquid it will slowly boil away a little each day, posing special safety problems if the container is in a closed space, like a garage. Hydrogen is explosive over very wide limits.

Hydrogen can be converted into electricity using fuel cells, the current means for providing electricity on manned spacecraft. Fuel cells resemble batteries more than they do engines: with no moving parts, they consume hydrogen and oxygen and produce electric power and water. They have conversion efficiencies of about 65 percent and would be an ideal means for burning hydrogen in vehicles because they would greatly increase vehicle efficiency and totally eliminate air pollution.

Meeting the Energy Challenge

In 1989 the industrialized world relied on fossil fuels to meet almost 90 percent of its energy needs. Present patterns of fossil energy supply have evolved over the past century as the result of many forces. Shortages of wood, and the development of coke and steam engines were essential elements in the first energy transition, to coal, in the latter half of the nineteenth century. Shortages of illuminating fuel in turn provided the initial impetus for oil exploration. Later, as the result of technological developments, petroleum products displaced coal in heating buildings and in transportation; convenience and cleanliness were important factors in the substitution of oil for coal. The development of modern pipeline technology enabled the widespread use of natural gas in buildings, industry, and power generation.

The twenty-first century will witness a third energy transition, this time to non-fossil energy sources. The move away from fossil fuels will be driven not by scarcity but by the urgent need to protect the earth's climate by reducing carbon dioxide emissions by 60 to 80 percent from current levels. Clearing the air of air pollution and reducing reliance on unstable suppliers of petroleum will be side benefits of changes that will be adopted primarily to curb global warming.

The industrialized countries are the world's largest consumers of fossil fuels. The OECD countries, alone, account for about half of global fossil fuel use. Yet, they cannot by themselves, change global energy patterns sufficiently to control greenhouse warming. International cooperation and agreements will be needed to reduce not only carbon dioxide emissions but those of other greenhouse gases such as methane and nitrous oxide. The long-term goal of these agreements must be fundamental — and comparatively rapid — reductions in global emissions in both developing and industrial countries.

For several reasons the industrialized nations have a special responsibility to help effect these changes. As the largest sources of energy-related carbon dioxide emissions they are a major part of the problem. And they have the wealth and the technological wherewithal to develop and use the alternative energy technologies that will be needed to reduce greenhouse gas emissions. The industrialized countries will also have to make available to developing countries the means to manufacture the renewable and high-efficiency technologies to meet their own growing needs. For their part, developing countries will have to redouble their efforts to stabilize their populations as well as move to the efficient, emissionless technologies of the 21st century.

As for the United States, the essential goals of a long-term national energy strategy are clear. It must simultaneously provide for meeting the nation's energy needs while reducing the threats of greenhouse warming, air pollution, and dependency on unreliable energy suppliers. The two primary elements of such a strategy are also clear. The nation must improve its overall energy efficiency, and support an accelerated transition to non-fossil energy sources along with the storage technologies to support their widespread use.

Effecting this transition will be difficult. There are institutional barriers to improved national efficiency and fossil fuel prices are still comparatively low compared with those of renewable sources. The greatest challenge will be to act before the symptoms overwhelm us. Doing so will require a willingness to adjust the way we live and to assume burdens now that will ultimately benefit our children later. It is already too late to avoid some degree of climate change or to undo the damage air pollution has caused. But it is not too late to contain those damages or to send the heirs to this planet the message that our was a generation that cared about how we lived in the world and how we left it for others.

References

Abrahamson, D. E. (ed.). 1989. *The Challenge of Global Warming*. Washington, D.C.: Island Press.

ALA (American Lung Association). 1989. *Health Effects of Ambient Air Pollution*. New York, NY: American Lung Association.

CCE (California Council for Environmental and Economic Balance). 1990. *Alternative Motor Vehicle Fuels to Improve Air Quality*. San Francisco, CA: California Council for Environmental and Economic Balance.

Cook, E. 1971. "The Flow of Energy in an Industrial Society." *Scientific American* (September): 135-144.

Elliott, D. L. et al. 1990. *U.S. Areal Wind Resource Estimates Considering Environmental and Land-Use Exclusions*. Paper presented at the American Wind Energy Association's (Washington, D.C.) 1990 Conference, September 28, 1990.

EPA (U.S. Environmental Protection Agency). 1989. *The Potential Effects of Global Climate Change on the United States*. Washington D.C.: U.S. Government Printing Office.

Flavin, Christopher et al. 1989. *Sustainable Energy*. Washington, D.C.: Renew America, Inc.

Foley, Gerald. 1987. *The Energy Question*. New York, NY: Viking Penguin, Inc.

Gribbin, John. 1990. *The Hothouse Earth*. London: Bantam Press.

Hansen, J. et al. 1988. "Prediction of Near-Term Climate Evolution: What Can We Tell Decision-Makers Now?" Pp. 35-47 in *Preparing for Climate Change*. Rockville, MD: Government Institutes, Inc.

Hansen, Kent et al. 1989. "Making Nuclear Power Work: Lessons from Around the World." *Technology Review* 30/40 (February/March).

Harrison, G. R. 1968. *The Conquest of Energy*. New York, NY: William Morrow and Company, Inc.

IPCC (International Panel on Climate Change), World Meteorological Organization/United Nations Environment Programme. 1990. *Climate Change: The IPCC Scientific Assessment*. New York, NY: Cambridge University Press.

Landsberg, H. H. and S. H. Schurr. 1968. *Energy in the United States: Sources, Uses, and Policy Issues*. New York, NY: Random House.

Lovins, Amory B. and L. Hunter Lovins. 1990. "Least-Cost Climatic Stabilization." Essay Submitted to the Mitchell Prize Competition. Old Snowmass, CO: Rocky Mountain Institute.

MacKenzie, James J. 1990. *Reducing U.S. Reliance on Imported Oil: An Assessment of Alternative Transportation Fuels*. Washington, D.C.: World Resources Institute.

_____. 1989. *Breathing Easier: Taking Action on Climate Change, Air Pollution, and Energy Insecurity*. Washington, D.C.: World Resources Institute.

MacKenzie, James J. and Michael P. Walsh. 1990. *Driving Forces: Motor Vehicle Trends and their Implications for Global Warming, Energy Strategies, and Transportation Planning*. Washington, D.C.: World Resources Institute.

MacKenzie, James J. and Mohamed T. El-Ashry. 1989. *Air Pollution's Toll on Forests and Crops*. New Haven, CT: Yale University Press.

Hansen, Kent et al. 1989. "Making Nuclear Power Work: Lessons from Around the World." *Technology Review* (Feb./March): 30-40.

Ogden, Joan M. and Robert H. Williams. 1989. *Solar Hydrogen: Moving Beyond Fossil Fuels.* Washington, D.C.: World Resources Institute.

ORNL, the Carbon Dioxide Information Analysis Center. 1990. *Trends '90, A Compendium of Data on Global Change.* Oak Ridge, TN: Oak Ridge National Laboratory.

OTA (U.S. Office of Technology Assessment). 1990. *Replacing Gasoline, Alternative Fuels for Light-Duty Vehicles.* OTA-E-364. Washington, D.C.: U.S. Government Printing Office.

Parker, Geoffrey (ed.). 1986. *The World: An Illustrated History.* New York, NY: Harper and Row.

Reddy A. K. N. and J. Goldemberg. 1990. "Energy for the Developing World." *Scientific American* (September): 63-72.

Schurr, S. H. et al. 1960. *Energy in the American Economy, 1850-1975.* Baltimore, MD: The Johns Hopkins Press.

Tomlinson, G. H. 1990. *Effects of Acid Deposition on the Forests of Europe and North America.* Boca Raton, FL: CRC Press.

UCS (Union of Concerned Scientists). 1990. *Cool Energy: The Renewable Solution to Global Warming.* Cambridge, MA: Union of Concerned Scientists.

Williams, Robert H. 1990. "Low-Cost Strategies for Coping with CO_2 Emission Limits." *The Energy Journal* 11/3: 35-59.

WRI (World Resources Institute). 1990. *World Resources, 1990-91.* New York, NY: Oxford University Press.

PART II

Historical Analysis

Chapter 2

The Neglected Challenge:
Energy, Economic Growth and
Environmental Protection in the
Industrial History of the U.S.

Martin V. Melosi

The industrialization of the United States during the nineteenth and early-twentieth centuries intensified the impact of energy use on the environment. The transition from a wood-based
economy to one dependent on fossil fuels resulted in intense air,
water and land pollution through extraction and burning of coal
(and later petroleum). The newly emerging economic order also
led to the concentration of factories and workers in urban areas which exacerbated environmental problems caused by the exploitation of fossil fuels. While most of the environmental problems were local in origin and impact in these early years, they
became chronic in every sector of the United States touched directly or indirectly by industrialization.

Current environmental threats from acid rain, global warming,
and hazardous waste originated in this era. At the same time,
the first major efforts to seek remedies for the array of industri-
ally induced pollutants also can be traced to the nineteenth and

Author's Note: The author would like to acknowledge the financial support
of the National Endowment for the Humanities and The Energy Laboratory
at the University of Houston in the preparation of this chapter.

early-twentieth centuries. The debate over economic progress versus environmental protection — so much a part of modern political
and social rhetoric — is but the most recent phase of a controversy more than 100 years old. Indeed, the discussion that follows
is meant to make explicit the importance of recognizing the historical context of industrial experience as a first step in addressing
politically the environmental problems and threats of our time.

Industrialization in the United States

Starting in the Middle Atlantic and North Central states, several factors contributed to the rise of large-scale industrialization.
New machinery replaced hand tools and muscle power in the fab-
rication of goods, and the harnessing of steam power allowed production to be centered in large urban-based factories. Mechanization undercut the need for workers with strong backs but required
a large labor force with specialized skills or, at least, the agility to
operate equipment. Migration from rural America and immigration from southern and eastern Europe helped provide this labor
force. Technological achievements, ranging from telegraph equipment to interchangeable machine parts, encouraged the expansion
and concentration of manufacturing. An organizational revolution
brought about better coordination between management and production functions in various business enterprises and encouraged
the formation of large, integrated companies, which exploited regional as well as national markets. In addition, state and federal governments actively promoted industrial development. And
westward expansion provided staple crops for export and gold and
silver for increasing the money supply (Klein and Kantor, 1976:
4-6; Russel, 1964: 186-199).

While agriculture was responsible for the largest single share
of production income before the Civil War, the growth and importance of manufacturing rose rapidly during the decades that followed. There were 140,000 industrial establishments in the United
States in 1859 — many of them hand or neighborhood industries.
Just forty years later, there were 207,000 — excluding hand and
neighborhood industries. In the 1880s, the value added to goods

by manufacturing and processing exceeded the value of agricultural products for the first time. About 1890, the United States surpassed Great Britain in industrial output, and by the turn of the century it was the world's leading manufacturing nation (Degler, 1967: 42-43; Russel, 1964: 338).

From Wood and Waterpower to Fossil Fuels

The transition from wood and waterpower to fossil fuels accelerated the industrialization process by the late-nineteenth century, and by doing so helped to transform the United States into a modern nation. The transition also meant the utilization of massive quantities of natural resources, and contributed significantly to the deterioration of the physical environment (Melosi, 1985: 17-18).

Fuelwood has the longest history of any energy source in the United States. Europeans marveled at the forests in America, since their own landscape had been denuded by centuries of intense cutting. Important in heating and cooking, wood also played an important role in the development of locomotives and steamboats, in the growth of a charcoal-fired iron industry, and in the emergence of stationary steam engines (Hindle, 1975: 3-5, 10-12). The development of motive steam power would have been delayed without abundant and accessible wood supplies and iron production (Taylor, 1951: 56-73; Cole, 1970: 355-356; Burlingame, 1946: 193-214; Petulla, 1977: 102-103, 122-124).

Waterpower was also an important energy source for some industrial uses throughout the nineteenth century. "Although the basic elements remained much the same...," historian Louis Hunter stated, "the scale, complexity, and refinement of details in design and operation found in such major hydropower installations as those of the New England textile centers bore slight resemblance to the water mills in which they had their origins." The importance of waterpower to burgeoning industry is no better illustrated than with the Merrimack River, which runs 110 miles through New Hampshire and Massachusetts. The "hardest working river in the world" provided approximately 80,000 horsepower to 900 mills and factories in 1880. The dramatic shift of manufacturing to major urban areas undercut the importance of waterpower, but its earlier vitality and that of wood suggests the undeniable importance of renewable energy sources throughout much of the nineteenth century (Hunter, 1979: 159-169, 181-184, 188).

Coal, however, soon became the preferred fuel of the Industrial Revolution. The dominance of fossil fuels was due less to the depletion of wood or waterpower sources than to the ability of coal — and later petroleum — to adapt more successfully to the demands of mechanization than the more territorially bound and less versatile renewable resources. While wood and waterpower maintained a portion of the industrial and domestic energy markets, the urban-based industrial economy, the expanding national railroad network, and the increasingly concentrated population came to rely more completely on coal.

Actual dependence took many years, but after certain barriers were overcome coal use grew steadily in importance. Business historian Alfred Chandler contended that anthracite — hard coal — from eastern Pennsylvania provided the basic fuel used for power and heat in the urban factories at mid-century. The availability of anthracite, advances in steam power, and new supplies of iron led to growth in several industries. While the factory system was essential to industrialization, "Why did factories" he queried, "which had become significant in British manufacturing by the end of the eighteenth century, not become a major form of production, except in the textile industry, in the United States until the 1840s?" Chandler concluded that the availability of more and better iron through the use of coal, in combination with the increasing use of steam power, changed the very nature of manufacturing in the 1830s. Early textile mills, powered by water and equipped with machinery constructed of wood and leather belting, were replaced by factories powered by steam, equipped with metal machinery, and located in major cities (Chandler, 1972: 141-181).

Changes in iron production provide only a partial answer to the dependence on coal. The initial use of American anthracite on a large scale originated with a major fuel crisis in Philadelphia during the War of 1812. Although residents in the anthracite region of Pennsylvania had used local hard coal before the war, Philadelphians relied on bituminous — or soft coal — from Virginia and Great Britain. The British blockade reduced supplies of trans-Atlantic coal, and forced consumers to seek out merchants who now willingly shipped coal from the anthracite region to Philadelphia and eventually other East Coast cities (Powell, 1980: 5-10).

The rise of bituminous coal as an industrial fuel soon surpassed anthracite. Soft coal became popular because of its versatility, high heat content, and relative compactness, and also because of the wide distribution of its deposits. (Bituminous was mined in at least 22 states.) The use of the Kelly-Bessemer process in the 1860s and the later adoption of the Siemens-Martin (or Open Hearth) process after about 1900, made bituminous coal a necessary ingredient in both steel and iron production. By World War I, sales of bituminous outpaced anthracite by about 450 percent (Kirkland, 1969: 302-304; Petulla, 1977: 178-180).

Coal in general achieved dominance because it was adaptable to more than industrial needs. By the 1830s, anthracite produced steam for factory machinery as well as steamboats and locomotives. The railroads, especially, helped to make coal preeminent among fuels because it became the railroads' primary source of revenue tonnage (Tarr and Koons, 1982: 72). In addition, coal invaded the domestic heating and lighting markets as early as the 1820s (Binder, 1958: 83-92).

At its peak in 1920, more than 658 million tons of coal were mined in the United States. Consumption increased seventy-seven times between 1850 and 1918. In fact, the growth of coal consumption outstripped energy consumption as a whole through the early-twentieth century. In the 1910s, coal represented more than 75 percent of the total energy consumption in the country, and exports exceeded 929,000 tons per year (Schurr and Netschert, 1960: 66-74).

The petroleum industry — the heir the energy market by the mid-twentieth century — was born in the age of coal. Like its fossil fuel counterpart, petroleum began as a specialized form of energy — first emerging as an important source of artificial light in the late-nineteenth century, then as a superior lubricant soon thereafter, and finally as the leading transportation fuel in the early-twentieth century.

The oil industry had its roots in the heart of Pennsylvania coal country. But its most dramatic impact grew out of the oil strikes in the Southwest and West at the turn of the century. The seemingly endless supplies of oil undercut the economic dominance of the Northeast and Midwest, as modernization and mechanization crossed the Mississippi River.

Until World War I, rise in demand for oil did not seriously threaten the dominant position of coal as the nation's leading energy source. In 1915, coal represented 74.8 percent of total aggregate consumption; oil represented only 7.9 percent. Yet the importance of oil grew steadily. Local experimentation with oil provided the necessary impetus for acquiring a much larger market and led to improved methods of transportation, efficient conversion of coal-burning equipment, and more sophisticated marketing techniques. While electricity eliminated the kerosene market in the twentieth century, the automobile turned petroleum refining toward gasoline. Since total energy consumption more than doubled between 1900 and 1920, oil became significant in absolute terms, if not as a percentage of overall consumption.

Building on its regional base, oil as fuel had some long-term advantages in its competition with coal. Foremost was price — oil was a bargain at less than $1.00 a barrel. Even when prices rose, the relatively low cost of equipment conversion and shipping gave oil an advantage over the more cumbersome coal. Furthermore, compared to the fragmented, financially weak, labor-intensive coal industry, the well-financed and effectively managed major oil companies were efficient forms of business enterprise. By the 1920s, the United States began to pass into a new energy era (Melosi, 1985: 35-50).

Energy Use and Pollution in the Industrial Age

Growing competition between coal and petroleum speaks profoundly to the vast energy abundance of the nation. Competing for markets took precedence over conserving resources; unrestrained economic growth was the credo of the day. But a concern about the environmental cost of energy development and use was ignored or relegated to a much lower priority than the desire for greater production. The concept of "environmental cost," as a consequence of doing business, did not find its way onto the balance sheet of companies in the nineteenth and early-twentieth centuries.

The development and use of any energy source is, by its very nature, environmentally intensive. The vast exploitation of wood as a fuel over the years led to deforestation and accompanying erosion in several parts of the country. The mining of anthracite scarred northeastern Pennsylvania. Many citizens in the region expressed concern about the effects of hard coal fires upon health. An irate New Yorker called for the abolition of anthracite furnaces because they "will hourly destroy the health of our women and children" (Binder, 1958: 96-97).

The increased use of bituminous coal raised great cause for concern because its dense, highly toxic smoke was a more serious threat than smoke from wood, anthracite or coal-gas. Unlike modern air pollution, coal smoke was more local in impact. From the 1870s through World War I, however, soft coal contributed significantly to pollution problems in many industrial cities — encroaching well beyond the city limits in some cases. It was most severe in areas where bituminous was a primary fuel for industry, transportation, and domestic purposes, and where temperature inversions were common. Particularly hard hit were Pittsburgh, Cincinnati, St. Louis, and Chicago.

The smoke problem was less significant in cities like New York, Boston, and Philadelphia, which relied on anthracite (or San Francisco which utilized natural gas). When anthracite was unavailable, however, cities like New York turned to bituminous. The Edison Company, which generated electricity for the city, periodically used soft coal to fire its boilers and was cited repeatedly by smoke inspectors. In order to escape the citations, the company placed scouts on the roof to warn the engineers to stop feeding coal into the furnaces when inspectors were photographing the plant (Melosi, 1985: 32).

Outside the city limits of several industrial communities, beehive ovens for producing coke belched out hydrocarbons, ash and waste heat, which killed foliage, trees and crops, and left layers of dust and ash everywhere (Tarr, 1991: 6-7). Steam locomotives sprayed vast amounts of dense smoke and cinders all along their routes. Industrial cities with dense smoke originating from stationary burners were often railroad centers as well, which exacerbated an already critical problem of air quality. Railroad coal use accounted for between 20 and 50 percent of the smoke in Chicago and Pittsburgh (Tarr and Koons, 1982: 73, 77).

The debilitating effects of smoke became quite obvious by the 1890s. Methods of burning coal were so primitive that great amounts of heat and various pollutants, especially sulfur, ash and dust went up the smokestacks and chimneys. Newspapers reported chronic "Londoners" — a combination of smoke and fog — in several cities, which led to work stoppages, the shortening of the school day, and myriad accidents. Although there were few scientific measures for smoke pollution, the assault on the senses were enough to set off protests. Citizens in Pittsburgh and St. Louis complained about frequent nasal, throat, and bronchial problems. Some observers speculated that fatalities from pneumonia, diphtheria, typhoid, and tuberculosis could be traced to smoke pollution, as could psychological trauma. The sooty walls of buildings, corroding marble statues, ash flakes on hanging laundry, and excessive grime on light-colored clothes were further testaments of the billowing black clouds (Grinder, 1980: 83-103).

By comparison, conservation and pollution problems in the oil industry rarely received the attention that smoke garnered. Part of the reason was that most of the oil fields were at a distance from major urban areas. However, the euphoria over striking oil in the mid-nineteenth century was not matched by foresight and restraint in producing and marketing it, resulting in substantial waste and serious spills.

The abundance of "black gold" appeared to be a permanent blessing; conservation was for the overly cautious. Waste and over-production was due to several factors: poor drilling and storing techniques, natural disasters, the competitive market, simple disregard, and greed. Some of the trial-and-error methods of discovery took effective conservation out of the hands of the oilmen, but others did not. In almost all cases, the ends seemed to justify the means.

Many of the problems oilmen encountered in fields across the continent were first experienced in Pennsylvania. While drilling practices steadily improved, storage of oil rarely was provided for until after a strike, and even then was usually inadequate. Part of the reason was that the search for oil was so expensive and so unscientific that it was impossible to finance storage facilities before the certainty of a strike. Seepage from wells was common because reliable casings were not employed. Earthen pits or wooden tanks were used to store oil, which resulted in substantial loss from evaporation or calamities such as fire. In June, 1892, Oil City experienced one of the worst fire and flood disasters in petroleum history. A dam burst on Oil Creek, knocking over a huge tank of naphtha which covered the water and filled the air with flammable gas. A spark from a passing train ignited the fumes, engulfing tanks of crude in flames. About 300 people were killed in the conflagration.

Inefficient transportation contributed to the substantial loss of oil. Poorly constructed barrels carted over bumpy roads led to spillage, and barge accidents on pond freshets were frequent. Less noticeable problems, such as infiltration of water into oil strata, plagued the Pennsylvania fields. A Local newspaper noted in 1861 that "So much oil is produced it is impossible to care for it, and thousands of barrels are running into the creek; the surface of the river is covered with oil for miles below Franklin" (Ise, 1926: 25).

The pattern of waste and the disregard for conservation measures were remarkably similar at Spindletop, Texas (struck in 1901), despite the years of experience in drilling for oil in other locations. Great fires periodically spread across the fields, such as one which burned 62 derricks and sent flames 1,000 feet into the air. Safety measures were eventually employed, but only after heavy losses.

The general squandering of oil at Spindletop was legendary. In 1902, the *Oil Investors' Journal* estimated that 10 million barrels had been wasted since the first strike. To impress investors, oil promoters opened up the wells, sending gushers of 125 feet into the air. In September 1901, 12 gushers were opened simultaneously for the benefit of 15,000 on-lookers. Gamblers placed bets on which well would gush the highest. In little time, the Spindletop field was ruined by such flagrant disregard.

Overproduction and squandering of supplies were not due simply to shortsightedness or recreational wastefulness; they were linked to the competitive economic system of the day. Several geologists in the 1870s warned about the dangers of extracting oil too rapidly, but few oilmen heeded the warnings. The traditional rights of landowners to exploit their real property encouraged immediate drilling. Unless a producer pumped as much of the resource as he was able, competitors could drain the oil on adjacent property.

The so-called "Rule of Capture" dominated the production of oil until the 1930s. It stated that those who owned the surface property over a common pool could take and keep as much oil and gas as possible — regardless of the drainage from adjoining property. However, it encouraged rampant drilling and pumping, which in turn led to severe overproduction (Melosi, 1985: 47-49).

Drilling and refining created other environmental problems by polluting the land, air, and water where oil was taken from the ground and where it was processed for marketing. This "localized pollution" — especially in refining areas such as Beaumont-Port Arthur, Texas — was serious, but it rarely attracted much attention from oil companies or state governments before World War I. In the fields, drain-offs of crude soaked the ground adjacent to the wells. Rapid pumping of oil introduced salt water into the underground pools as well as in the local water supply. In the pre-automobile days, oil even contributed to air pollution. Several days after the original well blew at Spindletop, a thick, yellow fog laden with sulfur engulfed the houses of Beaumont and continued to do so periodically until production slowed down. As historian Joseph Pratt argued, "At least as much oil probably found its way into the region's ground water and air in this period as found its way to market" (Pratt, 1978: 4).

Early refineries were built with little regard for environmental concerns. Often unrecovered petroleum was simply discarded in the most convenient location; open (sulfurous) flames from burning crude were noticeable everywhere. Floods along the coastal region washed oil into the rivers, streams, lakes, and the Gulf of Mexico.

With immediate profits in mind and industrial growth virtually a religion during this period, pollution control was a luxury at best. As with coal, the equation of oil with progress precluded serious attempts to understand, let alone address, its various environmental impacts. Ironically, one of the few conscious efforts at dealing with waste was the burning off of billions of cubic feet of natural gas — then considered a useless by-product of drilling for oil (Melosi, 1985: 49-50).

Factories as Polluters

The use of fossil fuels was not the only source of pollution in the burgeoning industrial age. The transformation of the economy brought with it a reshaping of the infrastructure in which goods were produced and consumed. The need for efficiency and

economies of scale in the production phase led to the development
of large and complex factories. Because of their size, operational
practices, and concentration near urban populations, modern factories — especially in the textile, chemical, and iron and steel
industries — became major sources of pollution. They were often
constructed near or on rivers, lakes and bays, since large quantities
of water were needed to supply steam boilers or for various production processes. Waterways also provided the easiest and least
expensive means of disposing of soluble or suspendable wastes such
as phenol, benzene, toluene, arsenic, and naphtha (Melosi, 1988:
753-761).

Studies of the impact of factories upon the environment suggest that in 1900, 40 percent of the pollution load on American
rivers was industrial in origin. (By 1968 that figure had increased
to 80 percent (Armstrong, 1976: 410).) The "death" of New Jersey's Passaic River in the late-nineteenth century was a classic
illustration of how factories defiled their surroundings. Before it
became badly polluted, the Passaic was a major recreational area
and also the center of a thriving commercial fishing industry. As
industrialization of the region accelerated after the Civil War, the
volume of sewage and industrial waste that poured into the river
forced the city of Newark to abandon the Passaic as a water supply. Pollution also ruined commercial fishing, and soon homes
along the waterway disappeared. During hot weather the river
emitted such a stench that many factories were forced to close
(Galishoff, 1975: 54-55).

The presence of a factory most often meant the deterioration of
physical surroundings. Factories usually employed the simplest —
if not the most sanitary — disposal methods for rubbish, garbage,
slag, ashes, and scrap metals. Meat packing, which began on farms
or in small rural slaughterhouses, concentrated in such cities as
Chicago and St. Louis, engulfing adjacent areas with foul smells
and simply dumping animal wastes on vacant lots. Tanneries contributed directly to water pollution by washing hides in available
water sources (Galishoff, 1975: 4-5).

Yet factories also contributed an even more insidious, if not so obvious, form of pollution — noise. Many factories produced excessively high noise levels from machinery that was inadequately lubricated or not equipped with mufflers or noise arresters. These high noise levels annoyed nearby residents, but more importantly impaired the hearing of employees. In time, businessmen began to realize that some loud factory noises were caused by mechanical problems and sought technical solutions. But more often they tolerated the din since profit came from production, not conservation (Smilor, 1977: 28-29).

The Industrial City and Population Growth

Human concentration in the major cities — encouraged by industrialization and related economic activity — contributed significantly to the pollution problems of the era, especially when city services lagged behind growth. Between 1850 and 1920, the world population increased 55 percent, while the population of the United States grew 357 percent. In 1850 the total population of the United States was approximately 23 million; by 1920 it was 106 million — 51 percent urban-based. Also by 1920, the number of urban areas increased from 392 to 2,722, and the number of cities with a population of 50,000 or more rose from 16 to 144 (Klein and Kantor, 1976: 69-71).

The rapid rise in the population was due primarily to spectacular increases in immigration and rural-to-urban migration. During these years almost 32 million people came to the United States largely from eastern and southern Europe. By 1910, 41 percent of all urbanites in the nation were foreign-born, and approximately 80 percent of the new immigrants settled in the Northeast. Migration from countryside to city was at least 15 million between 1880-1920. During those years, the proportion of the population living in rural America fell from 71.4 percent to 48.6 percent. One of the most obvious reasons for the urbanization of the American population was the dramatic shift of the labor force from agricultural to non-agricultural jobs. Between 1860 and 1900 the number of workers employed in manufacturing and construction quadrupled, while population increased less than 2.5 times (Dinnerstein and Reimers, 1975: 36-40; Klein and Kantor, 1976: 70-72).

Such population growth produced an incredible physical strain on most major cities. None suffered the repercussions more than the working class. Forced to live close to their place of employment, many workers found themselves crammed into the spreading slums in the central city. Neighborhood densities were staggering; the average block density in lower Manhattan increased from 157.5 persons in 1820 to 272.5 persons in 1850. New York City's Sanitary District "A" averaged 986.4 people to the acre for thirty-two acres in 1894 — or approximately 30,000 people in a space of five or six blocks. In comparison, Bombay, India — the next most crowded area in the world — had 759.7 people per acre (Brody, 1975: 133; Cochran and Miller, 1961: 264).

Such crowded conditions and limited city services offered fertile ground for health and sanitation problems. In one of the most widely publicized epidemics of its day, Memphis lost almost one-fifth of its population in 1873 to yellow fever — ostensibly originating in the slums. In New Orleans, typhoid was spread throughout the city by sewage that oozed from the unpaved streets. In "Murder Bay," not far from the White House in Washington, D.C., black families picked their dinners out of garbage cans and dumps. Mortality figures for the area were consistently twice as high as in white neighborhoods. Many workers had little choice but to live in the least desirable sections of the city, usually close to the factories where they worked or near marshy bogs and stagnant pools. Environmental services — water supply, sewerage, and refuse collection — often failed to keep up with demand. Smoke from wood-burning and coal-burning stoves and fireplaces fouled the air of the inner city, and the noise level in some areas was deafening (Melosi, 1986: 10-12).

Since the industrial city rose skyward at its core as well as expanding outward into the hinterland, not one but two distinct processes of growth contributed to its environmental problems. In the central city, the concentration of people, businesses and transit lines produced one pattern; rapid suburban sprawl produced another.

The pollution problems of the central city were much more obvious, and initially more serious, than those of the suburbs. City governments were ill-prepared to provide necessary services in the central city. Refuse accumulated in the streets faster than it could be collected in several neighborhoods, and a relatively primitive system of wastewater removal was in effect until the turn of the century. Sanitation systems, when introduced, often served the business districts and only the better residential areas. In many cases, sewage systems meant to eradicate effluents from the city proper, moved the wastes to nearby rivers and lakes, merely shifting the problem downstream (Tarr and McMichael, 1977: 47-61).

The technological advances that made possible the physical development of the central business district also contributed to pollution problems. The balloon frame, the steel girder, and the elevator made possible high-density building, which further strained meager city services and added to congestion problems. Advances in transportation — the omnibus, the horsecar, and electric streetcar — also exacerbated congestion and sometimes contributed directly to pollution — as in the case of horse manure. The wholesale uprooting of plants and trees to make way for future development reduced oxygen generation in the city's core and transformed the cities into "heat islands."

Outward expansion into the suburbs produced a variant to the environmental problems of the inner cities. The greatest cliche about suburbanization is that the middle class fled from the grimy inner cities to pristine suburbs where the urban blight could not engulf them. In reality, suburbs rarely escaped the pollution problems of the inner city. Early suburbs suffered because they often were too far removed from needed services; later they suffered from the proximity to the ubiquitous environmental problems radiating out from inner cities (Melosi, 1986: 14-18).

The Search for Remedies

While few contemporaries claimed that an environmental crisis was sweeping the country in the late-nineteenth and early-twentieth centuries, the confluence of air, water and land pollution in the era inspired a search for remedies. In many cases, environmental problems were treated as localized occurrences — linked to a specific polluter. But increasingly, especially in the case of energy use and water pollution, the source of the problem appeared to grow out of a larger set of circumstances, namely, the cost of industrialization. The primary dilemma was how to reconcile the vast economic benefits to the nation derived from industrial expansion with the threats to the health and well-being of the citizenry and the degradation of the natural environment.

To a large extent, the lines of this dilemma were not so clearly drawn. Few reliable tests existed to measure the extent of the pollution problems, with the possible exception of certain forms of water pollution. In the field of public health, the emergence of the bacteriological revolution in the 1880s offered the promise of successfully confronting epidemics. However, "contagionists" and "anti-contagionists" squabbled for several years over the proper ways to combat disease. Placing the various pollution problems in a larger environmental context was hampered by the lack of ecological or other natural science theory. And on a more mundane level, standards of environmental purity — or what actually constituted a liveable environment — had not been confronted, let alone determined.

Despite these limitations, and despite the significant economic achievements produced by industrialization, a search for remedies ensued. This took several forms: civic protests, education programs, court action, regulation and legislation. With some exceptions, the search for remedies primarily grew out of initiatives from environmental "consumers," that is, the receptors of the pollution or their agents (for example, government), rather than from "producers," i.e., the generators of the pollution. In the business community, there was no real dilemma for producers at this time;

pollution was an inevitable — and not completely preventable — consequence of economic growth. Without earnest cooperation from polluters or without the acceptance of "environmental cost" as a consequence of doing business, the achievements in pollution abatement and environmental regulation were most often in the setting of precedents rather than providing ultimate solutions.

Civic Protest

The earliest protests against pollution were responses to obvious irritations, such as bad-tasting water, billowing smoke, putrefying garbage, or noisy machinery. The concept of pollution as "nuisance" dominated these early complaints (and pre-date the industrial period). "Nuisance" was a popular contemporary term, which was applied arbitrarily to almost any recognizable environmental problem. Contemporary observers referred to the "smoke nuisance," the "garbage nuisance," the "hooting nuisance," and so forth. "The great majority of the dwellers in our cities have not, heretofore, taken any active personal interest in the sanitary condition of their respective towns," asserted sanitarian John S. Billings. "They may grumble occasionally when some nuisance is forced on their notice, but as a rule, they look on the city as a sort of hotel, with the details of the management of which they have no desire to become acquainted" (Billings, 1893: 304-305).

By the 1890s, however, sporadic protests against the irritations of a dirty city led to individual and group efforts to deal more forthrightly with smoke, sewage, garbage, and noise. Reform groups began to pursue changes in nuisance laws and city ordinances, to complain about industrial operations and municipal services, and to criticize public behavior and conduct.

As more was learned about the generation of pathogenic organisms and disease transmittal, the concept of "health hazard" replaced "nuisance" as a way to describe an environmental problem. Health hazards encompassed communicable diseases such as cholera, yellow fever, typhoid fever, and dysentery, but also included afflictions linked to a wider range of environmental factors, such as respiratory diseases associated with smoke pollution or emotional disorders attributed to high noise levels. The lack of medical sophistication throughout much of the nineteenth century sometimes produced unwarranted fears of fouls smells, miasmas, and water discoloration. But while environmental reformers sometimes exaggerated a potential threat, they at least faulted on the side of caution.

By the turn of the century, the concern for health expanded into a broader environmental perspective, indicating that reformers were beginning to see pollution not simply as an irritant but as an unwanted by-product of industrialization. Pollution was sometimes linked with wastefulness and inefficiency, but in such a way as to avoid the conclusion that industrial activity was intrinsically responsible for despoiling the environment. In many ways, reformers of the era were attempting to find ways to mitigate against the excesses of industrialization without abandoning its economic benefits — the ultimate dilemma of the time.

Some viewed pollution in more abstract terms: cleanliness was a sign of civilization, pollution was barbarity. Excessive noise, E.L. Godkin asserted, "invades the house like a troop of savages on a raid, and respects neither age nor sex" (Smilor, 1977: 26). Another observer noted that "there is no more significant distinction between ancient and modern cities than their respective attitude towards the evils of [the garbage problem]" (Melosi, 1973: 623).

Attitudes were changing, but equally important was that environmental issues was being incorporated into some portions of the urban bureaucracy and into the program objectives of many civic reform groups. Two strains of urban environmental reform developed in the late-nineteenth century. One was composed of professionals with technical and scientific skills — engineers, efficiency experts, sanitarians — who worked primarily within the municipal bureaucracy. Their role was developing systems to combat health hazards and pollutants, compiling statistics, and monitoring some forms of pollution. Sanitary engineers devised strategies for street cleaning and refuse disposal, designed sewers and drainage systems, and developed new methods of ventilating buildings. Efficiency experts established cost-accounting systems and organized personnel-management programs. Public health officials promoted environmental sanitation and epidemic control. As a group, they provided expertise never before available to municipal government.

Although the expert elite transmitted their ideas to municipal policy makers and through professional organizations, they were largely ineffective in communicating environmental concerns to the public. A second major group filled the void — they were citizen groups with strong civic and aesthetic values who usually operated outside city government, generating influence through organized protest or public awareness. Lacking the expertise to implement most changes themselves, they often supported the efforts of the technical elite. The heart of this civic movement — often with strong leadership from women — were voluntary citizens' associations, reform clubs, and civic organizations whose interest in urban life was broad and varied. Sometimes environmental pressure groups — such as smoke- and noise-abatement leagues — formed to combat a specific environmental threat. The membership of all of these groups came from the middle- and upper-middle classes, and cut across several professions. Given their economic status, they often were insulated from many of the worst environmental threats, thus their environmentalism was essentially a general concern for civic improvement (Melosi, 1982: 36-37).

Despite the fact that intermittent civic protest had been transformed into a more coherent form, pollution did not disappear. Public awareness certainly had been raised. However, mechanisms for turning protests into action had to be devised. Faith in technical experts to find solutions to pressing environmental problems was widespread. And, to some degree, technical and scientific methods made a difference. This was especially true in the case of public health, where bacteriological laboratories monitored water supplies and successfully battled communicable diseases. Engineering expertise applied to implementing environmental services and improving efficiency of machinery offered hope for reducing pollution. But faith in technology to solve problems was often overblown, and if cities or businesses were unwilling to utilize that technology, there was little chance to gauge its impact.

The most severe restriction on effective environmental reform in the early-twentieth century was the lack of a broad environmental perspective. Pollution problems were most often addressed as isolated cases with emphasis on the "end of the pipe" rather than the root causes. Furthermore, interrelationships among various forms of pollution seemed to escape attention. The smoke problem was considered independent of the noise problem, and the noise problem independent of the sewage problem. Rarely did protest groups confront them holistically, as part of an overall environmental problem or threat. In fact, other than civic groups, there were no organizations that were broadly concerned with environmental quality during these years. From the narrow vantage point of the consumer, eliminating the pollutant — rather than dealing with the source — was the primary goal (Melosi, 1986: 20-21).

Education

The hope that polluters would change their ways and that citizens could learn to act responsibly led to several experiments in environmental education at the turn of the century. Rather than a deterrent, this approach stressed changing behavior patterns as a long-term solution to pollution problems.

In the area of smoke abatement, in particular, debate raged over the viability of education as opposed to the prosecution of violators — a debate, for instance, that broke apart the coalition of anti-smoke groups in St. Louis in 1911. In several quarters the call for education prevailed because supporters argued that promoting efficiency and fuel economy would stimulate *additional* economic growth (Grinder, 1980: 95-96). In Chicago, the Society for the Prevention of Smoke — a group founded by local businessmen in 1892 — initiated an educational campaign for the city's downtown business community to reduce an unwanted nuisance, to minimize a costly economic problem, and to improve the city's

image (especially with the World's Fair scheduled to open in 1893).
The approach of this education program was to achieve voluntary
compliance through convincing businessmen to employ new boiler
designs and retrofit existing boilers with smoke consuming devices
(Rosen, 1989: 6ff).

Similar programs were instituted in other cities to help eradicate various forms of pollution. New York's Society for the Sup-
pression of Unnecessary Noise allied itself with the local press in a
publicity campaign meant to inform the public about the tyranny
of noise. The campaign had the broader purpose of also promoting
ordinances to curtail the most egregious forms of noise. One positive result was the establishment of quiet zones around hospitals
and schools (Smilor, 1980: 143-144).

Education programs which were not coordinated with more
coercive measures failed to produce many immediate or tangible
results. Relying on voluntary compliance after a presentation of
"the facts" was a rather unsophisticated use of education as a
persuasive device, and, as a result was often doomed to failure.

A potentially more effective — if not more insidious — use of
the education strategy was proselytizing among the young with
the hope that changing the behavior of children would immediately impact parents and also lead to more permanent changes
in attitude in the future. A good example was the establishment
of the Juvenile Street Cleaning League in New York, initiated by
Street Cleaning Commissioner George E. Waring. Taking note of
the participation of children in the local Civic History Club and
other patriotic organizations, Waring concluded that "it seemed
possible to enlist their interest in the cleanliness of the city." He
had two major goals in mind: First, the children could act as eyes,
ears and noses for the department in uncovering unsanitary conditions. Second, he wanted to educate the children — especially
in the working classes — in the ways of sanitation and civic pride,
which he hoped would be carried over to their parents.

In 1896 neighborhood leagues were established throughout the
city in settlements and in the public schools. By 1899 there were

75 leagues and 5,000 participants in New York City. Other cities around the country, including Philadelphia, Brooklyn, Pittsburgh, Utica, and Denver, established their own leagues (Melosi, 1981: 74-77). While the youth programs brought greater attention to the sanitation problems, they alone could not get to the heart of the pollution problems immediately facing the cities. The sources of pollution were not in the control of children or any civic group, but enmeshed in the transformation of the United States into a highly industrialized society.

The Courts

Some contemporaries believed that self-regulation and the proper application of technology were practical remedies as long as all parties were well-educated as to the nature and extent of pollution problems and their potential impacts on business efficiency and economy. But others placed their faith in the coercive power of government to contain the crass impulses of would-be polluters. And still others assumed that the courts would apply traditional principles of common law to protect property rights and public safety.

Through the end of the nineteenth century, common law doctrine failed to meet the demand for protective regulation of the environment, but in the application of nuisance law, it developed a legal form for addressing the issue of liability. It is generally understood that much of the legal history of the environment has been written by nuisance law. However, case law and statutes dealing with nuisances were not developed primarily to address environmental issues, and thus legal action essentially responded to a problem after it arose. And while no common law doctrine is wider in scope than nuisance law, its application to environmental issues has been less than systematic (Watrous, 1901: 98; Reynolds, 1978: 318-343; Krauss, 1984: 250; Bone, 1986: 1142-1226).

In the nineteenth century, especially, economic as opposed to ecological considerations shaped the application of nuisance law in cases affecting the environment. Lawrence Friedman and others asserted that judges deliberately structured tort doctrine to favor the economic interests of burgeoning industries. Morton J. Horwitz added that nineteenth-century tort law provided an indirect economic subsidy to entrepreneurial interests, but that nuisance law was slow to respond to the demand for economic subsidization (Horwitz, 1977: xi-xiv, 74).

There was, however, a substantial increase in actions for injunctions against industrial nuisances as early as 1837. Between 1871 and 1916, the number of private suits for nuisance injunctions increased at a rate comparable to the remarkable economic growth of the period. But the denial of injunctive relief persisted (Horwitz, 1977: 651-670).

The incidence of smoke pollution in the late-nineteenth century is a good example of the application of nuisance law in the wake of economic growth. The difficulty in addressing the smoke problem, especially for political leaders and the courts, was confronting the issue that smoke was a visible sign of economic prosperity and material progress in those cities most dependent on its use. Few courts were willing or able to determine the costs of smoke in hard economic terms, thus the relatively anemic legal response to air pollution at the time. Even when the law attached liability to a particular source of pollution, it treated the liability in narrow, particularist terms, rather than as a more general societal problem (Laitos, 1975: 66-70).

While the argument that the courts tended to protect entrepreneurs from nuisance actions is compelling, it can be taken too far. The application of existing legal remedies, especially nuisance, provided legitimate redress for plaintiffs against industrial defendants. After all, by defining liability — even narrowly — the courts left room for successful actions against industrial polluters (Schwartz, 1981: 1775). In some states — such as New York, Pennsylvania and New Jersey — victims of pollution won relief much more frequently than they were denied it, especially after 1871. Some laws were structured in such a way to accommodate the interests of parties injured by pollutants, as well as the interests of those who created pollution (Rosen, 1987: 8-11).

With respect to municipal and industrial wastes, a swing toward plaintiffs is not so evident. Part of the reason is that: (1) the courts in the nineteenth century were provided with no conclusive evidence that inorganic industrial waste posed a hazard to water supplies; (2) land disposal was treated as a relatively insignificant nuisance with little regard for its potential in contaminating groundwater; and (3) the introduction of municipal sewage into running water was not perceived as a public nuisance. The courts continued to uphold riparian rights — to have water quality and quantity protected for the owners — and dealt with nuisance cases as they arose rather than addressing them as part of a more generalized pollution problem. The courts generally held polluters liable for damage caused by waste disposal in streams — if the damage was understood — but the legal system provided few substantive prohibitions against the act of polluting itself (Fertig, 1926: 782-787; Besselievre, 1924: 217-219; Colten, 1987: 8).

Governmental Regulation

During the period of accelerating industrialization, not only the courts, but also the federal government — and most state governments — did their part to encourage rapid economic growth and large-scale extraction of energy sources. Because there were large reserves of fossil fuels on the public domain, federal officials realized the contradiction between promoting economic growth, on the one hand, and providing stewardship over the public lands, on the other. The "wise use" concept of resource conservation, which emerged at the turn of the century, was a happy compromise (Melosi, 1985: 79-85).

A major link between conservation and energy production was the disposition of mineral resources on public lands. Debate over coal-leasing measures during the Progressive Era involved questions of resource exploitation and control over the use of public lands (Hays, 1959: 82-90; Smith, 1966: 115; Ise, 1926: 324ff; Penick, 1968; 77ff). The controversy over waterpower also went to the heart of the "wise use" issue, one that was central to the question of exploiting energy sources. By the early twentieth century, America's waterways came to be viewed as multipurpose resources, including the generation of hydroelectric power. But private companies had already gobbled up western waterpower sites on most of the public domain. Not until the Water Power Act of 1920 did the federal government assert the principle of public regulation of hydroelectric power, including a clearer sense of waterpower development on navigable streams (Penick, 1968: 48-58; Hays, 1959: 74-81, 96-97, 160-165, 192-195). Both in the case of hydropower and the leasing of mineral lands, the issue at stake was controlling access to and the allocation of resources on the public domain.

By World War I the federal government began to restrain the unlimited exploitation of the public domain, but it did not broaden the "wise use" concept sufficiently to include those resources under private control. Oil production is a good example. State officials in particular explored remedies for potential oil depletion, but wasteful practices continued. By the late 1920s the realities of a glutted market encouraged the oil industry to develop an appreciation for conservation. Discoveries in California and in Oklahoma meant that the known reserves of crude had greatly outstripped demand for oil. The net result was incredibly low prices, a trend that worsened in the 1930s. But only after wanton exploitation of fields in east Texas and Oklahoma in the early 1930s was mandatory prorationing of wells enacted. At that point a semblance of order returned to the fields. State agencies, especially the Texas Railroad Commission, exercised greater influence over production controls than federal policies (Melosi, 1987: 169).

If the broadening of the "wise use" concept for energy sources was slow in coming, plans for protecting the environment was downright glacial. The federal government's approach was sporadic and particularistic, in a great degree reflecting the general perception that these were local problems best dealt with by ordinances or other local actions. Congress passed few laws that dealt with the environmental implications of energy. As late as 1955 government-sponsored environmental programs represented only 3 percent of the federal budget, with no financial support for pollution abatement (Rosenbaum, 1977: 12).

Despite the lack of federal leadership, industrial cities had begun to pay some attention to the environmental implications of energy exploitation and use by the turn of the century. The greatest success of smoke abatement proponents, for example, was the implementation of tougher local laws in almost every city by 1912. Yet local officials were unwilling to curb industrial development and selectively enforced the ordinances. During World War I, when unrestricted production became a patriotic duty, smoke abatement fell on hard times. Smoke pollution did not subside until the use of coal diminished in the 1920s. Not unlike the late 1940s — when Los Angeles began its long battle with smog — did the control of air pollution again invade local politics, and the issue did not achieve national status until the 1960s (Grinder, 1980: 83-103; Tarr and Koons, 1982: 71-92).

Pollution from oil production and transportation also remained mostly a local problem. The drilling and refining of oil, as mentioned, polluted local areas but rarely attracted attention from oil companies or state governments before World War I.

The federal government, however, established a precedent for combating oil pollution when it passed the Oil Pollution Control Act in 1924. The contamination of water from tanker discharges and seepage problems on land were the primary problems. The former attracted the most attention largely because the polluting of waterways and coastal areas affected commercial fishermen and resort owners. The oil industry at first treated the call to end polluting practices with grave apprehension. But the American Petroleum Institute, the major lobbying body for the industry, soon realized that the industry could control the flow of information to the government.

Herbert Hoover was the leading government proponent of oil conservation and of curbing pollution during the 1920s. As secretary of commerce he tried to protect American fisheries, despite his additional responsibility to commercial shippers. Hoover and his supporters wanted a comprehensive law to regulate land-based polluters as well as ships. But conflicting economic and political interests in Congress produced a much weaker bill. The 1924 Act had inadequate enforcement provisions and dealt only with dumping fuel at sea by oil-burning vessels. Although the act disappointed Hoover and the conservationists, it was the first serious attempt to deal with the issue on a national scale (Melosi, 1987: 170-171).

While the environmental implications of energy use and development received sporadic attention at the local, state, and federal levels before World War II, nineteenth-century American municipalities had placed on the books an array of ordinances regulating activities associated with health and sanitation, including the construction and emptying of privy vaults and cesspools, street cleaning, garbage collection, sewerage development and water supply. By the 1880s many cities passed statutes restricting "noxious" manufacturers to the outskirts, but few cities had specific regulations regarding the disposal of manufacturing wastes. If they were dealt with at all, these wastes were lumped under existing nuisance provisions (Tarr, 1985: 96; Colten and Breen, 1986: 54-55).

By comparison with state legislative action, municipal statutes and ordinances in the early-twentieth century did little to move beyond the courts in refining environmental liability. Under certain circumstances, municipalities found themselves as defendants, especially when the dumping of sewage threatened a riparian owner. In addition, the diversion of industrial wastes to municipal waste treatment facilities shifted the legal responsibility for stream pollution to the cities (Tooke, 1900: 87-90; Fertig, 1926: 786; Colten, 1987: 10).

While municipal ordinances did not frequently confront the broad problems associated with land and water pollution, the establishment of regulatory bodies in some cities worked to decrease pollution. The Chicago Drainage Districts, for example, attempted to prevent pollution in already badly contaminated watercourses. The Milwaukee Sewerage Commission was empowered under the statute which created it, to regulate the character and quantity of industrial waste discharged into the public sewer system (Jackson, 1924: 23; No author, 1937: 86).

The states, more than the municipalities or the federal government, were the centers of action for new legislation to control stream pollution — which remained in the early- and mid-20th century the major focus of concern over the disposal of municipal and industrial wastes. In general, public health and sanitation laws increased dramatically on the state level by the end of the century — particularly strong in the Northeast and slower in the South. The first state legislation to control stream pollution was written in 1878 in Massachusetts. It gave the State Board of Health the power to control river pollution caused by industrial wastes. Whereas in 1915 only eighteen state boards of health had divisions of sanitary engineering, all but four states established such divisions by 1927 (Vesillind, 1981: 26; Micklin, 1970: 131).

By World War I, states were establishing boards and commissions expressly designed to regulate water pollution, including the Sanitary Water Board of Pennsylvania, the Michigan Stream Control Commission, and the State Committee on Water Pollution of Wisconsin, plus similar boards in Ohio and Connecticut. These new bodies often were given expanded power over industrial pollution as well as municipal pollution (Warrick, 1933: 496; Monger, 1926: 790; Tobey, 1939: 1322).

As impressive as the efforts to develop state mechanisms for checking pollution appeared to be, the results were often disappointing. There were inconsistencies in the regulations and enforcement was lax. A survey conducted by the American Water Works Association in 1921 stated that only five states granted ample authority to its pollution agencies, and in nearly all cases enforcement was hampered by the lack of appropriations. Some experts believed that conditions improved by the late 1920s, citing the Ohio State Department of Health as an example of an effective regulator. However, the early laws made substantial accommodations to industry. Some laws failed to provide penalties

for infringements, and most laws exempted specific industries —
especially those central to their economy — or specific wastes,
such as petroleum, sawdust and wood wastes, acids, alkalis, and
white water from pulp mills. In some instances, certain streams
were exempted (Donaldson, 1921: 198; Besselievre, 1952: 325-344;
Fales, 1928: 715-717; Skinner, 1939: 1332).

Under the terms of state legislation the individual or company responsible for a nuisance, in theory at least, could be liable
to criminal action and a penalty for violating a law prohibiting
pollution by industrial wastes. In general, state boards preferred
cooperation to placing themselves in an adversarial relationship
with industry. The political and economic stakes were too high to
harass major employers in the states. Cooperation seemed safer
than legal sanctions, and it was a goal set by many public bodies in
the 1920s in the wake of public-private cooperation in World War
I. Trade associations, such as the American Petroleum Institute
and the Pulp and Paper Association, soon became involved in joint
projects for pollution control or waste utilization, although their
motives were sometimes questioned and questionable. State agencies often justified cooperation on the grounds that drastic control
by court action would hinder economic growth, and might result
in incomplete investigations of actual stream requirements and of
the applicability of treatment processes. In addition, action without adequate data would waste public and private funds. Among
the boards' functions, therefore, was providing the industries with
technical information and survey data to keep them abreast of the
most current disposal and recycling methods (Baity, 1939: 1302-
1303; Rue, 1929: 365-369; Besselievre, 1924: 217ff; Fertig, 1926:
786; Tobey, 1939: 1322).

Another important wrinkle in the evolution of environmental
liability at the state level was interstate conflict. On several occa-
sions one states brought action against another state (or industry
in that state) to restrain air and water pollution (Lay, 1931: 73-
85; Tobey, 1925: 707-710). It did not take long to recognize that
such chronic interstate rivalry could spill over into other areas.
One possible solution was interstate agreements or compacts to

control or abate pollution. Health departments and other agencies worked toward interstate compacts in several states including Pennsylvania, New Jersey, Ohio, West Virginia, Kentucky, New York, Maryland, Indiana, Illinois, Tennessee, and Michigan (No author, 1939: 58-60).

The interstate cooperative approach had practical and salutary benefits for dealing with stream pollution, but it was at best an incomplete tool. The interstate compacts did not serve as regional plans to abate municipal and industrial pollution, since they were drawn more narrowly to deal with the level of discharge into water. They also did little to further the definition of environmental liability, working instead to solve practical problems by avoiding litigation. And, even if taken collectively, they could do little to establish national standards of pollution control.

To a limited degree, federal regulation in the period sought to accomplish — for public health and water pollution at least — what state and court actions could not. There was, however, no overriding national vision or national policy for dealing with pollution. In 1912, the federal government began to give assistance to the states in evaluating water pollution through the Public Health Service's Stream Investigation Station in Cincinnati. In 1938 a loan and grant program for the states was set up through the PHS' Division of Water Pollution Control. The beginnings of concern about hazardous substances was noted in the passage of the Pure Food and Drug Act of 1906, the Insecticide Act of 1910, and the more substantial Food, Drug and Cosmetic Act of 1938, which limited the amount of additives and residues in agricultural products. In addition, industrial safety and hygiene began to receive a national hearing by mid-century (Davies, 1970: 38-40; Baity, 1939: 1300-1306; Tobey, 1926: 244-249).

Two pieces of legislation, although modest in the short-term, became important precedents for future action in dealing with water pollution and industrial waste: the Oil Pollution Control Act of 1924, mentioned above, and the so-called Refuse Act of 1899. Section 13 of the Rivers and Harbors Act of 1899, commonly called the Refuse Act, prohibited the discharge of wastes — other than sewer liquids — into navigable waters without a permit from the Army Corps of Engineers. Violations were punishable by fine or imprisonment. This provision superseded the Refuse Act of 1890 which prohibited dumping that would "impede or obstruct navigation."

The 1899 act suggested a strict prohibition against dumping which seemed to go beyond the primary goal of the law, that is, to simply preserve waterways for navigation. For several years, the Refuse Act functioned as a minor statute to protect navigation. In 1910, however, a New York group tried to invoke the act against a proposed sewer, but the Judge Advocate General ruled that pollution control was a function of the states alone. While one court in 1918 interpreted the act to forbid dumping per se — without regard to navigability — the courts in general interpreted the act literally in the early-twentieth century. By the 1960s the act was used, as one commentator noted, as a "*cause celebre* for the environmental movement." Or as another suggested, "a piece of legislation that was aimed at keeping carcasses of cows and other floating debris from obstructing the smooth flow of commerce seems to have been turned into a useful bit of antipollution legislation by some enterprising conservationists and politicians concerned with the environment." In many ways, the Refuse Act became a complement to existing federal water-quality legislation, beginning in the 1960s with the Water Quality Act of 1965. Here is a case where a modest proposal served as a significant legal tool largely because it found its way into national legislation (Cowdrey, 1975: 231-249; Rodgers, 1971a: 761-822, 1971b: 173-202).

Conclusion

The transformation of the American environment in the era of fossil fuels began without serious attention to "environmental costs" as a consequence of doing business. Until the early-twentieth century, environmental costs — if they were recognized at all — were missing from the economic balance sheet, a relatively low priority in the political arena, and inconclusively dealt with in the courts. Pollution was regarded as an aberration rather than as a predictable by-product of environmentally intensive economic activity. When pollution was not ignored or dismissed, it was considered an inevitable consequence of economic growth — rendering producers free of responsibility for its generation.

In time, piecemeal efforts to deal with specific, localized pollution problems arose in public forums and even political campaigns. In some cases, the courts began to address the difficult problem of determining liability. However, the national commitment to economic growth, the dominance of big business, and the limited power — and resolve — of government offered few opportunities to confront the problem of pollution in any serious way. Squandering of natural resources, inefficient burning of fuels, and the tainting of watercourses also worked against what was perceived as the long-range economic interests of the country.

Political solutions to environmental problems required broadscale acceptance of environmental costs as an integral part of the production process and as an unacceptable side effect of economic growth. But most politicians were no more receptive to promoting long-term goals than most businessmen were willing to sacrifice short-term profits.

When major pollution problems gained national attention in the latter years of the twentieth century, the question of economic growth versus environmental protection had not been successfully addressed, let alone resolved. The principle of "cost-benefit" represented only a tentative compromise in establishing policy. Controversy over "soft" and "hard" paths made it even clearer that environmental issues raised basic questions of values. In essence, the Industrial Revolution of the nineteenth century produced a fundamental dilemma in the twentieth: Should an economic future — consistently shaped by a series of short-term goals — be revised to embrace a less finite and possibly less certain outcome shaped by attention to environmental costs?

Not even the seemingly ominous projections of environmental disaster expressed in the controversy over global warming and other potential environmental calamities has moved the public debate much beyond the dilemma of economic growth versus environmental protection posed in the nineteenth century. This is unfortunate because the obstacles to political solutions of environmental problems caused by energy-intensive economic growth are the result of the nation's failure to recognize environmental degradation as an integral part of industrial capitalism.

An integrated policy approach requires a holistic appraisal of the net effects of industrialism — certainly economic, but also social and environmental. An equation built on the assumption of mutually exclusive goals — economic growth *versus* environmental protection — limits creative alternatives to the policy dilemma and certainly ignores the fact that decisions made simply in terms of short-term profit-taking may come at the expense of long-term economic security as well as environmental quality. The degradation of the physical environment benefits no one — not if those benefitting from the rewards of industrial capitalism look no farther than a few years into the future. It is imperative in successfully addressing global warming and other global change phenomena to understand the energy-environment-growth nexus put in place during the era of industrialism. The historical record demonstrates effectively that economic growth without attention to environmental cost is at best naive, at worst perilous.

References

Armstrong, Ellis C., Michael Robinson and Suellen Hoy (eds.). 1976. *History of Public Works in the United States, 1776-1976.* Chicago, IL: American Public Works Association.

Baity, Herman G. 1939. "Aspects of Governmental Policy on Stream Pollution Abatement." *American Journal of Public Health* 29 (December): 1297-1307.

Besselievre, E. B. 1952. *Industrial Waste Treatment.* New York, NY: McGraw-Hill.

_____. 1924. "Statutory Regulation of Stream Pollution and the Common Law." *Transactions of the American Institute of Chemical Engineers* 16: 217-230.

Billings, John S. 1893. "Municipal Sanitation: Defects in American Cities." *The Forum* 15 (May): 304-310.

Binder, Frederick Moore. 1958. "Anthracite Enters the American Home." *Pennsylvania Magazine of History and Biography* 82 (January): 82-99.

Bone, Robert G. 1986. "Normative Theory and Legal Doctrine in American Nuisance Law: 1850-1920." *Southern California Law Review* 59: 1101-1226.

Brody, David. 1975. "Slavic Immigrants in the Steel Mills." In Thomas R. Frazier (ed.), *The Private Side of American History*. New York, NY: Harcourt Brace Jovanovich.

Burlingame, Roger. 1946. *March of the Iron Men*. New York, NY: Charles Scribner's Sons, Ltd.

Chandler, Alfred D., Jr. 1972. "Anthracite Coal and the Beginnings of the Industrial Revolution in the United States." *Business History Review* 46 (November): 141-181.

Cochran, Thomas C. and William Miller. 1961. *The Age of Enterprise* (revised edition). New York, NY: Harper.

Cole, Arthur H. 1970. "The Mystery of Fuel Wood Marketing in the United States." *Business History Review* 44 (Autumn): 339-359.

Colten, Craig. 1987. "Industrial Wastes Before 1940." Durham, North Carolina.

Colten, Craig and G. Breen. 1986. "Historical Industrial Waste Disposal Practices in Winnebago County, Illinois, 1870-1980." Springfield, Illinois.

Cowdrey, Albert E. 1975. "Pioneering Environmental Law: The Army Corps of Engineers and the Refuse Act." *Pacific Historical Review* 44 (August): 231-249.

Davies, J. Clarence, III. 1970. *The Politics of Pollution*. New York, NY: Pegasus.

Degler, Carl N. 1967. *The Age of the Economic Revolution, 1876-1900*. Glenview, IL: Scott, Foresman.

Dinnerstein, Leonard and David M. Reimers. 1975. *Ethnic Americans*. New York, NY: Dodd, Mead.

Donaldson, Wellington. 1921. "Industrial Wastes in Relation to Water Supplies." *Industrial Wastes in Relation to Water Supplies II* (March): 193-198.

Fales, Almon L. 1928. "Progress in the Control of Pollution by Industrial Wastes." *American Journal of Public Health* 18 (June): 715-727.

Fertig, John H. 1926. "Legal Aspects of the Stream Pollution Problem." *Journal of the American Public Health Association* 16 (August): 782-788.

Fuller, George W. 1926. "Administrative Problems in the Control of Pollution of Streams." *Journal of the American Public Health Association* 16 (August): 777-804.

Galishoff, Stuart. 1975. *Safeguarding the Public Health: Newark, 1895-1918*. Westport, CT: Greenwood Press.

_____. "Sanitation in Nineteenth and Early Twentieth Century Urban America: An Overview." Atlanta, Georgia.

Grinder, R. Dale. 1980. "The Battle for Clean Air: The Smoke Problem in Post-Civil War America, 1880-1917." In Martin V. Melosi (ed.), *Pollution and Reform in American Cities, 1870-1930*. Austin, TX: University of Texas Press.

Hays, Samuel P. 1959. *Conservation and the Gospel of Efficiency: The Progressive Conservation Movement, 1890-1920*. New York, NY: Atheneum.

Hindle, Brooke. 1975. *America's Wooden Age*. Tarrytown, NY: Sleepy Hollow Restorations.

Horwitz, Morton J. 1977. *The Transformation of American Law, 1780-1860*. Cambridge, MA: Harvard University Press.

Hunter, Louis. 1979. *Waterpower in the Century of the Steam Engine*. Charlottesville, VA: University Press at Virginia.

Ise, John. 1926. *The United States Oil Policy*. New Haven, CT: Yale University Press.

Jackson, J. Frederick. 1924. "Stream Pollution by Industrial Wastes, and Its Control." *American City* 31: 23-26.

Kirkland, Edward C. 1969. *A History of American Economic Life* (4th edition). New York, NY: Appleton-Century-Crofts.

Klein, Maury and Harvey A. Kantor. 1976. *Prisoners of Progress: American Industrial Cities, 1850-1920.* New York, NY: Macmillan.

Krauss, E. P. 1984. "The Legal Form of Liberalism: A Study of Riparian and Nuisance Law in Nineteenth Century Ohio." *Akron Law Review* 18 (Fall): 223-251.

Laitos, Jan G. 1975. "Continuities from the Past Affecting Resource Use and Conservation Patterns." *Oklahoma Law Review* 28 (Winter): 60-96.

Lay, George C. 1931. "Suits by States to Abate Nuisances." *United States Law Review* 65 (February): 73-85.

Melosi, Martin V. 1988. "Hazardous Waste and Environmental Liability: An Historical Perspective." *Houston Law Review* 25 (July): 741-779.

_____. 1987. "Energy and Environment in the United States: The Era of Fossil Fuels." *Environmental Review* 11 (Fall): 167-188.

_____. 1986. "Environmental Crisis in the City: The Relationship Between Industrialization and Urban Pollution." In M. V. Melosi (ed.), *Pollution and Reform in American Cities.* Austin, TX: University of Texas Press.

_____. 1985. *Coping With Abundance: Energy and Environment in Industrial America.* New York, NY: Alfred Kropf.

_____. 1982. "Battling Pollution in the Progressive Era." *Landscape* 26: 35-41.

_____. 1981. *Garbage in the Cities: Refuse, Reform and the Environment: 1880-1980.* College Station, TX: Texas A&M University Press.

_____. 1973. "'Out of Sight, Out of Mind': The Environment and the Disposal of Municipal Refuse, 1860-1920." *Historian* 35 (August): 621-640.

Micklin, Philip P. 1970. "Water Quality: A Question of Standards." In Richard A. Cooley and Geoffrey Wandesforde-Smith (eds.), *Congress and the Environment.* Seattle, WA: University of Washington Press.

Monger, John Emerson. 1926. "Administrative Phases of Stream Pollution Control." *Journal of the American Public Health Association* 16: 788-804.

No author. 1939. "Control of Pollution in Interstate Waters." *American City* 54 (April): 58-60.

_____. 1937. "Industrial Wastes in City Sewers-I." *American City* 52 (May): 85-87.

Penick, James, Jr. 1968. *Progressive Politics and Conservation.* Chicago, IL: University of Chicago Press.

Petulla, Joseph M. 1977. *American Environmental History.* San Francisco, CA: Boyd and Fraser Publishing Company.

Powell, Benjamin H. 1980. "The Pennsylvania Anthracite Industry, 1769-1976." *Pennsylvania History* 47 (November): 3-27.

Pratt, Joseph A. 1978. "Growth or a Clean Environment?" *Business History Review* 52 (Spring): 1-29.

Reynolds, Osborne M., Jr. 1978. "Public Nuisance: A Crime in Tort Law." *Oklahoma Law Review* 31: 318-343.

Rodgers, William H., Jr. 1971a. "Industrial Water Pollution and the Refuse Act: A Second Chance for Water Quality." *University of Pennsylvania Law Review* 119: 761-822.

_____. 1971b. "The Refuse Act of 1899: Its Scope and Role in Control of Water Pollution." *Ecology Law Quarterly* 1: 173-202.

Rosen, Christine. 1989. "Chicago's Society for the Prevention of Smoke: Education and the Law in the Fight Against Air Pollution in the 1890s." Berkeley, California.

_____. 1987. "A Litigious Approach to Pollution Regulation: 1840-1906." Berkeley, California.

Rosenbaum, Walter A. 1977. *The Politics of Environmental Concern,* second edition. New York, NY: Praeger Publishers.

Rue, John D. 1929. "Disposal of Industrial Wastes." *Sewage Works Journal* 1 (April): 365-369.

Russel, Robert R. 1964. *A History of the American Economic System.* New York, NY: Appleton-Century-Crofts.

Schurr, Sam H. and Bruce C. Netschert. 1960. *Energy in the American Economy, 1850-1975.* Baltimore, MD: Johns Hopkins Press.

Schwartz, Gary T. 1981. "Tort Law and the Economy in Nineteenth-Century America: A Reinterpretation." *Yale Law Journal* 90 (July): 1717-1775.

Skinner, Harvey J. 1939. "Waste Problems in the Pulp and Paper Industry." *Industrial and Engineering Chemistry* 31 (November): 1331-1335.

Smilor, Raymond W. 1980. "Toward an Environmental Perspective: The Anti-Noise Campaign, 1893-1932." In Martin V. Melosi (ed.), *Pollution and Reform in American Cities.* Austin, TX: University of Texas Press.

_____. 1977. "Cacophony at 34th and 6th: The Noise Problem in America, 1900-1930." *American Studies* 28 (Spring): 23-38.

Smith, Frank E. 1966. *The Politics of Conservation.* New York, NY: Pantheon Books.

Tarr, Joel A. 1991. "Searching for a 'Sink' for an Industrial Waste: Coke Production and the Environment." Pittsburgh, Pennsylvania.

_____. 1985. "Historical Perspectives on Hazardous Wastes in the United States." *Waste Management and Research* 3: 95-102.

Tarr, Joel A. and Kenneth E. Koons. 1982. "Railroad Smoke Control: The Regulation of a Mobile Pollution Source." In George H. Daniels and Mark H. Rose (eds.), *Energy and Transport.* Beverly Hills, CA: Sage Publishers.

Tarr, Joel A. and Francis Clay McMichael. 1977. "Historical Decisions About Wastewater Technology, 1850-1932." *Journal of the Water Resources Planning and Management Division, ASCE* 103 (May): 47-61.

Taylor, George Rogers. 1951. *The Transportation Revolution, 1815-1860.* New York, NY: Rinehart.

Tobey, James A. 1939. "Legal Aspects of the Industrial Wastes Problem." *Industrial Engineering Chemistry* 31: 1320-1322.

_____. 1926. "Federal Control of Hazardous Substances." *American Journal of Public Health* 16 (March): 244-249.

_____. 1925. "Public Health and the United States Supreme Court." *American Bar Association Journal* 11 (November): 707-710.

Tooke, C. W. 1900. "Pollution of Running Streams by Sewage." *Municipal Engineering* 19 (August): 87-90.

Vesillind, P. Aarne. 1981. "Hazardous Waste: Historical and Ethical Perspectives." In J. Jeffrey Peirce and P. Aarne Vesillind (eds.), *Hazardous Waste Management.* Ann Arbor, MI: Ann Arbor Science Publishers.

Warrick, L. F. 1933. "Relative Importance of Industrial Wastes in Stream Pollution." *Civil Engineering* 3 (September): 495-498.

Watrous, George D. 1901. "Torts, 1701-1901." In Faculty, Yale Law School, *Two Centuries' Growth of American Law, 1701-1901.* New York, NY: Charles Scribner's Sons, Ltd.

Chapter 3

Fueling the Illusion of Progress:
Energy and Industrialization
in the European Experience

Dolores Greenberg

According to new studies of environmental damage, the past
is very much with us. Recently the Stockholm Environment Institute reported that carbon emissions take a century or more to
disappear naturally. In other words, what was released in the
1880s as toxic byproducts of fossil fuel combustion and of deforestation have mixed with toxins released in the 1980s. Moreover,
each ton of carbon in the air resulted in 3.7 tons of carbon dioxide, the greenhouse gas associated with global warming (W. Clark,
1990: 71).

Much more than we may have realized, understanding the past
is essential for meeting current energy challenges. However, as this
chapter emphasizes, an array of fixed ideas about energy patterns
has long clouded accurate assessments of the industrializing process. First of all, since the 19th century coal and steam have
been extolled as the catalysts of the Industrial Revolution. By
the 1780s, according to most accounts, fossil fuels had edged out
wood fuel, muscle, and water power in England, a pattern then
emulated on the Continent and in the United States by the 1870s.
Secondly, the Industrial Revolution has been accepted as synony-
mous with progress. In what can be described as an "energy stage
theory" of history, the transition to coal has been equated with

the "take off" to mechanization, factory organization, and productivity. This evolutionary cornucopian construct presumed serial transitions with coal giving way to electricity, oil, and gas — supposedly even better sources for continuing improvements in living standards and human welfare. Or to put it another way, a single-source fossil-fuel mentality has been seen as the critical component of dynamic, positive, modernization and social change (Cippola, 1962: 35-36; Landes, 1969: 32, 41, 99; Rostow, 1971; Cook, 1976: 2-25; Hunter, 1985: 102-117; Kuznets, 1966; Kenwood and Lougheed, 1982: 3-26).

This mentality is so deeply entrenched in Western culture that the important compilation of historical data published in 1971 by *Resources For the Future* limited its coverage to what are labelled "modern, commercial" sources — that is, coal, oil, natural gas, and hydroelectricity. Except in passing, it excludes so-called "noncommercial" sources — fuelwood, wastes, and the power of draft animals and people (Darmstadter, 1971: 1-5).

Despite this model of development, a far more complex pattern prevailed in which adoption of coal-fueled technologies supplemented rather than replaced renewable energy sources (Greenberg, 1982: 29-58; Kanefsky, 1979: 360-375; Von Tunzelmann, 1978: 8, 98-115). Widespread adoption of coal came later in the 19th century than is often supposed and coal continued to dominate the "commercial" fuel mix in industrialized nations until the 1950s. Coal use, the source of much of today's carbon emissions, was not, as is widely supposed, edged out by oil after the introduction of the automobile. Even in Western Europe the dramatic swing to oil did not occur until the 1960s (Maull, 1980: 17).

This chapter, in reexamining the energy patterns which accompanied industrial change from England to Eastern Europe, demonstrates the distortions fostered by the single-source mentality and places in historical perspective the biases fueling our "illusion of progress" (Brown, 1990: 3-16).

Western Europe and the Costs
of the Single-Source Mentality

Only recently have we begun to deal with the challenges posed by the connections between energy and industrialization. And only in the last decade have historians begun to reexamine the traditional view that Britain's industrial ascendancy was based on coal and steam. What we have uncovered as a consequence is the delayed and uneven transition to fossil fuels and the fact that in Britain, as in continental Europe, the types of power were as varied as the organization of industrial activity. Indeed wood, water, and muscle power figured more importantly for the dynamics of British economic development from the 1780s through the 1870s than coal and steam. Even the "leading sectors" such as textiles, iron, and railways relied on a mix of wood, water, and muscle power supplemented by coal. While we have no precise data on the amounts or sources of mechanical power consumed before 1914, waterpower appears to have been the primary determinant of industrial activity both in Britain and on the Continent until the late 19th century. Its increasingly efficient utilization did more to transform the scale of production and levels of industrial output than coal-generated steam. In addition, wood continued to be used past mid-century for charcoal smelted iron, for industrial heat, and for fueling railroads, as well as for space heating and cooking (Berg et al., 1983; Greenberg, 1982: 29-52; Greenberg, 1990: 693-714; Crouzet, 1982: 84-86; Quataert, 1988: 4-23; Reynolds, 1983).

Significant adoption of fossil fuels dates from the "second Industrial Revolution" of the 1880s. Instead of the traditional model of coal's adoption in the 1780s, largely tied to textiles, extensive coal use was coupled to urban growth, science-based technology, and energy-intensive heavy industry — phenomena which occurred simultaneously in the United States, Britain, Germany, and France from the 1880s. The all-steel Eiffel Tower on the Paris horizon of 1889 stood as a dramatic symbol of new urban industrial resource use in these Western nations as did the electrical grid of 300,000 volt current built to span an entire region of western

Germany by 1891 (Tipton and Aldrich, 1987: 167). Both foretold
the possibilities of new social systems and industrial organization
which would consume unprecedented amounts of fossil fuels.

But even by the turn of the century fossil fuels did not account for the only, nor the primary, source of pollution. Very
probably in 1900 deforestation added even more carbon to the atmosphere than coal. According to one estimate, consumption of
fuelwood in 1900 was still more important than the combined total consumption of oil, gas, and hydro (Parker, 1984: 21; see also
Putnam, 1953: 439-440). Not only was wood burned for cooking
and heating, it continued to be used in small-scale industry. In
addition, local timber was burned commercially for river and rail
transportation, for smelting iron, even for electric power generation. Since deforestation released carbon dioxide stored in plants
and reduced the capacity of forests to reconvert carbon dioxide to
oxygen, wood, like coal, must be counted as a source of long-term
global environmental problems.

As late as 1914 coal-fueled energy-intensive industry represented only one type of industrial production and, moreover, a
form that was spatially concentrated. In fact, outside of particular regions of France and Germany, Europe was largely untouched
by so-called modern, commercial energy systems (Pounds, 1985:
355-407). Into the interwar period and in "advanced" countries,
industrial production continued to depend on a diverse fuel mix
of coal and wood plus human, animal, and water power.

Nevertheless, two factors had insured increasing coal consumption by the turn of the century: the needs of new industries and
accelerating urban concentration. In Britain as on the Continent
the manufacture of steel, machine tools, steel ships, automobiles,
chemicals, heavy electrical equipment, and the refining of non-
ferrous metals — lead, zinc, copper — devoured solid fuel. The
demands of heavily populated urban centers for power, lighting,
transportation, and consumer goods also accounts for the creation
of energy-intensive systems. Growing urban centers not only escalated the demand for energy, but catalyzed development of a new

power source, coal-fueled electricity. Electric street cars replaced horsedrawn omnibuses; steps were taken for electrifying railways; and electric lamps were introduced in streets, houses, and in the growing numbers of urban factories electric motors mounted on industrial machines revolutionized the workplace. With the construction of long-distance systems of power distribution within expanding cities, to reach suburbs, and to link metropolitan centers, electricity became a determinant of continued coal combustion.

Energy sources were hardly uniform from West to East, nor was there a linear sequence of adoption. But the shift to coal occurred in critical energy using segments of the industrial sector. While old industries increased solid fuel consumption, new industries, preeminently iron, steel, chemicals, and electric power generation became dependent on coal. By the 1880s charcoal smelting, once located near heavily forested woodlands, had been replaced largely by the use of coal for coking. And after 1880, according to Richard Gordon, coal was "Europe's only well-developed resource" (Gordon, 1970: 19). The opening of exceptional reserves in part reflected a reaction to the high price of preferred traditional fuels, timber, charcoal, and small units of available water power since bituminous, among the most polluting types of coal, was plentiful and cheap. By World War I, process heat industries such as copper, lead, zinc and clay products, cement, glass, and chemicals are estimated to have used much the same quantities of coal as transportation. Besides its use in the industrial sector, coal became a significant, even if not the dominant fuel for households, transportation, and commerce in western Europe suggested by our limited data (Berend and Ranki, 1974a: 117; Parker, 1984: 57-71; Tipton and Aldrich, 1987: 1-9).

Increasing demand for this new primary energy source brought changes in national suppliers. Britain had been the world's preeminent industrial power and the world's primary producer of coal in the 19th century. Since the nation's most important supply areas were near the coast, this geological benefit allowed easy transport to European markets. In response to rising demand, thousands of British firms mined high quality bituminous coal suitable for coke, and at lower prices than competitors in France and Germany. Although Britain led in absolute coal output, by the end of the century production was growing faster in continental countries (Gordon, 1970: 20; Mitchell, 1984). The Saar and Lorraine basins on the German-French border, important in their own right, were second to the Ruhr, the undisputed coal center of Europe. Organized as the Rhenish Westphalian Coal Syndicate in 1893, RWCS cartel members produced hugh supplies of medium volatile bituminous. Continued mapping of these deposits, combined with deeper mining, produced a sizable growth in known reserves of good coking coal and added significant new reserves.

After the 1880s, industrial enterprise increasingly spread north, south, and east, from the core areas of Britain and northwestern Europe, to the periphery. On the Continent, coal burning industries extended in a narrow belt from northern France to northwest Germany so that by 1914 the coal output and ranking of industrial areas had changed significantly from a half-century before. Continental Europe, particularly the northwest, emerged as the dominant industrial region in the world. It far outstripped Great Britain which, though still the leader in bituminous production and cotton textiles, had lost ground to Germany, the nation where coal mining together with iron and steel production expanded rapidly until World War I (Pounds, 1985: 305-507).

In contrast to western European nations, until World War I Britain remained self-sufficient in coal. Not only did it lead in absolute coal output, but also in exports. Indeed, so much coal was exported that merchant vessels in the pre-war period burned some 21 million metric tons as fuel for transporting the shipments. Exports continued as the decisive factor in the industry's growth and until 1913 the largest share of these export earnings derived from the trade with continental Europe, including shipments to Britain's major competitors, France and Germany. By contrast, ten years later Britain's poor equipment coupled to worker resistance contributed to curtailed output, bringing a steady decline in its world market share. Output per man-hour-shift rose by barely 10 percent between 1913 and 1936, compared to a rise of

117 percent in Holland, 81 percent in Germany, and 50 percent in Belgium (J. Clark, 1990: 9, 23-27; Crouzet, 1982: 265; Elbaum and Lazonick, 1986: 275, 287).

The usual focus on the 20th century transition to oil and natural gas should not obscure the central importance of coal, which from 1900 to the 1950s remained the preeminent "commercial" fuel of industrial Europe. At the turn of the century coal had accounted for 95 percent of the consumption of the four primary commercial energy sources — coal, oil, gas and hydro — used in the West and 83 percent of world "commercial" energy consumption. In the very period when these other sources were increasingly adopted, from 1900 to the eve of World War I, world coal production rose a startling 74 percent (Gordon, 1970: 20). Although we do not know the actual energy consumption by fuel category, by use, and by nations, certain critical industries clearly consumed the greatest proportions, with iron and steel burning the largest tonnage. Blast furnace and coke oven technology had long linked coal use to pig iron production and steel. Rising iron and steel production and coal use corresponded because coal was an essential chemical input as well as a needed fuel. Consequently, in Germany coal production rose by 283 percent between 1886 and 1913 as pig iron output rose by 533 percent. Equally spectacular was the growth in chemicals, electricity, and heavy electrical machinery using brown coal. After World War I coal output continued to grow in large measure because of steel's coke requirements. Efficient use further insured the market, resulting at the same time in increased coal consumption for transporting this bulky solid fuel. Coal would remain the most widely available "commercial" energy resource and the one around which these industries were organized into the 1920s (Jensen, 1990: 32-42; Parker, 1984: 106-109; Pounds, 1985: 45-47, 332-345; Tipton and Aldrich, 1987: 156).

The configuration of energy-market interdependence which emerged in the 20th century reinforced as it reflected the steadily rising demand for coal. By the interwar era, Western Europe, a prolific energy producer, served both its own needs as well as export markets. Both Britain and Germany engaged in an extensive export trade. Primarily intra-European, it also included overseas shipments — a profitable way to provide ballast for ships picking up foreign cargo (J. Clark, 1990: 9-88, ff.; Gordon, 1970: 260; Darmstadter, 1971: 24-32).

Despite changing international business conditions during the first half of this century, increasing production figured as the coal industry's long-term strategy. While national coal industries of the 1920s have been described as "sick" and in decline, the trouble often reflected excess capacity. The leading producing nations, Great Britain and Germany, increased output both to achieve self-sufficiency and to increase foreign sales. Production grew at an especially rapid rate in the two immense basins of Germany and France. Germany's coal industry, despite territorial losses and the need to provide reparations in coal, had recovered remarkably quickly after World War I. By the late 1920s, it was functioning at a high level of productivity, capturing British markets in France and in Italy. When depression struck in 1929, cutthroat competition brought only temporary declines in production. By 1937 coal output in western Europe had regained its 1929 levels (J. Clark, 1990: 59-70; Gordon, 1970: 19-20).

Indeed, coal's prominence lasted past World War II as the energy resource around which most large-scale industries were organized. Although historians place considerable emphasis on the post-war shift to petroleum, total coal consumption continued to rise until the 1950s. As electric power output expanded from the 1920s so did the market for coal. Besides providing the major fuel for generating electricity and coke for pig iron production, it also provided a major fuel for space heating. As late as 1950 Western European nations such as Britain, Germany, and Belgium depended on coal for some 90 percent of commercial energy, France for 70 percent (Darmstadter, 1971: 15; Gordon, 1970: 19; Gordon, Jacoby and Zimmerman, 1987: 81).

The delayed interfuel substitution of petroleum for coal points to the relation of technology, costs, and convenience in fuel choices.

Initially oil, like gas and electricity, was developed more because it seemed clean and convenient than because it was necessary. Important since the 1870s for kerosene and as a lubricant for machines, not until 1900 did industries begin experimenting with oil as a fuel. Cleaner to handle and to burn, it left no ash, was easier to transport, and was more heat efficient. But while major industrial nations such as Britain, Germany, and France each contained enormous coal reserves which shaped fuel preferences, Western Europe possessed little oil. Oil remained scarce and expensive, at least until the large finds of the 1930s. In 1936, Germany relied on foreign oil sources for some 70 percent of its liquid fuels. The dependence, interestingly, proved the reason for German research on liquid hydrocarbons which during World War II supplied most of its military fuel (Stokes, 1985: 254-277; Stranges, 1984: 643-647).

Initial demand for petroleum came primarily from its qualities as a liquid fuel which met technological innovations in transportation. Although in the case of the internal combustion engine the necessity for liquid energy is obvious, nevertheless, oil's challenge to the supremacy of coal was not immediate. Automobiles did not capture a mass market until the 1920s. And Norman Pounds maintains that if it weren't for the internal combustion engine, oil's importance might never have escalated (Pounds, 1985: 64-65). In fact, diesels did not replace steam locomotives on railroads until improvements in the operating efficiency of diesel engines led to their substitution for coal-fueled steam locomotives in the 1920s. Similarly, merchant marine reliance on coal-burning steamships did not start declining until the 1920s (Darmstadter, 1971: 19; Thomas, 1987). (Despite the adoptions of oil-fired and motorized vessels, even by mid-decade over one-third of U.S. registered vessels burned coal.)

The steel industry located in the Ruhr coal fields illustrates the possibilities of diverse supplies within an industry which continued to emphasize coal. For example, gas engines — run on blast furnace gas — were used to run dynamos. Coal-fueled electric power was introduced both as a source of heat in electric steel furnaces for smelting and also for many tasks in the mines. Moreover, these power plants became an integral part of the economy and functioning of the mines and steel mills. Connections were made with regional grids so that excess power was sold to help defray costs and to meet peak load requirements.

As in the case of oil, there were delays in the adoption of electricity. Introduction of long-distance power lines did not result in immediate acceptance of this new source of energy for at least two reasons. Construction of electrical grids required enormous capital outlays. Some metropolitan centers such as Berlin moved to electric lighting and power by the 1920s, but English cities continued to rely on gas. Costs for users, even with the introduction of alternating current, remained high (Hughes, 1983; Schivelbusch, 1988; Wilson, 1988).

Rapid growth of electrical systems accelerated only after 1929. And since fuel constituted the largest cost for thermal generation of electricity, coal, which was cheap, figured as the preferred fuel. Into the 1940s, the preference of electric utilities for coal provided the single most important stimulus to production. By the 1930s, electricity supplied almost 70 percent of inanimate factory motive power in Germany and more than 40 percent in the U.K. and Belgium. Even though electricity often functioned as a direct substitute for coal, the growth in the demand for electricity sustained demand for coal (Hughes, 1983: 404-464; Crouzet, 1982: 259-260). So important was the tie-in between electric power generation and the coal market that in 1938 the International Labour Office estimated that three quarters of the demand for coal that was affected by fuel economies resulted primarily from its use in electric power generation (J. Clark, 1990: 62).

As for hydroelectricity, it remained relatively insignificant for most regions of Europe into the 1940s. Hydro had a very different spatial distribution and it too supplemented rather than replaced coal, sometimes fostering development of new industrial areas like the Swiss Alps. Also, new industries such as electro-chemicals and electro-metallurgical, which were extremely energy intensive, became important where water power resources were most abundant, but may not have developed otherwise.

Although the 1920s marked the beginning of a transition to an expanded fossil fuel base, reliance on coal persisted into the 1950s. Coal's long duration as Western Europe's major fossil fuel source coupled to the extraordinary volume of its combustion had environmental and economic costs which need to be recognized in any calculus of progress. However, they are too often still barely acknowledged in accounting for "how the West grew rich" (Rosenberg and Birdzell, 1986).

Eastern and Central Europe: An Alternative Industrial Experience

Turning to Eastern and Central Europe, we find an interesting case study of the bias which has governed our collection of data and the consequent distortion of the relation of energy to the industrializing process. Throughout this region, rural home and craft shop production constituted the dominant form of industrial organization and outside of new heavy industry, manufacturing relied on wood, people, animals, and water. However, data on renewable and animate power consumption in manufacturing have never been collected or even estimated. The available statistics, like those for the West, only report fossil fuels and electric power. This limited information is the basis for concluding that the Austro-Hungarian Monarchy produced only 6 percent of Europe's industrial production in 1900. Based on the same criteria — the low output of production resulting from fossil-fueled mechanization — the nations of the area are designated as "backward" or "underdeveloped" (Berend and Ranki, 1974a: 112-119, 131; Kaser and Radice, 1985: 262-274).

Although statistics are lacking on the contribution of rural households and small-scale manufacturing to the output of textiles, clothing, or food processing, we do have descriptive accounts that highlight their persistence as an alternative to inanimately powered large-scale production. Domestic flax spinning remained an important source of income in the hills of Silesia where it supplemented earnings from poor agriculture. A domestic cotton industry was carried out in peasant cottages from northeastern Bialystock to the Polish estates of the southeast. Hand looms were reported in every other house in the villages of Bulgaria and spinning wheels were another source of wages for women. Domestic and cottage industry also existed along with the many small-scale and local establishments in food processing such as butchers and bakers. To these must be added the shops of skilled craftsmen in glass cutting, cabinet making, and leather (Pounds, 1985: 304-306, 317).

The data not only omit the most dominant organization of manufacturing, home and workshop industry, but as important, they mask the importance of muscle and water-power in large-scale production. Industrial pockets with factories employing hundreds of workers date to the 18th century in the flourishing western provinces of the Hapsburg Monarchy. By the mid-19th century the growing Austrian textiles, food processing, and coal industries depended on a mix of wood, water, and muscle power joined to coal-fueled steam engines. In Czech lands, water-powered mechanization of spinning and weaving had been completed in the 1870s. In eastern Poland, where there had been no significant industrialization before the 1870s, an important water-powered large-scale textile industry emerged along the streams of Lodze. And in Hungary, water-powered flour milling flourished using the most advanced techniques (Berend and Ranki, 1974a: 123-134; Berend and Ranki, 1974b: 51-53; Pounds, 1985: 304, 309, 331, 425-426).

It is the growth of large-scale "commercially"-fueled enterprise which has been the model used to categorize the nations of the region. And when we turn to the emergence of energy-intensive new industries devouring coal and coke we find a pattern paralleling that in Britain and Western Europe. Measured by mining and factory output using inanimate motive power, industrialization in the Czech lands seems most closely to correspond to the Western prototype. From the 1880s, its steel and engineering capacities and its chemical and power industries placed Czechoslovakia on a par with Europe's major industrial nations. By 1931, the country compared favorably with France. By contrast, Hungary and Poland are categorized as "developing" nations, with Romania, Yugoslavia, and Bulgaria cited as "less developed." Albania, where 80 percent of the population remained dependent on agriculture as late as 1939, is labelled "backward" (Enyedi, 1976; Berend and Ranki, 1974a: 112-119; Trebilcock, 1981: 300-301, 308; Kaser and Radice, 1985: 30-33, 226-228).

What is most striking in those areas designated "less developed" or "developing" is the skewed emphasis on energy extraction. Rapid growth of what were foreign-dominated energy industries — coal, oil, electricity, and electrical equipment — necessitated such large quantities of energy consumption that on the eve of the war, the Dual Monarchy ranked fifth in terms of the value of its fuel and it figured as the third largest European producer of coal — ahead of France. Investment in coal-fueled electric generation remained one of Eastern Europe's most significant areas of expansion. Power plants rose from 835 in 1925 to over 3000 in 1938 and the region's total output of electric current more than doubled. In Hungary, electric energy is said to have shown the most impressive growth of all basic industry, rising more than four-fold between 1921 and 1938 (Berend and Ranki, 1974b: 134; Kaser and Radice, 1985: 140, 210-219, 261). In addition, the building of railway networks to meet the market needs of energy distribution, and increased mechanization of agricultural techniques, increased demand for "commercial" fuels.

Like South America and the Middle East, Eastern Europe served as a foreign-controlled resource provider to fuel Western industrialization. Romania and Russia emerged as net energy exporters, developed under the direction of multinationals which supplied capital from the 1880s. Their coal exports moved west where they supplemented coal supplied by Britain and Germany, Europe's leading coal producers and consumers. In the case of oil, the West depended exclusively in this era on imports from Romania, Poland, and Russia (Kaser and Radice, 1985: 210-219).

Foreign control went hand in hand with long-term strategies to increase extraction. Beneath the forests of Upper Silesia, extending from Prussia through Austria to Russia, lay a coal basin second only to the Ruhr. This area quickly became competitive with western Europe and, by 1913, the lowest pit-head prices for coal were found in Upper Silesia. After the war, Poland, which had the highest output per man-hour-shift in Europe, offered the cheapest coal. It became a preeminent producer and exporter of hard coal for markets in Scandinavia, France, and Italy. Total exports rose from under 500,000 metric tons in 1922 to some 12.5 million metric tons annually from 1923-31. Domestic consumption took two-thirds of production in 1930, but the rest was exported. Despite the shrinking international market during the world-wide depression, Poland increased production and its share of world exports rose from 6 percent in 1929 to 18 percent in 1937 (Pounds, 1985: 398, 507-508; Kaser and Radice, 1985: 32-34, 210-214, 260-61; J. Clark, 1990: 69-70).

In Czechoslovakia, coal fueled domestic industrialization while excess production went into international markets. Although the country had smaller reserves than Poland, it had the right mix for heavy manufacturing, especially the high-grade coking coal so important for steel production. In addition to hard coal, large deposits of low-energy lignite (also known as brown coal) were mined for export to Germany. In Hungary, too, brown coal output, mainly from Esztergom, expanded significantly over the interwar period (Berend and Ranki, 1974: 125-131; Kaser and Radice, 1985: 286-288).

In the less industrialized poorer nations to the East, governments intervened to retain foreign private companies. In Russia in the 1880s the government had sought European capital to develop its important western Donetz coal basin. In Romania, by the late 1930s the state encouraged increased output, paying foreign companies in advance and buying about 70 percent of coal production (Kaser and Ranki, 1985: 30-33, 255, 286-287).

Oil development reflected a similar pattern. From the turn of the century, when oil was still largely used for kerosene and as a machine lubricant, Western Europe sought out petroleum supplies from lesser developed and colonial areas in a world-wide competition for oil concessions. By 1900, even before the future demand for automobile fuel was clear, the industrialized nations of the West, in particular Britain and Germany, had secured petroleum supplies from concessions on its eastern periphery. Foreign capital, especially in Poland, Romania and Russia, dominated development and explains why by 1913 Eastern Europe and Russia ranked just below the United States as the world's most important suppliers. Even in Albania, Italians developed the oil deposits of Selenca (J. Clark, 1990: 28-31; Kaser and Radice, 1985: 214; U.S. Department of Energy, 1981: 89). Growth of the region's energy output for foreign use meant profits went abroad, a situation that did not stimulate significant regional growth rates or broad economic change.

By the inter-war period Romania ranked fifth among the leading oil producers in the world. Romania offers a dramatic example of a dual economy where a modern foreign-dominated extractive sector, mainly for international trade, coexisted beside traditional technology in non-farm production. Even compared to the western provinces of the Monarchy, where mining and manufacturing clustered only in selected areas, Romania was overwhelmingly rural, agricultural, and characterized by domestic and small-scale industry. But in this country, whose population primarily relied on biological and renewable power sources, fossil fuel extraction became the nation's first big business. Oil alone was responsible for 20-25 percent of fossil-fueled industrial output (Berend and Ranki, 1974a: 141; Kaser and Radice, 1985: 255-256, 268-272, 294).

Large-scale concentrated enterprise had initially appeared and remained restricted to the foreign development of oil, natural gas, and coal. While Romania's oil production in 1884 represented 5 percent of world production, the change came in 1900 when British and Belgian interests received concessions to establish the

Telega Oil Company. By 1905 German, Dutch, French, American, Austrian, Italian, and Swiss investors were also supplying much needed capital. Despite protests by local oil interests aimed at foreign control, and legislation to regulate exploitation on state lands, by 1914 only 4.5 percent of the capital invested in the industry was domestic. Three foreign firms produced about 70 percent of total output and monopolized internal and export markets — Steaua Romana owned by Deutsche Bank, Romana Americana, a Standard Oil subsidiary, and the largest producer, Astra Romana, a subsidiary of Royal Dutch Shell. By 1925, Hugo Stinnes, the German power magnate, had also acquired 49 brown coal works and 37 oil fields and petroleum factories. And in 1927, AGIP, an Italian mixed enterprise funded by the Italian government, purchased some 90 percent of Prahova.

By 1930, Romania was exporting three-quarters of its petroleum production. Much of the rest was used domestically for energy-related industry. When the depression brought an enormous drop in prices — which halved the value — Western companies, to make up for lower prices, almost doubled extraction. Production rose from 4.8 million tons in 1929 to 7.4 in 1933 (Berend and Ranki, 1974: 106-107, 141; J. Clark, 1990: 33; Kaser and Radice, 1985: 235; Tipton and Aldrich, 1987: 243; U.S. Department of Energy, 1981: 89).

Romanian oil enterprise stimulated the industrialization of a region which spread from Bucharest to Brasov and attracted related industries, transport, and commerce. As in the West, chemicals and electricity, were offshoots of energy development and were heavily energy intensive. The chemical industry, for example, consisted largely of refineries connected with the oil fields. But in terms of large-scale industry (it must be remembered that we know very little of small-scale operations), Romania remained a backward nation with oil exported to serve the raw material needs of the West. The growth of extractive industry did not result in broader economic development, and processing remained at comparatively low levels. Employment, measured motive power, and value of output remained so narrowly concentrated that in

1930 the value of estimated industrial production totaled only 7 percent of the economy as a whole (Pounds, 1985: 269).

When we turn to Russia again we find a similar pattern. Industry remained small compared to figures on total population, but at the turn of the century Czarist Russia was the world's largest oil producer, responsible for 55 percent of world supplies. As in Romania, large-scale industrial enterprise centered on energy extraction, in this case from the Donetz coal basin of southwestern Russia, from the oil fields of the Ukraine, and from the Baku fields near the Caspian sea. The capital and machinery supplied by the West was then paid for with exports of primary products. In Russia, as elsewhere in the East, the proportion of industrial output seems small compared to total economic activity, but here too the figures largely ignore textiles, food processing, and clothing manufacture in rural areas using traditional technologies and power sources (Tipton and Aldrich, 1987: 38-41; U.S. Department of Energy, 1981: 262).

Foreign commercialization of Russian fossil fuel dates from the Crown leases in the Baku district of Transcaucausan Russia in the 1870s where, by 1877, a 19-kilometer foreign-funded pipeline had been laid. By 1899, some three-quarters of Russia's soft coal was extracted by fifteen companies, ten of which were foreign. Railways, also built with foreign funds to transport fuel, further stimulated rising energy demand. For example, petroleum exports date from completion of the Baku-Batum line in 1883, connecting the Caspian and Black Seas and opening the export route. In 1885, the Ekaterine railway linked the coal resources of the Donetz basin with the iron ore of Krivoi Rog, bringing rapid industrialization in southern Russia in the 1890s. In the prerevolutionary period, Produgol, the giant coal mining syndicate, cornered more than 70 percent of the fuel business with the railroads. In another energy connection, the government-initiated "crash program" for industrialization in the 1890s relied on petroleum exports to pay for the heavy foreign railway loans and for armaments. Then, too, the Baku-Batum Kerosene Pipeline, completed in 1906, was under the direction of the Rothschilds and this pipeline, the longest, most technologically advanced in the world, kept Russian oil competitive (Trebilcock, 1981: 266; Cadieux, 1986: 335-344; Parker, 1984: 106; U.S. Department of Energy, 1981: 261-264).

Although Russia produced large tonnages of coal, by 1913 high consumption made it a net importer. Two decades later the same was true of oil. Until World War I the oil industry had suffered from a scarcity of capital, skilled labor, and technology. It was especially injured by the revolution and civil war. After the revolution, although adding to production, the nation also increased its liquid fuel consumption. Rising oil output in the late 1920s allowed for substantial increases in exports, but oil consumption was still strikingly high — the largest among all areas of the world, except Latin America, in 1925. Moreover, not until 1927 did oil production return to 1900 levels. The output of coal and petroleum doubled from 1927 to 1932, and from 1932 to 1937 the output of coal more than doubled again. Petroleum supplies, however, fell short of expectations. Even though oil production increased steadily until World War II, in 1933, the U.S.S.R. became a net importer of oil to meet the needs of rapid industrialization (Tipton and Aldrich, 1987: 194; U.S. Department of Energy, 1981: 261-262).

In most of Eastern Europe the rate of measured industrial output was restored to pre-war levels by the late 1920s. Except for Romania, power production of electricity expanded quite rapidly, in line with the world-wide trend, and in the early 1930s there were comparatively high rates of industrial growth in Yugoslavia, Romania, and Bulgaria, with significant recovery in Hungary. These patterns were interrupted by world economic crises, but the war buildup of the 1930s, by reinforcing the demand for fossil fuels, reinvigorated economies from Austria to Czechoslovakia, Romania, Poland and Russia (Tipton and Aldrich, 1987: 171).

The Need for a New Paradigm

The growing awareness that fossil fuels are poisoning the atmosphere, that their accelerating use over the last century represents a threat — a hazard to society — demands an extraordinary

readjustment of long-held premises about the benefits of nonre-
newables to work, abundance, and the nature of social "advance"
(Greenberg, 1990: 693-714).

According to a still significant strain in public discourse, cut-
backs in accelerating use of fossil fuels would bring an inevitable
decline in the growth of goods and services and contraction of the
possibilities for prosperity (Riker, 1975: 145-146; Alchian, 1975:
1-25; Winger and Nielson, 1976: 2-3: *Nuclear Industry*, 1977; Stobaugh and Yergin, 1979: 167-230; Simon and Kahn, 1984). Little
more than a decade ago President Carter's call for energy efficiency and less use, conservation, was interpreted as dangerous to
the nation; as a policy that meant "freezing in the dark." Despite
considerable evidence to the contrary, we continue to emphasize
supply development of oil and coal as the "commercial" fuels essential for growing GNP. In 1991, President Bush, claiming to be
the environmental president, nevertheless strongly advocated oil
supply development as an economic necessity.

By contrast, traditional energy sources, what we call renewables, have been identified both as a cause and as a reflection
of backwardness. As recently as the energy crises of the 1970s,
economists, business executives, and political leaders ridiculed
proposals to reduce rising oil consumption by turning to energy
alternatives. Renewables such as water, wood, biomass, and solar
were dismissed as primitive and inefficient for industrial economies
(Alchian, 1975: 1-25). Consequently their replacement by fossil
fuels has been regarded as vital to more productive technologies
and to sustained economic growth.

The idea that renewables are primitive and inefficient has en-
dured, although it is as simplistic and historically inaccurate as the
premise that fossil fuels replaced renewables in a linear sequence
of progress-wood, water, then coal and oil. Both are constructs
derived from the long-time equation of productivity and progress
which reflects an economic paradigm for evaluating energy systems
and their efficiency. Just as thermodynamic criteria for energy efficiency were disregarded, omission of data on renewables was said

to be "minimized by the low efficiency with which such fuels are traditionally used" (Darmstadter, 1971: 1, 3-5).

If one challenge before us is to recognize the environmental costs of the extended and extensive burning of timber, coal, and oil, the second is to come to a more accurate understanding of renewables. But not only are historical data on wood fuel consumption lacking, more to the point, wood is hardly referred to as a source of heat in historical scholarship on rural manufactures. Direct use of water power, so critical historically in industrial activity, has only recently been estimated. Similarly, the fragmentary statistics on the useful work performed by draft animals and people is in keeping with a point of view which disregards muscle power as a significant source for production and economic growth. Studies such as that by the End-Use Oriented Global Energy Project have recently attempted to remedy the deficiency, but we still have only selective information on renewables even though wood and plants are used today as an energy source by some 80 percent of world population (Goldemberg et al., 1987: 190-234; Dunkerley et al., 1981: 45-64).

It seems time to reconsider basic premises about the multiple costs of energy use for society and to face the cultural biases which have resulted in extraordinary gaps in our knowledge. We need to reevaluate long-standing assumptions about "modern" power sources, as well as the corresponding claims that renewables are not "commercial," or that they cannot be used efficiently for sustained development.

In evaluating the relation of energy to the well-being of people and the planet, perhaps the basic challenge is to ask new questions about the past and the future.

References

Adams, Richard. 1982. *Paradoxical Harvest: Energy and Explanation in British History, 1870-1914.* Cambridge, MA: Cambridge University Press.

Alchian, Arman A. 1975. "An Introduction to Confusion." Pp. 1-25 in Morris A. Adelman et al. (eds.), *No Time to Con-*

fuse: A Critique of the Final Report of the Energy Policy Project of the Ford Foundation. San Francisco, CA: Institute for Contemporary Studies.

Ashton, T. S. 1965. *The Industrial Revolution: 1760-1830*. New York, NY: Oxford University Press.

Berend, Ivan T. and Gyorgy Ranki. 1974a. *Economic Development in East-Central Europe in the 19th and 20th Centuries*. New York, NY: Columbia University Press.

_____. 1974b. *Hungary, a Century of Economic Development*. New York, NY: Barnes and Noble Books.

Berg, Maxine et al. (eds.). 1983. *Manufacture in Town and Country Before the Factory*. Cambridge, MA: Cambridge University Press.

Brown, Lester R. 1990. "The Illusion of Progress." Pp. 3-16 in Lester R. Brown et al. (eds.), *State of the World*. New York, NY: W. W. Norton and Company.

Cadieux, Francois. 1986. "Western Technology and Early Russian Pipelines, 1877-1917." *Journal of European Economic History* 15 (Fall): 335-344.

Cippola, Carlo. 1962. *The Economic History of World Population*. Baltimore, MD: Penguin Books.

Clark, John G. 1990. *The Political Economy of World Energy: A Twentieth Century Perspective*. Chapel Hill, NC: University of North Carolina Press.

Clark, William C. 1990. *Usable Knowledge for Managing Global Climate Change*. Stockholm, Sweden: The Stockholm Environment Institute.

Cook, Earl. 1976. *Man, Energy, Society*. San Francisco, CA: W. H. Freeman and Company.

Crouzet, Francois. 1982. *The Victorian Economy*. New York, NY: Columbia University Press.

Darmstadter, Joel. 1977. *How Industrial Societies Use Energy: A Comparative Analysis*. Washington, DC: Resources For The Future.

_____. 1971. *Energy in the World Economy: A Statistical Review of Trends in Output, Trade, and Consumption Since 1925*. Baltimore, MD: Johns Hopkins University Press.

Dunkerley, Joy et al. 1981. *Energy Strategies for Developing Nations.* Baltimore, MD: Johns Hopkins University Press.

Elbaum, Bernard and William Lazonick (eds.). 1986. *The Decline of the British Economy: An Institutional Perspective.* Oxford: Oxford University Press.

Enyedi, Gyorgy. 1976. *Hungary: An Economic Geography.* Boulder, CO: Westview Press.

Goldemberg, Jose et al. 1987. *Energy for a Sustainable World.* Washington, DC: World Resources Institute.

Gordon, Richard. 1970. *The Evolution of Energy Policy in Western Europe: The Reluctant Retreat From Coal.* New York, NY: Praeger.

Gordon, Richard, Henry Jacoby and Martin Zimmerman. 1987. *Energy: Markets and Regulation.* Cambridge, MA: The MIT Press.

Greenberg, Dolores. 1990. "Energy, Power, and Perceptions of Social Change in the Early Nineteenth Century." *American Historical Review* 95 (June): 693-714.

_____. 1982. "Reassessing the Power Patterns of the Industrial Revolution: An Anglo-American Comparison." *American Historical Review* 87 (December): 1237-1261.

_____. 1980. "Energy Flow in a Changing Economy, 1815-1880." Pp. 29-58 in Joseph R. Frese and Jacob Judd (eds.), *An Emerging Independent American Economy, 1815-1875.* Tarrytown, NY: Sleepy Hollow Press.

Holmes, Douglas R. and Jean H. Quataert. 1986. "An Approach to Modern Labor: Worker Peasantries in Historic Saxony and the Friuli Region Over Three Centuries." *Comparative Studies in Society and History* 3 (April): 191-216.

Hughes, Thomas. 1983. *Networks of Power: Electrification in Western Society: 1880-1930.* Baltimore, MD: Johns Hopkins University Press.

Hunter, Louis C. 1985. *History of Industrial Power in the United States, 1780-1930. Vol. II: Steam Power.* Charlottesville, VA: University of Virginia Press.

Jensen, W. G. 1990. *Energy and the Economy of Nations.* Cambridge, MA: G. T. Foulis & Co.

Jones, Eric L. 1981. *The European Miracle: Environments, Economies, and Geopolitics in the History of Europe and Asia.* Cambridge, MA: Cambridge University Press.

Kanefsky, John. 1979. "Motive Power in British Industry and the Accuracy of the 1870 Factory Return." *Economic History Review*, 2nd series, 32 (August): 360-373.

Kaser, Michael C. and E. A. Radice (eds.). 1985. *Economic Structure and Performance Between the Wars.* New York, NY: Oxford University Press.

Kenwood, A. G. and A. L. Lougheed. 1982. *Technological Diffusion and Industrialization Before 1914.* New York, NY: St. Martin's Press.

Kuznets, Simon. 1966. *Modern Economic Growth: Rate, Structure, and Spread.* New Haven, CT: Yale University Press.

Landes, David. 1969. *The Unbound Prometheus: Technological Change, 1750 to the Present.* London: Cambridge University Press.

Lloyd-Jones, Roger and M. J. Lewis. 1988. *Manchester and the Age of the Factory: The Business Structure of Cottonopolis in the Industrial Revolution.* New York, NY: Routledge, Chapman Hall.

Maull, Hanns. 1980. *Europe and World Energy.* London: Butterworths.

Mitchell, Brian R. 1984. *Economic Development of the British Coal Industry: 1800-1914.* New York, NY: Cambridge University Press.

Morris, Cynthia Taft and Irma Adelman, 1988. *Comparative Patterns of Economic Development, 1850-1914.* Baltimore, MD: Johns Hopkins University Press.

Nuclear Industry. 1977. "Conservation: Its Role in the Energy Debate" (March): 9-12.

Parker, N. 1984. *Europe and the Wider World: Essays on the Economic History of Western Capitalism.* New York, NY: Cambridge University Press.

Pollard, Sidney. 1981. *Peaceful Conquest: The Industrialization of Europe, 1760-1970.* Oxford: Oxford University Press.

Pounds, Norman. J. G. 1985. *An Historical Geography of Europe, 1800-1914.* New York, NY: Cambridge University Press.

Putnam, P. C. 1953. *Energy in the Future.* New York: Van Nostrand Press.

Quataert, Jean. 1988. "A New View of Industrialization: 'Proindustry,' or the Role of Small-Scale, Labor Intensive Manufacture in the Capitalist Environment." *International Labor and Working Class History* 33 (Spring): 3-22.

Reynolds, Terry. 1983. *Stronger Than a Hundred Men: A History of the Vertical Water Wheel.* Baltimore, MD: Johns Hopkins University Press.

Riker, William H. 1975. "The Ideology of a Time to Choose." Pp. 145-156 in Morris A. Adelman et al. (eds.), *No Time to Confuse: A Critique of the Final Report of the Energy Policy Project of the Ford Foundation.* San Francisco, CA: Institute for Contemporary Studies.

Rosenberg, Nathan and L. E. Birdzell, Jr. 1986. *How the West Grew Rich: The Economic Transformation of the Industrial World.* New York, NY: Basic Books.

Rostow, Walt W. 1971. *The Stages of Economic Growth: A Non-Communist Manifesto* (second edition). Cambridge, MA: Cambridge University Press.

Sabel, Charles and Jonathan Zeitlin. 1985. "Historical Alternatives to Mass Production: Politics, Markets, and Technology in Nineteenth Century Industrialization." *Past and Present* 108 (August): 133-176.

Schivelbusch, Wolfgang. 1988. *Disenchanted Night: The Industrialization of Light in the Nineteenth Century.* Berkeley, CA: University of California Press.

Schmeichen, James. 1984. *Sweated Industries and Sweated Labor: The London Clothing Trades, 1860-1914.* Champaign, IL: University of Illinois Press.

Simon, Julien L. and Herman Kahn (eds.). 1984. *The Resourceful Earth: A Response to Global 2000.* New York, NY: Oxford University Press.

Stobaugh, Robert and Daniel Yergin (eds.). 1979. *Energy Future: Report of the Energy Project at the Harvard Business School.* New York, NY: Random House.

Stokes, Raymond G. 1985. "The Oil Industry in Nazi Germany, 1936-1945." *Business History Review* 59 (December): 254-277.

Stranges, Anthony. 1984. "N. Friedrich Bergius and the Rise of The German Synthetic Fuel Industry." *ISIS* 75 (December): 643-667.

Thomas, Donald E. 1987. *Diesel: Technology and Society in Industrial Germany.* Auburn, AL: University of Alabama Press.

Tipton, Frank B. and Robert Aldrich (eds.). 1987. *An Economic and Social History of Europe, 1890-1939.* Baltimore, MD: Johns Hopkins University Press.

Trebilcock, Clive. 1981. *The Industrialization of the Continental Powers, 1780-1914.* New York, NY: Longman, Inc.

U.S. Department of Energy. 1981. *Energy Industries Abroad.* Washington, D.C.

Von Tunzelmann, G. N. 1978. *Steam Power and British Industrialization to 1860.* New York, NY: Oxford University Press.

Wilson, J. F. 1988. *Ferranti and the British Electrical Industry, 1864-1939.* New York, NY: Manchester University Press.

Winger, John G. and Carolyn A. Nielson. 1976. "Energy, the Economy, and Jobs." *Energy Report From Chase* (September): 2-3.

PART III

Contemporary Issues

Chapter 4

Climatic Change and Energy Supply:
A Comparison of Solar and Nuclear Options

Dean Abrahamson

Climatic Change:
The End of the Fossil Era

The world faces a threat potentially more catastrophic than any other threat in human history — climate change and global warming...nothing less than a complete change in attitudes and lifestyles will succeed in averting potentially catastrophic impacts from climatic change and global warming.

Mostafa Tolba, Executive Director UNEP, 1990

A Limit to Growth

A century ago, when my grandparents were beginning their adult lives, pollution was primarily a matter of trash in the backyard. Environmentalism found its expression through the preservation of unique landscapes as parks, and creating zoos and monuments. Various institutions, governmental and nongovernmental, were created to encourage and manage these activities. This work continues as does that necessary to protect past gains from bull-dozers, drill rigs, and population pressures (Abrahamson, 1990).

During my parents' lifetimes pollution began to impact large areas, river basins, and entire airsheds. The 1950s saw the first serious efforts to address these insults, and the 1970s brought realization that pollution was a major threat to health, to economic well being, and to our natural heritage. Institutions established at that time — the United Nations Environmental Programme and the United States Environmental Protection Agency and its counterparts in other countries, a host of public interest organizations — yet have much to do.

It is distressing to realize that the conventional pollution issues which shape the agenda of these agencies — water management, solid waste, urban air pollution, acid rain, and such — are in a sense trivial and that our management of them has been tragic. They are trivial not in their consequences but because we have known the causes, we have known the effects, we have had the technology in hand to prevent or greatly diminish the impacts, and we have known the economic costs of both impacts and remedies. We have dealt with these issues by tradeoffs at the margin — piece by piece casting our irreplaceable biological capital into the bonfires stoked by short-sighted economic interests rationalized through conventional necroeconomic [sic] benefit-cost analyses (Office of the President, 1990: 207-224; Daly, 1990).

Global climatic change, stratospheric ozone depletion, and loss of biological diversity are now among the issues thrusting themselves onto the policy agenda. These are fundamentally different from conventional pollution issues. They threaten the integrity of the global systems which sustain all living things and our political economies. They are global, making all countries vulnerable to the actions of all others. They are irreversible in times of social, political, and economic relevance. And these problems can not be solved by adding a device at the end of the pipe or smokestack. Remedy requires reducing the level of the activities which produce the pollutants.

If the present understanding of the greenhouse effect is even approximately correct, avoiding potentially catastrophic climatic change will require stabilization of the concentration of greenhouse gases in the atmosphere. Stabilization of these concentrations will require that anthropogenic greenhouse gas emissions be reduced greatly: carbon dioxide emissions by more than 60 percent, perhaps much more (Marston et al., 1991); methane emissions by 15 to 20 percent; nitrous oxide by 70 to 80 percent; emissions of the major chlorofluorocarbons (CFCs) essentially eliminated; and large reductions be made in emissions of the other greenhouse gases (IPCC, 1990).

This seems benign so long as the issue is cast in the abstract terms of chemical pollutants as we don't relate to them very well. We relate intimately, however, to the activities which give rise to these gasses (IPCC, 1990):

- Fossil fuel burning produces about 46 percent of global heating;
- Emissions of CFCs and other industrial chemicals produce about 27 percent of global heating;
- Destruction of old-growth forests produces about 18 percent of global heating;
- Greenhouse gas emissions from agriculture produce about 10 percent of global heating.

And the levels of these activities are causing the release of greenhouse gases at rates far in excess of those which can be removed by natural sinks — hence their concentrations in the atmosphere and the consequent greenhouse forcing are increasing rapidly.

The greenhouse effect and resultant climatic change provide clear evidence that the human enterprise, as presently conducted, has grown to the point that its waste products are poisoning global systems upon which life, and the political economy, depend. A limit to growth has been exceeded.

As the fossil fuels are far and away the largest single source of greenhouse gas emissions, and as there is no practical way known to burn these fuels even at the present rate without releasing more greenhouse gases than can be assimilated, it must be concluded that replacement of fossil by non-fossil primary energy sources are among the measures necessary to limit global climatic change.

The Consequences of Inaction

The Intergovernmental Panel on Climate Change (IPCC) has summarized the impacts expected were business-as-usual emissions of greenhouse gases to continue into the early part of the 2000s. These include (IPCC, 1990):

- ...irreversible changes in the climate could be detectable by the end of this century [by 2000];

- ...The [climate] changes will not be steady and surprises cannot be ruled out. The severity of the impacts will depend to a large degree on the rate of climate change;

- Sufficient evidence is now available to indicate that changes in climate would have an important effect on agriculture and livestock... Patterns of agricultural trade could be altered by decreased cereal production in some of the currently high-production areas... On balance, the evidence suggests that in the face of estimated changes of climate, food production at the global level can be maintained... however, the cost of achieving this is unclear;

- The rotation period of forests is long and current forests will mature and decline during a climate in which they are increasingly more poorly adapted... Large losses in the form of forest declines can occur. Losses from wildfire will be increasingly extensive;

- Natural terrestrial ecosystems could face significant consequences... Projected changes in temperature and precipitation suggest that climate zones could shift several hundred kilometers toward the poles over the next fifty years... These rates are likely to be faster than the ability of some species to respond and responses may be sudden or gradual...Most at risk are those communities in which the options for adaptability are limited and where climate changes add to existing stresses...The socioeconomic consequences of these impacts will be significant...

- Relatively small climate changes can cause large water resource problems in many areas...a one to two degree Celsius temperature increase, coupled with a 10 percent reduction in precipitation, [could result in] a 40 to 70 percent reduction in annual runoff...Changes in drought risk represents potentially the most serious impact of climate change on agriculture at both regional and global levels (Waggoner, 1991);

- Changes in precipitation and temperature could radically alter the patterns of vector-borne and viral diseases by shifting them to higher latitudes...Global warming and increased ultraviolet radiation resulting from depletion of stratospheric ozone may produce adverse impacts on air quality...An increase in UV-B radiation intensity at the earth's surface would increase the risk of damage to the eye and skin and may disrupt the marine food chain...climate change, pollution, and ultraviolet-B radiation from ozone depletion can interact, reinforcing their damaging effects on materials and organisms;

- Global warming will accelerate sea-level rise, modify ocean circulation, and change marine ecosystems, with considerable socioeconomic consequences...A 30 to 50 cm sea-level rise, projected by 2050, will threaten low islands and coastal zones. A one meter rise by 2100 would render some island countries uninhabitable, displace tens of millions of people, seriously threaten low-lying urban areas, flood productive land, contaminate fresh water supplies, and change coastlines...Reductions in sea-ice will benefit shipping, but seriously impact on ice-dependent marine mammals and birds...regional shifts in fisheries will have major socio-economic impacts.

The Consequences of Action

The present understanding of the greenhouse effect is that total global anthropogenic carbon emissions must be reduced to less than three billion tonnes per year, perhaps much less, to stabilize the atmospheric concentration of carbon dioxide. The global population is now about 5.3 billion individuals. So, if the allowable carbon releases with stabilization were allocated to all humans equally each would have an annual budget of no more than 570 kilograms of carbon per year.

The global anthropogenic carbon emission rate from fossil fuel burning is now about 1,100 kilograms of carbon per person per year. The distribution varies greatly between countries. In India the average release is about 200 kilograms of carbon per person per year: in Kenya and Pakistan about half that of India. Canadian emissions are about 4,600 kilograms of carbon per person per year, and they are 5,300 kilograms in the United States (Boden et al., 1990).

There is also a wide disparity in greenhouse gas emissions between individuals. As an indicator of individual emissions for some individuals, a family of four flying for a vacation from New York to Hawaii would cause the emission of approximately 2,900 kilograms of carbon from their air travel. A person who travels 100,000 miles per year by scheduled airline would have his or her personal emission budget credited with about ten tons of carbon per year (Abrahamson and Sørensen, 1991). This is about 9 times the total global annual average per-capita emissions, 18 times the average allowable per capita annual emissions under a stabilization regime, or 50 times as much as the annual per-capital releases in India and yet it would not qualify the individual for the highest category of frequent flyer perks on some airlines.

It is not that we must give up the gratification provided by activities such as these, but we must learn how to achieve the same ends without the services provided by fossil fuels. Airplanes, as other modes of transport, can use fuels derived from non-fossil primary energy sources. Yet, measures which are sufficient to achieve stabilization of atmospheric greenhouse gases are likely to impinge upon western life-styles in the short term — or further exacerbate distributional inequities which may, in turn, lead to activities which impinge upon western life-styles (Heilbroner, 1974).

When Must We Act?

Previously our main concern centered on the effects of development on the environment. Today, we need to be equally concerned about the ways in which environmental degradation can dampen or reverse economic development.

Brundtland et al., 1987

It is our lot to be living when humankind is recognizing that its activities are destroying the resource base upon which its well-being depends. Human activities now can cause major changes in global climate within a few decades. Current rates of greenhouse gas emissions are committing the Earth to temperature increases of about 0.3 to 0.5 degrees Celsius per decade with significantly more warming in high northern latitudes. Business-as-usual emissions could commit the earth in only another 60 years to a climate not seen since the Pliocene epoch one to five million years ago (IPCC, 1990).

Many indices of human activities are growing exponentially: population, energy use, economic activity. Exponential growth is common in nature, but can continue only so long as the system exhibiting such growth remains small compared with its surroundings. Exponential growth is ended when the system exhibiting such growth runs out of space, of food, or is poisoned by its own wastes. This is as true for humans as it is for yeasts, fruit flies, or rabbits.

Global consumption of fossil fuels increased by more than 4 percent per year from the 1940s through the late 1970s. Growth rates declined in the late 1970s but rose again during the 1980s. At an annual growth rate of only 3 percent per year, the annual consumption of fossil fuels, and hence the releases of carbon dioxide, doubles each 23 years. Were a 3 percent growth rate in global fossil fuel consumption to be maintained, the amount of fuel consumed and carbon dioxide released during the next quarter century would be comparable to the releases from the beginning of the industrial revolution to today.

This is why things are happening quickly. This is why we cannot delay and leave the hard decisions to the next generation.

Required Actions

If our understanding of the science is approximately correct, the prevention of climatic change which could be catastrophic means (IPCC, 1990):

- Reducing the rate of growth of the world population is essential.

- Reducing global carbon dioxide emissions from fossil fuel use to a small fraction of present levels by shifting from oil and coal to natural gas in the very short run and to non-fossil primary energy sources early in the next century; improving the efficiency with which energy is used and converted; management and behavioral changes (e.g., increased work in homes through information technology); and structural changes (e.g., modal shifts in transportation).

- Full implementation of the Montreal Protocol phasing out CFCs, and other long-lived industrial greenhouse gases.

- Limiting agricultural emissions through: reducing methane emissions from livestock husbandry; reducing the use of nitrogenous fertilizers; shifting marginal lands to fodder, forest, etc.; and moving toward sustainable agriculture practices.

- Stopping the destruction of old growth forest, whether in the tropics or elsewhere and starting, and sustaining, large reforestation programs.

And, we must do these things in ways that do not make the cure worse than the disease.

These measures will also go a long way toward resolution of many traditional environmental insults. Acid precipitation will be reduced in parallel with the reduction in coal and oil use. Stratospheric ozone depletion will be reduced as are the emissions of the CFCs. Efficient energy use will carry with it recycling and waste source reduction. Halting destruction of old growth forests will do much to slow the rate of species extinction as will reducing the total energy flows used to sustain humans and their artifacts.

Selecting Primary Energy Sources

...a shift to renewable [energy sources] and nuclear in the first half of the next century reduces the emissions of carbon dioxide, initially more or less stabilizing emissions in the industrialized countries...stringent controls in industrialized countries, combined with moderate growth of emissions in developing countries could stabilize atmospheric concentrations. Carbon dioxide emissions are reduced to 50 percent of 1985 levels by the middle of the next century.

> Intergovernmental Panel
> on Climate Change, 1990

Energy brokers all change in the physical and biological worlds, as money brokers transactions in the economic world. These worlds are linked tightly.

Energy policy is an evolving art. Less than twenty years ago energy policy was almost exclusively concerned with energy supply, energy consumption was regarded as being a measure of all things good, and quality of life was taken as being directly proportional to *per capita* energy consumption.

Energy consumption had grown exponentially for several decades. Total energy consumption in the United States was increasing at about 4 percent per year, the consumption of electricity at about 7 percent per year. These growth rates were regarded as a natural characteristic of modern industrial economies and it was assumed that they would continue for the foreseeable future — certainly for the several decades life of investments in new energy supply.

The Ford Foundation Energy Policy Project (FFEPP, 1974) legitimized including considerations of energy end-use in energy policy as was emphasized at the time by Joseph L. Sax:

> This is an important document by the only true test of importance; it requires us to alter the questions we ask about energy problems. No one who reads this report will ever again be able to view energy policy as merely a matter of developing supplies to meet demands projected into the future from unquestioned historical patterns of use (Sax, as quoted in FFEPP, 1974: 398).

The Energy Policy Project's final report, and accompanying technical analyses, began to demolish the dogma that continued increases in energy consumption at historic rates were either necessary or desirable.

Energy policy is no longer constrained to considerations of energy supply. It has now been demonstrated that economic activity can continue to grow with *decreasing* energy inputs (U.S. DOE, 1991). It is also known that the same energy services can be provided with a fraction of current energy consumption, with large accompanying economic savings for those who must pay the energy bills, and with large accompanying reductions in environmental impacts and risks to national security (Goldemberg et al., 1988; Johansson et al., 1989).

Increasing the efficiency with which we use energy, however necessary, can not sufficiently reduce emissions to stabilize atmospheric greenhouse gas concentrations. The choice of primary energy supply is of vital importance.

Energy use has been an index of industrial production which has grown nearly fifty-fold in the last 100 years. Four-fifths of that growth has come since 1950, almost all of it based on fossil fuels — coal, oil, and natural gas. The menu of primary energy sources available to replace the fossil fuels is short: fission, fusion, tides, geothermal, and solar.

The fission fuel — uranium and thorium — resource base is comparable to that of the solid hydrocarbons if plutonium is separated from spent reactor fuel and recycled. The technology is available for the conversion of nuclear fuels to useful energy carriers. Nuclear fission, with breeder reactors, could supply sufficient energy to displace the fossil fuels from a narrow technical perspective, e.g., leaving aside questions of cost, safety, and links with nuclear weapons.

Nuclear fusion has been the Holy Grail of energy supply. Fusion has a very large fuel base as it is essentially isotopes of hydrogen found in water. Determining the appropriate resources to allocate to controlled fusion research is an important element of research and development policy, but fusion does not yet lie within the realm of energy supply policy as fusion power could not penetrate the supply market for decades. Fusion, particularly if deployed as fusion-fission hybrid reactors, could also carry with it the risks which continue to plague nuclear fission (Abrahamson, 1974).

Tidal power drops from the menu because there is not enough energy in tides to be of interest even were the technology for its capture available. The total energy of global tides and tidal currents is only equal to about a quarter of present global commercial energy use (Davis, 1990 and Holdren, 1990), only a minute fraction of which could, even theoretically, be harnessed for man's purposes.

Geothermal power suffers from both resource and technological constraints. The total geothermal energy of the world's volcanoes and hot springs is only about 2 percent of today's global commercial energy use. This energy flux can be utilized in hyper-thermal areas, for example Iceland, but cannot be of more than local or regional importance. The geothermal heat conducted by rocks is two and a half times today's commercial energy use, but the technology is not available to use the dry geothermal heat flux which, like that of waves and tides, is too diffuse to be effectively exploited (Kerr, 1987).

The solar energy falling on the earth's continents is more than 2,000 times the total annual commercial energy now being used by man. The solar energy flux can be captured by many means: hydropower, biomass, wind, waves, photovoltaic conversion, ocean thermal conversion, direct heating, and others (Weinberg and Williams, 1990). There is but limited potential for hydropower expansion in most industrial countries in contrast to many developing countries. Further, the environmental costs of large hydropower schemes is hampering their growth generally. Windpower has large potential, as do biomass and photovoltaic solar energy conversion systems. Renewable energy sources could soon supply all of today's global commercial energy use in a cost-effective manner.

Conclusion: Solar vs. Nuclear

If the hydrocarbons must remain in the ground the only available primary energy sources are nuclear power with breeder reactors, and solar power converted primarily through biomass cycles, windpower, or with photoelectric cells, and augmented by other renewable energy where it is locally available.

Nuclear Power

The Atomic Energy Dream

There is understandable drive on the part of men of good will to build up the positive aspects of nuclear energy simply because the negative aspects are so distressing.

Alvin M. Weinberg, 1969

During the 1950s and 1960s atomic energy was regarded with what now seems to be naive optimism. Claims were made that its use would solve the world's problems of hunger, poverty, and pollution. The abundance and security which it would provide would allow the more noble aspects of human nature to ascend and permit the full development of the brotherhood of man (Seaborg and Corliss, 1971).

Reactors would provide enough energy to make bread from rocks with electricity that was too cheap to meter — and power our ships, military vehicles, airplanes, and space rockets.

Atomic explosives would make planetary engineering practicable. We would move mountains, stabilize geological faults, change the climate, reverse the flows of rivers, create harbors and canals, and release mineral resources previously locked tight far below the ground.

Radioisotopes recovered from reactor by-products would supply: radioactive isotopes of cesium to sterilize the world's sewage and eliminate water-borne diseases; plutonium-238 sources to provide heat for our coffee percolators, warm diving suits, and power totally implantable artificial hearts; tritium to dope latex for condoms which would glow in the dark; our food and building products would be irradiated, as would much, much, more.

This was the scientific power dream — and it has not been forgotten.

The Ghosts in the Machine

> We nuclear people have made a Faustian bargain with
> society. On the one hand we offer in the catalytic
> burner [breeder reactor] an inexhaustible source of
> energys...But the price that we demand of society for
> this magical energy source is both a vigilance and a
> longevity of our social institutions that we are quite
> unaccustomed to.
>
> Alvin M. Weinberg, 1972

Nuclear energy is a technology of the state. When, in the
late 1960s and early 1970s, efforts were made to move it from the
laboratories into the community it failed the tests of public and of
market acceptance in most, but not all, countries (Novick, 1976;
Patterson, 1983).

When it was announced that nuclear explosives would be used
to blast a new transisthmus canal and new harbors in Alaska
and Australia, and that 20,000 explosives each the size of the Hi-
roshima bomb would be detonated in Colorado to stimulate natural gas production, questions were raised about safety (Lewis,
1972 and Metzger, 1972). These programs were soon abandoned.

Most of the ambitious radioisotope schemes were curtailed or
abandoned. The safety of some, such as food irradiation, are still
being debated. The space program continues to place large radioactive sources in orbit — and occasionally into the atmosphere.

The proposals to build power reactors on the San Andreas
Fault, in mid-town New York City, and in hamlets throughout the
land brought questions about reactor safety. When tens of power
reactors were ordered by electric power utilities with no prior experience with nuclear power, each reactor ten-fold larger than the
largest demonstration reactors, the entire fuel cycle began to be
examined.

And, hovering in the background was the specter of the diversion of nuclear fuels into clandestine weapons programs.

One by one these, and other, issues were examined by independent scientists. As unresolved problems were uncovered the general public became aware of the ghosts in the machine. A lively debate resulted — lasting from the late 1960s through the 1970s — leading to the rejection of the nuclear dream in most, but not all, countries.

But, the issue is not yet resolved.

Conditions Have Changed

What this country needs to dramatize our energy crisis is a good twenty-four hour blackout.

Chet Holifield, Chairman, U.S. Congress
Joint Committee on Atomic Energy, 1972

During the debates of the 1960s and 1970s coal and energy shortfalls were regarded as the only alternatives to atomic power. Oil and natural gas resources were recognized as being limited, and it was argued that a higher and better use for these hydrocarbons was as feedstock for the manufacture of plastics and other products. Solar power was dismissed as being outrageously expensive and, even if costs would come down, as being unable to provide the need for power, assumed to be doubling each 10 years.

The recognition of the importance of the anthropogenic impacts on greenhouse effect and the resultant risk for climatic change has, however, changed the context within which atomic power is considered. Coal can no longer be considered an acceptable alternative. Means to provide needed energy services with a fraction of present energy consumption are now available. And, renewable energy supply technologies have advanced far beyond those of the 1970s.

But the Major Issues
Remain Unresolved

> The nuclear industry must come to recognize that its long-term viability depends on being able to convince the public that it can offer a peaceful atom that is unambiguously distinct from the military atom. Unless this is accomplished, nuclear power is doomed as a major long-term energy option. While nuclear power might get a second chance, in light of greenhouse concerns, it would not be likely to get a third if there were a major diversion incident somewhere in the world that could be plausibly linked to nuclear power.
>
> R. H. Williams and H. A. Feiveson, 1990

Nuclear power is subject to indisputable imperatives. One is to safeguard potential nuclear explosives, particularly the plutonium created as an inevitable by-product of the fission process. The other is the imperative to contain radioactivity in reactor and nuclear fuel cycle operations (Carter, 1987).

These imperatives are expressed in several, intimately linked, issues:

- Assuring that the radioactive waste products are isolated from contact with the biosphere for hundreds of thousands of years;

- Assuring that catastrophic releases of radioactive materials as a result of accidents at reactors or other fuel cycle facilities will occur very infrequently;

- Assuring that plutonium or other weapons-usable nuclear fuels are not diverted from the nuclear fuel cycle for use as atomic explosives or plutonium contamination weapons;

- Restructuring our society and institutions to make the above possible.

The need to demonstrate that wastes can be isolated, major accidents avoided, plutonium contained, and new institutions created to manage atomic power has been evident since the dawn of the atomic age. Thousands of talented scientists and other professionals have devoted their lives to the resolution of these intrinsic problems of atomic power. These unsolved problems were the reason that the market and the community have rejected atomic power. They remain unsolved.

Nuclear power is simply not poised to play a role in the avoidance of potentially catastrophic climatic change. There is yet no high-level radioactive waste repository anywhere in the world. Reactors characterized by their promoters as being inherently-safe are on the drawing boards, but the first demonstration plant to test the concepts will not be built until the early 21st century at the soonest (Mårtensson, 1992). Criteria for a diversion-resistant nuclear fuel cycle have been developed (Williams and Feiveson, 1990), but there is no evidence that they are being implemented. Pleas for new international institutions to manage atomic power are again being heard, but the issue has yet to be joined in national or international political fora (Nilsson and Abrahamson, 1992).

Solar Power

A transition to an efficient, sustainable [renewable] energy system is both technically possible and socially desirable.

Dennis Hays, 1977

There are many solar energy technologies now available. Biomass derived from energy plantations or residuals from agriculture, forestry, or waste streams can be converted to heat, electricity, alcohols, or methane. Windpower is now widely available at a tenth the cost of only a decade ago. Hydropower can be expanded in developing and developed countries alike. Photovoltaic cells are now the technology of choice for many remote or specialized locations and are expected to find wide general application within the decade.

Of fundamental importance is that solar energy systems require essentially no net emissions of carbon dioxide or the other greenhouse gases.

Solar power is not totally free of environmental impacts. There are potential land-use conflicts associated with several solar energy techniques, including, but certainly not limited to, hydropower impoundments. Growing crops for energy rather than for food or fiber can involve all of the considerations characteristic of monoculture agriculture. There are occupational health and toxic waste issues associated with some photovoltaic cells.

The environmental, social, and occupational health considerations for solar power are, however, both qualitatively and quantitatively different from those intrinsic to the use of nuclear power in that they do not pose the global risks comparable to those of major reactor accidents, the failure of high-level radioactive waste repositories, or the linkage between civilian and military nuclear energy.

John Holdren summarized:

> The only other external energy cost that might match the devastating impact of global climate change is the risk of causing or aggravating large-scale military conflict. One such threat is the potential for conflict over access to petroleum resources. The danger is thought to have declined since the end of the 1970s, but circumstances are easily imagined in which it could reassert itself — particularly given the current resurgence of U.S. dependence on foreign oil. Another threat is the link between nuclear energy and the spread of nuclear weapons. The issue is hardly less complex and controversial than the link between carbon dioxide and climate; many analysts, including me, think it is threatening indeed (Holdren, 1990).

Not only do solar and nuclear power differ greatly in their environmental and health risks, they differ in scale and structure as well. Nuclear power is inherently centralized and demands major involvement by the state. Attempts to minimize the risks associated with waste management, accidents, and the possible diversion of nuclear fuel into use as weapons will necessarily require large sites each with many reactors and associated sensitive facilities.

Solar and other renewable energy supply technologies are, on the other hand, intrinsically diversified. Some countries or regions will use a mix of biomass, hydropower, and windpower, for example. Other regions would use photovoltaic systems almost exclusively. Further, solar energy facilities would be individually small compared with the thousands or tens of thousands of megawatts of power at individual nuclear power sites.

The issue was summarized in an insightful essay by Måns Lönnroth, which included:

> Electricity gives people power over their everyday life. Power over electricity is, on the other hand, firmly vested within the core of the present electricity industry.

> The electricity industry has come full circle in the hundred years after Edison. Then, the fall in distribution costs triggered by the AC system made energy services a less attractive idea. Centralization and economies of scale promised to resolve all supply problems. Now, environmental pressures make the electricity industry face a juncture: the industry will evolve either toward a large scale expansion of nuclear energy or toward a large degree of diversification and, possibly, decentralization.

> The nuclear expansion would reinforce the tendency of centralization, nationally as well as internationally... Diversification, on the other hand, would reinforce the emerging tendencies of a much wider range of technologies, first based on natural gas and then later based on various solar technologies.

...Somewhat blasphemously, the electricity industry of the late 20th century can be compared with the Catholic Church of the mid-15th century. Then, the great cathedral building was over. Most cathedrals had been completed. One or two had collapsed. Some were still under construction — the Kölner dome, started in the 13th century, was not completed until the 19th century.

The 1000 MW steam turbine is the electrical industry equivalent of the 15th century cathedral. It is the material manifestation of an ideology and a world view which promises cheap electricity in return for dependency (Lönnroth, 1989).

The analogy is no less apt for the industries supplying liquid, gaseous, and solid energy carriers.

The inherent centralization and the requirements for governmental control of nuclear power are regarded as major advantages of nuclear over solar power by some. Other individuals regard these characteristics of atomic power as being sufficient for its rejection.

Discussion and Conclusions

Nothing makes sense unless its continuance for a long time can be projected without running into absurdities...there cannot be unlimited, generalized growth... Ever bigger machines, entailing ever bigger concentrations of economic power and exerting ever greater violence against the environment do not represent progress: they are a denial of wisdom.

E. F. Schumacher, 1976

Like it or not, the era of planetary management is upon us. The human enterprise as now conducted exceeds the carrying capacity of the earth. The evidence is plain for all to see: widespread forest loss and other ecosystem damage caused by acid precipitation; stratospheric ozone depletion caused by emissions of CFCs and other industrial gases; a rate of species loss which is greater even than that during the great extinction of the dinosaurs more than 50 million years ago; and, rapidly increasing atmospheric concentrations of greenhouse gases.

Fossil fuel use is the major cause of these, and other, threats to our welfare. Fossil fuel use has also permitted the growth in services and artifacts which define that welfare.

Avoiding an irreversible commitment to potentially catastrophic climatic change within only a very few decades requires that we reduce our rates of consumption of the fossil fuels to a small fraction of those of the present. The only non-fossil primary energy sources which have the potential to replace the fossil fuels are atomic power, with commercialization of plutonium, or solar power.

Clarion calls for a renaissance of the nearly moribund global nuclear power programs to help avert the threat of climatic change are being heard from many quarters. Yet, evidence is lacking that control of the intrinsic hazards of atomic power is any closer than it was 20 years ago. No high-level radioactive isolation facility exists anywhere in the world and even the most optimistic estimates to not anticipate the first of them until well into the next century. Reactors claimed to be less prone to major accidents remain on the drawing boards and have yet to be demonstrated. The web of technical, institutional, and political measures which have been created to control the spread of nuclear weapons is in disarray. New international institutions and security measures which would make atomic power immune from national politics and isolated from influence by public opinion are hinted at (Häfele, 1990; MacLachlan, 1990), but have yet to be subjected to the tests of the market and of the community. And, if all of this were not enough, new nuclear power is, even by conventional criteria, more expensive than other available measures to reduce greenhouse gas emissions from the energy sector (Keepin and Katz, 1988; Financial Times, 1990).

It would be highly imprudent to rely on atomic energy to get us out of our dilemma.

There are, however, two options open to us, both of which avoid the threat of large climatic change and the inherent risks of atomic power. Means are now available to reduce greatly our energy consumption without loss of energy services and while meeting conventional tests of economic efficiency for those who must pay the energy bills. The technologies for large-scale utilization of solar power are also now available, at competitive prices.

Atomic power and solar power futures would both avoid continued emissions of greenhouse gases and the resultant climatic change. It appears that either of them would result in increased energy costs as conventionally measured. Either could supply global energy needs.

Atomic power and solar differ, however, in two fundamental respects. Atomic power carries with it several inherent and very large risks to health and welfare. Solar power is free of these hazards. Atomic power is inherently highly centralized and minimizing accident risks and diversion of weapons, usable atomic fuels will require major governmental involvement in the fuel cycle. Solar power is inherently diversified and decentralized. Solar power and atomic power differ greatly in degree of centralized control over energy supply.

But, making the decisions between the plutonium economy and a renewable energy economy — and implementing the transition from fossil to non-fossil energy systems — is not the only challenge before societies. We are not committed to a considerable climatic change because of greenhouse gas emissions of the past and those certain to occur while new policies and programs are debated and deployed. The IPCC analyses have shown that even with the most vigorous policy responses considered, including a shift to non-fossil energy sources within the next fifty years, there is likely to be an increase in global annual average temperature of at least two degrees Celsius within the next century. Responding to this climatic change, which is unprecedented in historic times, will severely stress society. Slower implementation of measures necessary to stabilize greenhouse gas emissions could result in global heating of three or more degrees Celsius.

These are the challenges of global warming. Science has shown us what must be done if we are to avoid major global disruption. What remains is the much more difficult task of showing that the necessary changes in our behavior can be realized.

Acknowledgement

Financial support from the Joyce Mertz-Gilmore Foundation is gratefully acknowledged as are constructive review comments from Thomas B. Johansson, Bo Wiman, and several other colleagues at the Department of Environmental and Energy Systems of Lund University, and Steve Cornelli, University of Minnesota. Mead Data Central, producers of the LEXIS and NEXIS research service is gratefully acknowledged. Use was made of Focus on Global Change, a service of the Institute for Scientific Information.

References

Abrahamson, D. 1990. "The New Environmental Agenda." *Bench and Bar of Minnesota* (July): 22-26.

_____. 1974. "Controlled Fusion: Another Mistake?" *Environment* 16/2: 3-4.

Abrahamson, D. and Morten Sørensen. 1991. "Carbon Emissions for Air Travel Between Selected Cities," in manuscript.

Boden, Thomas A. et al. 1990. *Trends '90: A Compendium of Data on Global Change.* Oak Ridge, TN: Carbon Dioxide Information Center, Oak Ridge National Laboratory.

Brundtland et al. 1987. World Commission on Environment and Development. *Our Common Future.* New York, NY: Oxford University Press.

Carter, Luther. 1987. *Nuclear Imperatives and the Public Trust.* Washington, DC: Resources for the Future.

Daly, Herman E. 1990. "Boundless Bull." *Gannet Center Journal* (Summer): 113-118.

Davis, G. R. 1990. "Energy for Planet Earth." *Scientific American* 263 (September): 21-27.

Financial Times. 1990. "Plutonium in Surplus." *Financial Times Energy Economist* (July): 6-8; and "World Status Report: Nuclear Power." *Financial Times Energy Economist* (January): 11-18.

Ford Foundation Energy Policy Project (FFEPP). 1974. *A Time to Choose America's Energy Future.* Cambridge, MA: Ballinger.

Fulkerson, W., R. R. Judkins and M. K. Sanghvi. 1990. "Energy from Fossil Fuels." *Scientific American* 263 (September): 83-89.

Goldemberg, José, Thomas B. Johansson, Amulya K. N. Reddy and Robert H. Williams. 1988. *Energy for a Sustainable World.* New Delhi: Wiley Eastern.

Häfele, W. 1990. "Energy From Nuclear Power." *Scientific American* 263 (September): 90-97.

Hayes, Denis. 1977. *Rays of Hope: The Transition to a Post-Petroleum World.* New York, NY: W. W. Norton and Company.

Heilbroner, Robert. 1974. *An Inquiry into the Human Prospect.* New York, NY: W. W. Norton and Company.

Holdren, J. P. 1990. "Energy in Transition." *Scientific American* 263 (September): 109-115.

Holifield, Chet. 1972. As quoted in: Allen L. Hammond et al., 1973. *Energy and the Future.* Washington, DC: American Association for the Advancement of Science.

Intergovernmental Panel on Climate Change Working Group I (IPCC). 1990. *Policymakers Summary of the Scientific Assessment of Climate Change.* Geneva: World Meteorological Organization.

Johansson, Thomas B., Birgit Bodlund and Robert H. Williams (eds). 1989. *Electricity: Efficient End-Use and New Generation Technologies and Their Planning Implications.* Lund, Sweden: Lund University Press.

Keepin, B. and G. Katz. 1988. "Greenhouse Warming: Comparative Analysis of Nuclear and Efficiency Abatement Strategies." *Energy Policy* (December): 538-561.

Kerr, R. A. 1987. "Hot Dry Rock: Problems, Promise." *Science* 238: 1226-1228.

Lewis, Richard S. 1972. *The Nuclear Power Rebellion.* New York, NY: Viking Press.

Lönnroth, Måns. 1989. "The Coming Reformation of the Electric Utility Industry." Pp. 765-786 in Thomas B. Johansson, Birgit Bodlund and Robert H. Williams (eds), *Electricity.* Lund, Sweden: Lund University Press.

MacLachlan, A. 1990. "Nuclear Revival Seen When Public Knows, Accepts, Nuclear's Edge." *Nucleonics Week* (June 28, 1990): 9.

Marston, J. B., M. Oppenheimer, R. M. Fujita and S. R. Gaffin. 1991. "Carbon-Dioxide and Temperature." *Nature* 349/6310: 573-574.

Mårtensson, Anders. 1992. "Inherently Safe Reactors." *Energy Policy*, in press.

Metzger, H. Peter. 1972. *The Atomic Establishment.* New York, NY: Simon and Schuster.

Nilsson, Lars J. and Dean Abrahamson. 1992. "Safeguarding and Internationalizing Nuclear Power." *International Journal of Global Energy Issues*, in press.

Novick, Sheldon. 1976. *The Electric War: The Fight Over Nuclear Power.* San Francisco, CA: Sierra Club Books.

Office of the President. 1990. "Global Environmental Issues." *Economic Report of the President.* Washington, DC: U.S. Government Printing Office.

Patterson, Walter C. 1983. *Nuclear Power.* London: Penguin.

Schumacher, E. F. 1976. *An Economics of Permanence.* Palo Alto, CA: Institute for the Study of Non-Violence.

Seaborg, Glenn T. and W. R. Corliss. 1971. *Man and Atom: Building a New World Through Nuclear Technology.* New York, NY: E. P. Dutton.

Tolba, Mostafa. 1990. Opening remarks at Second World Climate Conference, Geneva, October 29, 1990, as quoted by Randall Palmer, Reuters.

Toronto Conference. 1989. *The Changing Atmosphere: Implications for Global Security* WMO-No. 710. Geneva: World Meteorological Organization.

U.S. Department of Energy (U.S. DOE). 1991. *Monthly Energy Review* DOE/D-0035. Washington, DC: U.S. Department of Energy.

Waggoner, Paul A. 1991. "U.S. Water Resources Versus an Announced but Uncertain Climate Change." *Science* 251/1002.

Weinberg, Alvin. 1972. "Social Institutions and Nuclear Energy." *Science* (July 7).

_____. 1969. As quoted by Sheldon Novick, *The Careless Atom.* New York, NY: Houghton Mifflin Company.

Weinberg, Carl A. and Robert H. Williams. 1990. "Energy From the Sun." *Scientific American* (September) 98-106.

Williams, R. H. and H. A. Feiveson. 1990. "Diversion-Resistance Criteria for Future Nuclear Power." *Energy Policy* (July/Aug): 543-549.

Chapter 5

The Social Costs of Electricity Generation:
Wind and Photovoltaic vs. Fossil and Nuclear Energy

Olav Hohmeyer

The following chapter presents the results of a research project on the total costs to society induced by different technologies for electric power production in the Federal Republic of Germany (FRG) and the conclusions of the latest international discussion on the topic. This is to say that the problem of electricity costs is looked upon from a macroeconomic perspective including the internal or private costs as well as the social costs of electricity production. The chapter focuses on conventional electricity generation on the basis of fossil and nuclear fuels on the one side and on wind and photovoltaic electricity as examples for renewable energy sources on the other.

Introduction to the Problem

In a market economy, the basic economic problem of allocating scarce resources to competing uses is solved through the market mechanism based on the market prices of the resources. A

Author's Note:The original study on the "Social Costs of Energy" (Hohmeyer, 1988) was conducted under a research contract for the EC Commission, Directorate General XII.

precondition for the optimal functioning of this allocation process is that the market prices reflect all costs involved in production. If this situation is assured, the microeconomic calculations of the economic agents involved may lead to a macroeconomic optimum of the allocation process for society. If, however, substantial costs of the production process are not reflected in the market prices because such costs are passed on to third parties not involved as consumers or producers of a product (in the instance of external or social costs), the market mechanism cannot secure an optimal macroeconomic allocation. Such sub-optimal allocation leads to considerable losses to society. Decisions on the use of competing energy systems are regularly based upon the relative costs at which the energy service desired can be delivered. Utilities or households making such decisions are considering the costs occurring to them. These costs reflected by the market prices of the energy technologies and the operation and maintenance costs are referred to as internal costs.

Since late in the 1970s the exclusive reliance on internal cost considerations for choices concerning competing energy systems seems to have become increasingly questionable. Since the 1970s, air pollution from combustion processes has caused serious damage to the forests of many European countries, as has been documented by official studies and annual statistics. While more than 50 percent of all German trees show traces of damage, a considerable portion of them are virtually dying. These and other environmental damages do not show up in the price of the energy generated by combustion processes. Thus, the seemingly cheap source of energy may be relatively expensive for society. The environmental costs induced can be handed on to third parties not involved in the production or consumption of the energy as in the case of the forest owners or in the case of people suffering from respiratory diseases due to air pollution from combustion processes.

Authors like Solow (1982) or Wicke (1986) have pointed out such discrepancies between the energy costs of a business (internal costs) and the total energy costs to society. This discrepancy which was first pointed out by Pigou (1912) has been named 'social costs' by Kapp (1979), a pioneer in this field of analysis.

The climate catastrophe due to the use of CFCs but also due to the imbalance of the production and natural absorption of CO_2 is another example of possible social costs from the use of energy, which are handed on to future generations by today's energy consumers. Again, the costs of a possible climate change do not show up in the market prices of energy generated on the basis of fossil fuels.

The nuclear accident at Chernobyl has shown that electricity production based on nuclear fuels may induce vast social costs due to the release of radioactivity from nuclear accidents in power stations or other parts of the nuclear fuel cycle. Nobody will get any compensation due to the health damages caused by the Chernobyl accident outside the U.S.S.R. Although thousands of cancer incidents have to be expected, the people hit will have to bear the costs without getting any financial assistance. Again this is an indication of massive social costs of energy consumption not taken into account in the price of nuclear electricity.

Since the reports of the Club of Rome in the 1970s we know that non-renewable energy resources are rather limited as compared to the present and foreseeable future energy consumption of the world. Energy price developments of the last thirty years show in the case of crude oil, for example, that long-term scarcity is not adequately reflected in present oil prices (Schneider, 1980: 835). If this is the case, such energy sources are only seemingly cheap today due to the fact that future generations will pay high opportunity costs for present use. Again, we have a case of social costs not included in the market prices of energy.

From the examples given we can conclude that electricity production based on fossil or nuclear fuels induces substantial social costs, whereas it would appear that the use of renewable energy sources involves far fewer and lower social costs. If this is the case, then in terms of a macroeconomic optimum, there may be too little investment in technologies utilizing renewable energy sources, resulting in high costs to society.

The Social Costs of Electricity Generation: The First Analysis

The question arises — how large is the difference between the social costs (and benefits) of photovoltaics or wind energy and those of conventional electricity generation? Is this difference large enough to affect the competitive position of photovoltaics or wind energy? If so, how does it affect the market introduction and diffusion of photovoltaic and wind energy systems?

The following discussion will deal only with the direct competition between wind and photovoltaic electricity and electricity supplied by the public grid. Special markets will not be taken into consideration. Although it is difficult, if not impossible, to quantify and monetize certain social costs, particularly those in the area of health and environmental damage, the estimated minimum net social costs of conventional electricity are compared with those of wind energy and photovoltaics. Even though full monetization can at best remain an estimate, awareness of the minimum net social costs (the lowest possible realistic figures) cannot but help to improve an allocation process which hardly ever takes into account social costs. The results given should be interpreted as a first systematic overview producing very crude figures which can nevertheless be used as a base for some initial, corrective economic policy measures.

Wherever doubt exists, assumptions have been made counter to the underlying hypothesis, namely, that the social costs of systems using renewable energy sources are considerably lower than those of systems using conventional energy. Thus, although suggested corrective measures may not be optimal, they err only in so far as they are insufficient.

The study upon which this chapter is based has been conducted within the climatic, economic, and administrative framework of the Federal Republic of Germany. Although the quantitative and monetary results are not directly applicable to other countries, the general approach is valid for any market-oriented economy.

Four principal areas of social costs of energy systems have been considered:

- environmental effects, including effects on human health;

- depletion of non-renewable resources;

- general economic effects such as changes in gross value added or employment; and

- subsidies paid by government agencies directly or indirectly as public provisions in kind.

Public expenditure for research and development on energy technologies has been subsumed under the general heading of public subsidies.

In each of these general areas, there are a variety of single social costs which are discussed in the final report of the research project (Hohmeyer, 1988 and 1989) which has been published in English and German and which is internationally available through Springer publishers.

The following effects could not be quantified and monetized:

- the psycho-social costs of serious illness or deaths as well as the costs to the health care system;

- the environmental effects of the production of intermediate goods used for investments in energy systems and the operation of these systems;

- the environmental effects of all stages of the fuel cycles (specifically in the case of nuclear energy);

- the full cost of climatic changes;

- the environmental risks of routine operation of nuclear power plants; and

- hidden subsidies for energy systems given under other titles.

Methodological Remarks
on the Results Derived

The *environmental and health damages* due to the use of *fossil fuels* have been quantified on the basis of numerous German studies on the matter. Most of the time, possible damage ranges for certain types of damages resulted. The aggregated damage costs have been attributed to electricity production according to its share of emissions of the most important air pollutants after weighing these pollutant emissions with their relative toxicity. The resulting share of electricity-caused damages is about 28 percent of all environmental and health damages attributed to air pollution. The costs of climatic changes have only been included with a vastly underestimated figure including only the reinforcement of coastal dams and fortifications in West Germany. As figures for the control of CO_2 in power stations quoted by Koomey for the United States (0.8 - 2.6 cents/kWh) show, this leads to an extreme underestimation of the costs relating to CO_2 (Koomey, 1990).

Table 5.1 summarizes the calculated social costs in the area of environmental and health damages for conventional electricity generation based on fossil fuels.

In the area of environmental and health damages from *nuclear electricity*, only the health damages of major nuclear accidents have been taken into account. These damage costs have been calculated on the basis of the reactor accident at Chernobyl. Taking into account the population density of the FRG, the probability of radiation-induced cancer, the probability of such a nuclear accident and the losses in production potential due to cancer incidents

Table 5.1
Estimated External Cost of Air Pollution
(1982 prices — all figures rounded to ten millions)

Damages to	Total quantified damages (million DM_{82}/yr.)			Share of damages due to electricity generation based on fossil fuels (28 %) (million DM_{82}/yr.)		
Flora	6,030	—	9,090	1,690	—	2,540
Fauna		90			30	
Mankind	1,620	—	40,350	450	—	11,300
Materials	2,230	—	4,000	620	—	1,090
Climate	60	—	110	20	—	40
Total (simple addition)	10,030	—	53,640	2,810	—	15,000
Total range based on independent errors	31,840	±	19,450	8,910	±	5,450
Willingness to pay[a]		44,540			12,470	

Note: [a]Wicke 1986. Figures recalculated to 1982 prices.

caused, we have tried to monetize these costs. The value of human life is set at 1 million DM (about 0.5 million US$) according to the lost production potential. This, of course, is rather cynical and does not nearly reflect the real losses and human hardship involved. Based on industry figures for avoided deaths, Buchanan (1988) calculates 3 - 10 million US$ per human life, six to twenty times more than our calculations. Not considering all other social costs involved with nuclear accidents and all other parts of the nuclear fuel cycle, we derived social costs in the order of 0.012 - 0.12 DM/kWh. Table 5.2 shows these calculations. The top part gives all thinkable parameter variations, the second part looks at the Chernobyl accident itself and the bottom part gives our calculation for Germany on the basis of the most likely parameter values.

Table 5.2
Estimated External Costs of Nuclear Power Due to the Risk of Nuclear Accidents

Cases considered	Percentage of released radioactive inventory 1 - 50% (0.25 - 12.5)[1]	Possible variations of important parameters — Population density (0.5 - 10.0)[2] Result in million pers. rem	Cancer incidents per 1 million pers. rem (200 - 3 700)[3]	Cancer incidents per nuclear accident	Production losses per nuclear accident (750 000 DM per cancer incident) million DM	Probability of nuclear accidents (one accident per 2 000-20 000 years of operation)	Electricity produced per nuclear accident (7.5 TWh per year and installation)	Production losses per kWh nuclear electricity produced 10^{-2} DM/kWh
	0.25 x 240	x 0.5 = 30	200 x 30 =	6,000	4,500	20,000	150,000 TWh	0.0030
						2,000	15,000 TWh	0.030
			3,700 x 30 =	111,000	83,250	20,000	150,000 TWh	0.0555
						2,000	15,000 TWh	0.5550
		x 10.0 = 600	200 x 600 =	120,000	90,000	20,000	150,000 TWh	0.06
						2,000	15,000 TWh	0.6
General case of nuclear accident based on the radioactive impact of Chernobyl: 240 million pers. rem, 4% release			3,700 x 600 =	2.22 million	1,665,000	20,000	150,000 TWh	1.11
						2,000	15,000 TWh	11.10
	12.5 x 240	x 0.5 = 1,500	200 x 1,500 =	300,000	225,000	20,000	150,000 TWh	0.15
						2,000	15,000 TWh	1.50
			3,700 x 1,500 =	5.5 million	4,126,500	20,000	150,000 TWh	2.75
						2,000	15,000 TWh	27.51
		x10.0= 30,000	200 x 30,000 =	60 million	4,500,000	20,000	150,000 TWh	3.0
						2,000	15,000 TWh	30.
			3,700 x 30,000 =	111 million	83,250,000	20,000	150,000 TWh	55.5
						2,000	15,000 TWh	555.

Table 5.2 (continued)
Estimated External Costs of Nuclear Power Due to the Risk of Nuclear Accidents

Cases considered	Possible variations of important parameters			Production losses per nuclear accident (750,000 DM per cancer incident) million DM	Probability of nuclear accidents (one accident per 2,000-20,000 years of operation)	Electricity produced per nuclear accident (7.5 TWh per year and installation)	Production losses per kWh nuclear electricity produced $10^{**(-2)}$ DM/kWh
	Percentage of released radio-active inventory 1 - 50% (0.25 - 12.5)[1]	Population density (0.5 - 10.0)[2] Result in million pers. rem	Cancer incidents per 1 million pers. rem (200 - 3,700)[3]	Cancer incidents per nuclear accident				
Chernobyl (5 TWh/a) 1,000 cancer incidents per 1 million pers. rem	1.0 x 240	x 1.0 = 240	1,000 x 240 =	240,000	180,000	3,000	15,000 TWh	1.2
Accident like Chernobyl in the FRG. 1,000 cancer incidents per 1 million pers. rem	1.0 x 240	10.0 x 240 = 2 400	1,000 x 2,400 =	2.4 million	1,800,000	‖ 20,000 - ‖ 2,000	150,000 TWh 15,000 TWh	1.2 12.0

1) 0.25 - 12.5 times the percentage released at Chernobyl
2) 0.5 - 10.0 times the population density of the western part of the USSR
3) 200 - 3,700 cancer incidents per 1 million person rem

For small and medium sized wind turbines (up to 250 kW) placed in moderately sized wind parks (up to 35 MW each) only the generated noise seems to be an environmental infringement. Based on Danish noise measurements and average rural locations in northern Germany we have calculated social costs of 0.00009 DM/kWh.

In the case of *photovoltaic installations* we have considered accidents of maintenance personnel for decentralized roof installations (50 percent of all assumed installations) amounting to 0.00007 DM/kWh and opportunity costs for the land use of centralized installations of 30 DM/m^2 amounting to 0.00876 DM/ kWh. Assuming 50 percent of each type of installation the average social costs of photovoltaics amounts to 0.00441 DM/kWh.

The *depletion of non-renewable energy resources* does not show up sufficiently in the energy prices. The present energy prices do not secure that future generations will have access to energy services at fair prices. Present price signals and the short-sighted economic utility theory discounting future needs at incredible rates while rejecting the notion of intertemporal justice considering only one non-renewable energy source lead to a waste of energy today at the expense of future generations. In contrast to present economic paradigms, justice in the distribution of energy resources over time is possible as soon as renewable energy sources are taken into consideration. If we consider the non-renewable energy resources of the world as energy capital inherited by mankind and solar energy as our daily energy income which we may harvest by technologies utilizing renewable energy sources, a very simple idea can be applied to secure justice in the distribution of energy services across all present and future generations, achieving long term sustainability by very simple means.

Energy services can be supplied by drawing on our energy capital or on our energy income. Today the second is the more expensive way, but it does not diminish future availability of energy services as does our use of part of our energy capital. To keep this availability constant when we are reducing our energy capital, we need to set aside funds for additional future investments in technologies utilizing renewable energy sources. This is what is meant by the idea of 'reinvestment.'

Based on the costs of a renewable backstop technology and the fact that the funds set aside will be needed when the non-renewable energy sources are depleted, we can calculate the present value of the necessary reinvestment surcharge as:

$$S(t_0) = S(t_n) \times (1 + i)^{-n} \qquad (5.1)$$

S is the reinvestment surcharge and i is the real interest rate which can be earned by long term assets. The strategic life span (n) of the resource may be calculated by dividing all reasonably assured resources through the present annual consumption (depletion). To fully achieve intertemporal justice we have to consider equal energy services per capita. This demands the extrapolation of the present total energy consumption based on the future development of the world population. From the following function the strategic life span can be derived:

$$R(t_0) = \sum_{n=t_0}^{te} q(t_0) \times \frac{P(n)}{P(t_0)} \qquad (5.2)$$

Where –

$R(t_0)$ = resource today
$q(t_0)$ = annual consumption today
$P(t_0)$ = population

Population growth rates are assumed to decline from the 1.65 percent annual growth rate in 1990 to a zero rate of growth in 2100. During this time frame, total world population is projected to increase from 5.233 billion in 1990 to 11.868 billion in 2100.

The average real interest rate on long term financial assets has been 2.14 percent in the FRG over the last thirty years. Using

annual figures for the FRG results in the strategic life spans of the
different non-renewable energy sources as follows:

Hard Coal – 200 years
Lignite – 1,034 years
Crude Oil – 65 years
Natural Gas – 86 years
Uranium – 67 years

On the basis of the life spans calculated and the reinvestment
cost of the backstop technology assumed, the reinvestment surcharges given in Table 5.3 have been calculated.   For all non-
renewable energy sources a weighted average of 0.0322 DM/kWh
results for 1985 and of 0.1275 DM/kWh for 2050.

Table 5.3
"Reinvestment" Surcharges for Non-Renewable Energy Sources

Energy source	Portion of electricity generated 1985 in %	Surcharge $0.01DM_{82}$/kWh	
		1985	2050
Crude oil	2.1	9.794	38.785
Natural gas	9.6	6.278	24.864
Hard coal	33.0	0.561	2.387
Lignite	25.8	1.2×10^{-9}	4.8×10^{-9}
Fossil fuels total	70.5	1.405	5.568
Uranium	23.7	9.388	37.177
Conv. electricity generation with 5.5 % other sources without surcharge	94.5	3.220	12.753

Figure 5.1 shows the development of these surcharges over time
assuming constant per capita consumption for the future.

These surcharges secure even access to energy services of all
generations through their reinvestment in backstop technologies.

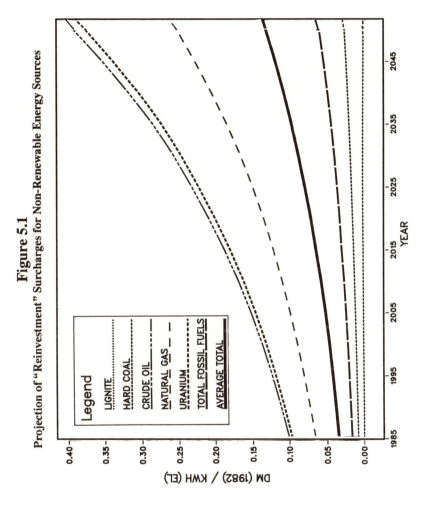

Figure 5.1

Projection of "Reinvestment" Surcharges for Non-Renewable Energy Sources

Legend

LIGNITE

HARD COAL

CRUDE OIL

NATURAL GAS

URANIUM

TOTAL FOSSIL FUELS

AVERAGE TOTAL

DM (1982) / KWH (EL)

YEAR

1985 1995 2005 2015 2025 2035 2045

0.40 0.35 0.30 0.25 0.20 0.15 0.10 0.05 0.00

The *macroeconomic impact* on production, employment and growth has been analyzed with the help of an enlarged input-output table which has been supplemented by technology-specific production functions of the energy technologies under analysis. To derive net effects, a direct comparison of the new and the substituted energy technologies is necessary. Figure 5.2 shows the structure of the approach used.

Table 5.4 gives the results for wind and Table 5.5 the results for photovoltaic solar energy.

Wind energy results in social benefits in the range of 0.0053 - 0.0094 DM/kWh whereas photovoltaics, not including the exaggerated results for 1982, result in social benefits of 0.0296 - 0.0850 DM/kWh.

The *direct and indirect subsidies* for different energy technologies given in the FRG are summarized in Table 5.6. This does not include non-R&D subsidies for wind energy and photovoltaics, as these should be measured against the overall net social benefits of these systems. The R&D subsidies for these technologies take into account necessary future subsidies (factor 5 - 10 of all R&D subsidies so far). The largest subsidy per kWh are the R&D subsidies for nuclear power, while the R&D subsidies for fossil fuels are very small and the total R&D subsidies for wind and photovoltaics are substantial.

Aggregated First Results
and Comparison of Social Costs

When the quantified social costs of conventional energy systems for the production of electricity based on fossil fuels are summed up and standardized for the production of 1 kWh, gross social costs in the range of 0.04 - 0.09 DM_{82}/kWh result. For electricity generated in nuclear reactors (excluding breeder reactors), social costs in the range of 0.1 - 0.2 DM_{82}/kWh have been calculated. A weighted average for these gross social costs according to the fuel composition found in the electricity generation of the

Figure 5.2
Structure of Macroeconomic Net Effects of Energy Technology Choice

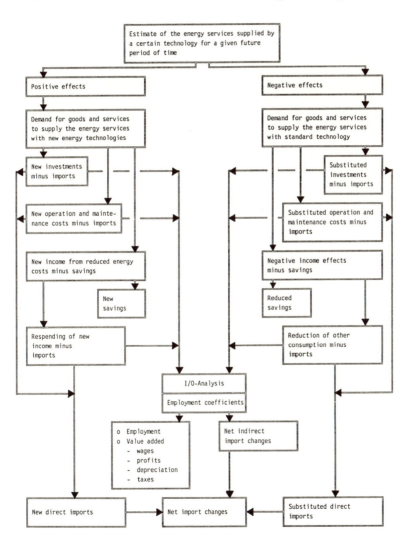

Table 5.4
Annual External Economic Effects of Wind Energy—1986–2030
(1982 prices and productivities based on 1975 input-output table for FRG)

Changes in	1986	1990	2000	2010	2020	2030
Savings (million DM_{82})	−73.4	+21.8	+124.2	+224.3	+329.6	+461.2
Imports (million DM_{82})	−234.2	+209.8	+212.7	+227.5	+252.6	+295.5
Gross value added (million DM_{82})	−160.0	−231.5	−337.9	−453.6	−584.8	−767.2
of which:						
wages and salaries (million DM_{82})	+134.4	+112.0	+104.0	+102.6	+106.3	+114.7
other income (million DM_{82})	−29.6	−74.8	−132.5	−192.4	−258.2	−345.4
depreciation (million DM_{82})	+47.6	+61.6	+84.5	+110.1	+139.7	+179.7
taxes (million DM_{82})	−312.7	−330.0	−393.1	−472.4	−570.4	−713.1
Employment effect (person years 1975)	+15,170	+14,040	+14,770	+16,270	+18,480	+22,020
Lowered bill for government and public agencies due to increased employment (million DM_{82})	340.5	315.1	331.5	365.2	414.7	494.2
Domestic external economic net effects in:						
million DM_{82}/yr.	+107.1	+105.4	+117.8	+135.9	+159.5	+188.2
0.01 DM_{82}/kWh	0.0054	0.0053	0.0059	0.0068	0.0080	0.0094

Table 5.5
Annual External Economic Effects of Photovoltaic Electricity—1982–2050
(1982 prices and productivities based on 1975 input-output table for FRG)

Changes in	1982	1990	2000	2010	2020	2050
Savings (million DM_{82})	−3,446.4	−1,183.3	−191.5	+204.9	+461.8	+1,128.4
Imports (million DM_{82})	−929.9	−249.5	+63.6	+171.8	+264.4	+510.2
Gross value added (million DM_{82})	+4,406.0	+1,064.3	+129.6	−378.3	−729.9	−1,647.7
of which:						
wages and salaries (million DM_{82})	+4,270.8	+703.5	+819.6	+507.4	+397.2	+382.8
other income (million DM_{82})	−760.8	−504.3	−454.8	−478.1	−543.9	−930.0
depreciation (million DM_{82})	+1,515.3	+708.7	+389.3	+325.2	+300.9	+476.7
taxes (million DM_{82})	−619.3	−565.3	−624.5	−732.7	−884.1	−1,577.2
Employment effect (person years 1975)	+135,120	+64,530	+38,430	+32,180	+33,310	+49,480
Lowered bill for government and public agencies due to increased employment (million DM_{82})	3,032.1	1,448.0	862.5	722.1	747.5	1,110.4
Domestic external economic net effects in:						
million DM_{82}/yr.	+3,991.7	+1,329.0	+800.6	+548.7	+479.1	+591.1
0.01 DM_{82}/kWh	0.1996	0.0665	0.0400	0.0274	0.0240	0.0296

Table 5.6
Comparison of Annual Public Expenditures for
Conventional Electricity and Wind and Photovoltaic (1982 prices)

	Public expenditure (million DM_{82})	Relevant amount of electricity produced[1] in 1984 (10^6 kWh)	Public expenditure ($10^{-2} DM_{82}$/kWh)
Public provisions in kind			
a) Fossil fuels	161	245 800[2]	0.0655
b) Nuclear	90	84 400[3]	0.1066
Monetary public subsidies			
a) Hard coal	563	245 800	0.2290
b) Oil, gas	11	245 800	0.0045
c) Nuclear	116	84 400	0.1374
d) Accelerated depreciation	205	245 800	0.0834
R& D grants			
a) Hard coal	95	245 800	0.0385
b) Oil, gas	0.4	245 800	0.0002
c) Nuclear	1968	84 400	2.3531
Total	3210	356 200[4]	0.9012

Assumed future annual public R&D expenditure for wind and photovoltaic energy (prospective expenditure until the technologies have reached maturity) (1982 prices)

	Estimated annual expenditure (million DM_{82})	Relevant amount of electricity produced[1] (10^6 kWh)	Public expenditure ($10^{-2} DM_{82}$/kWh)
a) Wind energy	52 to 104	20 000	0.26 - 0.52
b) Photovoltaics	104 to 208	20 000	0.52 - 1.04

[1] Figures do not include own use and distribution losses
   (source: Arbeitsgemeinschaft Energiebilanzen 1985, Table 2.10.2)
[2] Total electricity produced from fossil fuels in 1984
[3] Total electricity produced from nuclear fuels in 1984
[4] Total electricity produced from all sources in 1984

Federal Republic of Germany in 1984 is 0.05 - 0.12 DM_{82}/kWh electricity generated.

Table 5.7 gives a summary of the social costs of the different means of electricity generation monetized in our study, which should be consulted for detailed information (Hohmeyer, 1988 and 1989).

Table 5.7
Comparison of Social Costs of Electricity Generation for Fossil, Nuclear and Renewable Energy Sources
(DM_{82}/KWh)

a) Gross social effects of electricity generated from fossil fuels (all figures are estimated minimal external costs)		
1. Environmental effects	0.0114 -	0.0609
2. Depletion surcharge (1985)		0.0229
3. Goods and services publicly supplied		0.0007
4. Monetary subsidies (including accelerated depreciation)	0.0032	
5. Public R&D transfers		0.0004
Total	**0.0386 -**	**0.0881**
b) Gross social costs of electricity generated in nuclear reactors, excluding breeder reactors (all figures are estimated minimal external costs)		
1. Environmental effects (human health)	0.0120 -	0.1200
2. Depletion surcharge (1985)	0.0591 -	0.0623
3. Goods and services publicly supplied		0.0011
4. Monetary subsidies		0.0014
5. Public R&D transfers		0.0235
Total	**0.0971 -**	**0.2083**
c) Average gross social costs of the electricity generated in the FRG in 1984		
1. Costs due to electricity from fossil fuels (weighting factor 0.7444)	0.0287 -	0.0656
2. Costs due to electricity from nuclear energy (weighting factor 0.2556)	0.0248 -	0.0532
Total (conventional electricity)	**0.0535 -**	**0.1188**

d) Net social costs of wind energy			
1. Environmental effects (noise)		(-)	0.0001
2. Public R&D transfers (estimate)	- 0.0026 -	(-)	0.0055
3. Economic net effects	+ 0.0053 -	(+)	0.0094
4. Avoided social cost of present electricity generation	+0.0535 -	(+)	0.1188
Total social benefits rounded to three digits	+ 0.056 -	(+)	0.123
mean		(+)	0.089
e) Net social costs of solar energy (photovoltaics)			
1. Environmental effects (noise)		(-)	0.0044
2. Public R&D transfers (estimate)	- 0.0052 -	(-)	0.0104
3. Economic net effects (not including 1982 figures)	+ 0.0240 -	(+)	0.0665
4. Avoided social cost of present electricity generation	+ 0.0535 -	(+)	0.1188
Total social benefits rounded to three digits	+ 0.068 -	(+)	0.171
mean		(+)	0.119

When the social costs and benefits of electricity generated on the basis of wind energy are considered (with the social costs of present electricity generation included as avoided costs), total social benefits in the range of 0.06 - 0.12 DM_{82}/kWh result. This is an estimate of a probable range for the minimum social net benefits of wind energy. The sum of social benefits of photovoltaics lies in a range of 0.07 - 0.17 DM_{82}/kWh. Again this is only an estimate of a probable range for the minimum social net benefits. Since all assumptions in our study minimized the advantages of renewable energy sources, in cases of doubt, the probable social benefits are considerably higher than these figures show.

Even without the inclusion of all social costs, and with a deliberate bias against renewable energy sources, the monetized net social costs of wind and photovoltaic energy systems are of the same order of magnitude as the basic market prices of conventionally generated electricity. The handling of the social costs has a considerable effect on the allocation process and the current market introduction of wind energy as well as the future market introduction of photovoltaic solar energy.

The Effect of Social Costs on the Competitive Situation and Market Diffusion

How can we analyze the impact of the consideration of social costs on the competitive position of a new versus an established technology? For this we look at a two-product market, as shown in Figure 5.3.

The costs of the established technology are gradually increasing due to, for example, rising exploration and mining costs, while the costs of the new technology based on renewable energy sources are decreasing considerably over time due to technological learning. Such developments can empirically be shown for conventional electricity and wind or solar energy. At the point t_0 the new energy technology reaches cost-effectiveness if no social costs are considered. The substitution process can start at t_0.

Figure 5.3
Comparison of Electricity Generating Cost Over Time by Renewable and Conventional Technologies
(No Social Costs Considered)

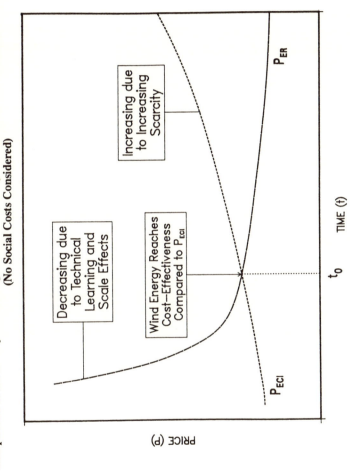

P_{ER}: Wind Energy
P_{ECI}: Conventional Electricity, Only Internal Costs

Figure 5.4 shows the effect of including the net social costs. These are defined as the difference between the social costs of the conventional electricity generation and the new technology.

A static application of the social costs of a base year (e.g., 1985) results in a parallel projection of the market price curve of conventional electricity. This results in a new intersection with the energy cost curve of the renewable energy source, showing that the new energy technology reaches cost-effectiveness at ($t_0 - \Delta t = t_1$). If the social costs reach a sizable order of magnitude we get a distorted competitive situation, giving the wrong price signals for the choice of energy technologies. If we consider that cost-effectiveness does not lead to instant technology substitution, but that we find a substitution (or market diffusion) process which may stretch over 20 or more years, we can picture the impact of not considering social costs as a shift of the market penetration curve of the new technology by Δt. If social costs are not considered, the diffusion process is delayed by this time span as compared to the best possible diffusion time schedule for society (Figure 5.5).

In the following, the social costs quantified above are applied to the analysis of the future competitive position and market diffusion of wind and photovoltaic solar energy. Figure 5.6 shows the impact of including social costs of electricity generation on the competitive situation and the resulting market introduction of wind energy systems in the FRG. An electricity price of 0.25 DM_{82}/kWh is assumed for small consumers, and is applied to private production of electricity by wind energy which substitutes electricity otherwise bought from public utilities. An electricity price of 0.065 DM_{82}/kWh is assumed for the electricity sold to the grid by decentralized installations. It is also assumed that WEC owners will consume only 20 percent of the electricity produced by wind energy systems, and 80 percent will be sold to the public grid. This results in an average electricity price of 0.102 DM_{82}/kWh for the conventionally generated electricity to be substituted by the wind energy systems. A real price increase of 2 percent annually for the substituted electricity has been taken into account. This price development is shown as the lowest price

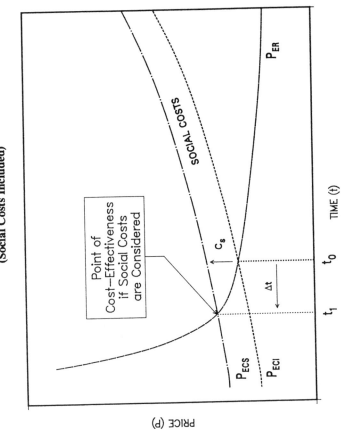

Figure 5.4
Comparison of Electricity Generating Cost Over Time by Renewable and Conventional Technologies
(Social Costs Included)

P_{ER} : Wind Energy
P_{ECS} : Conventional Electricity Including Social Costs

Figure 5.5
Market Diffusion of Wind Energy Systems

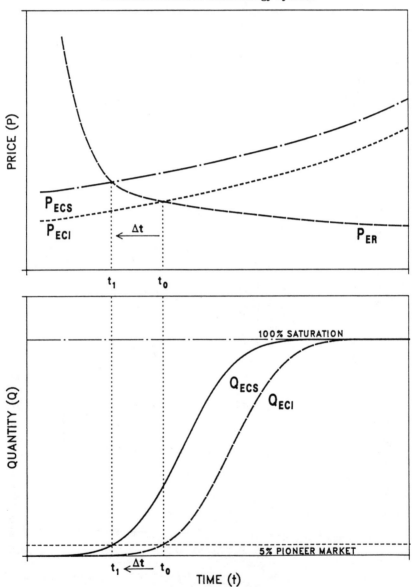

Q_{ECI}: Market Diffusion Curve Without Considering Social Costs
Q_{ECS}: Market Diffusion Curve Taking into Account Social Costs

curve for substituted electricity in Figure 5.6a. For the electricity price of wind energy systems (small wind energy systems of 50 to 100 kW nominal power), a cost curve has been derived, based on the few available German wind energy cost figures of the period 1980-86, and on the very reliable Danish wind energy prices of the years 1979-85. The data given as investment costs have been recalculated as cost per kWh, assuming yearly capital costs of 9.63 percent (annuity) based on a real interest rate of 5 percent, which slightly exceeds the long term real interest rate of the last 30 years in the FRG, and an operational life span of 15 years, which is clearly below the generally assumed 20 years.

There is an intersection of the wind energy cost curve with the market price curve of the electricity to be substituted (termed A) in Figure 5.6a. At this point of intersection, wind energy is competitive with the electricity to be substituted at market prices which do not include social costs. Adding the lower range of the estimated minimum net social costs (0.06 DM/kWh) to this market price curve results in a second curve for the substituted electricity which gives the new point of cost-effectiveness for wind energy at B. The inclusion of these social costs shows that wind energy is competitive with the electricity to be substituted considerably earlier than market prices show. Accordingly, the market introduction of wind energy systems starts considerably earlier. This is shown in Figure 5.6b for German wind energy price conditions.

It has been assumed that the pioneer market for wind energy systems not oriented towards cost-effectiveness amounts to about 5 percent of a technically feasible potential of about 20 TWh wind electricity produced per year in the Federal Republic of Germany. This potential translates into about 100,000 wind energy systems of 100 kW nominal power. After wind energy systems become cost-effective, market penetration should begin, reaching 95 percent of the technical potential 20 years after achieving cost-effectiveness, as shown in Figure 5.6b.

The addition of the upper range of the minimum net social costs of electricity generation (0.12 DM/kWh) to the market price

Figure 5.6
Influence of Social Costs on Market Penetration of Wind Energy Systems

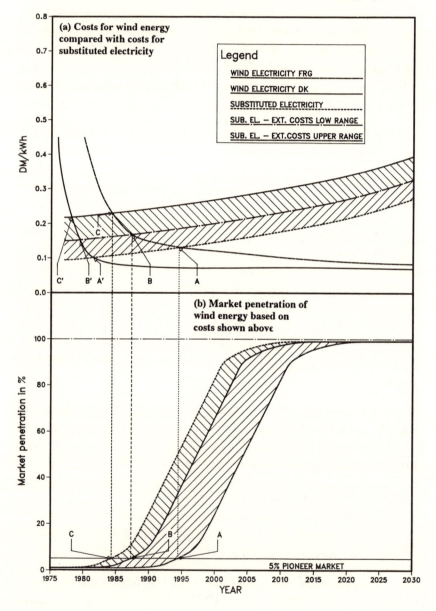

of substituted electricity results in a third cost curve for the substituted electricity. This curve again gives a point of cost-effectiveness for wind energy systems as the intersection with the wind energy cost curve at C. The change in the market penetration of wind energy systems resulting from this altered cost situation is shown in Figure 5.6b in the same way as the effect discussed above. The inclusion of social costs in the market allocation process would already have led to a substantial shift in the market penetration of wind energy systems.

Depending on how social costs are taken into account in the near future, the point of cost-effectiveness of wind energy systems in the FRG varies overall from 7 to 10 years. Thus, it is clear that if social costs are not included, a serious misallocation of resources results, causing substantial costs to society.

Figure 5.7 illustrates the situation for photovoltaic solar energy. In the FRG, 1982 photovoltaic prices amounted to approximately 2.7 DM/kWh, about 15 times the price of the electricity to be substituted. The inclusion of the estimated social costs shown in Figure 5.7 will affect the competitive situation of solar energy in about 10 to 15 years from now, if the estimated cost degression curve for photovoltaics is realistic. Based on the figures for photovoltaics given by several authors, electricity costs of 0.62 DM_{82}/kWh were estimated for the year 2000 and of 0.26 DM_{82}/kWh for the year 2050. On the basis of production by decentralized systems, with 50 percent of the electricity produced being used for private consumption and 50 percent being sold to the public grid, the combined market price of the electricity to be substituted will be about 0.19 DM_{82}/kWh in 1990 in the FRG. A real price increase of 2 percent annually is assumed for the electricity to be substituted.

As in the case of wind energy, there is an intersection for the photovoltaic electricity cost curve with the market price curve of the electricity to be substituted termed A in Figure 5.7a and 5.7c. At this point of intersection, photovoltaic solar energy is competitive with the electricity to be substituted at market prices

Figure 5.7
Influence of Social Costs on Market Penetration of Photovoltaic Systems

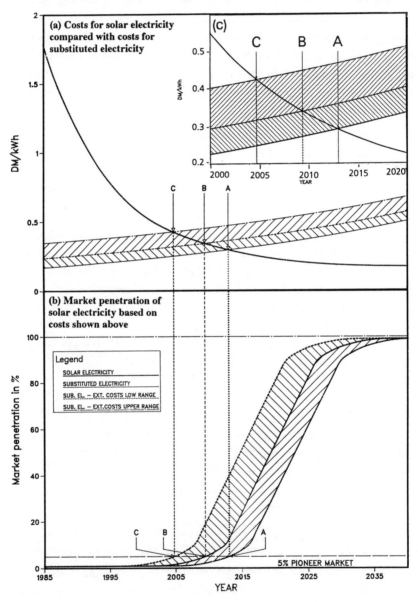

which do not include social costs. Adding the lower range of the minimum net social costs (0.07 DM/kWh) to this market price curve results in a second price curve for the substituted electricity which gives the new point of cost-effectiveness for photovoltaics at B. The inclusion of these social costs shows that photovoltaics are competitive with the electricity to be substituted earlier than market prices show. Accordingly, the market introduction of photovoltaic energy systems starts earlier. This is shown in Figure 5.7b. It has been assumed that a pioneer market for photovoltaic systems not oriented towards cost-effectiveness amounts to about 5 percent of an assumed technically feasible potential of about 20 TWh/year in the Federal Republic of Germany, which translates into approximately 2.25 million decentralized installations of 10 kW peak load each. After photovoltaic systems become cost-effective, market penetration should begin, reaching 95 percent of the technical potential 20 years after achieving cost-effectiveness, as shown in Figure 5.7b.

The addition of the upper range of the minimum net social costs of electricity generation (0.17 DM/kWh) to the market price of substituted electricity results in a third cost curve for the substituted electricity. This curve again gives a point of cost-effectiveness for photovoltaics as the intersection with the photovoltaic electricity cost curve C. The change in the market penetration of photovoltaic systems resulting from this altered cost situation is shown in Figure 5.7b in the same way as discussed above. The inclusion of social costs in the market allocation process leads to a substantial shift in the market penetration of photovoltaic systems of about eight years. If these social costs are not included, a serious misallocation results.

The International Discussion
following the Publication
of the First Results in 1988

The results of this first study have led to new hopes concerning the market introduction of renewable energy sources on the side of the proponents as well as to irritation and doubts on the side of the promoters of conventional electricity generation and supply side energy strategies. With a general public placing high priority on the solution of environmental problems, the results of this first publication have led to the demand of a practical consideration of social or external costs and a correction of the energy policy in the Federal Republic of Germany.

Specifically in the Federal Republic of Germany, different States of the U.S.A., Great Britain, and the Netherlands this discussion has induced a number of national studies trying to analyze whether the results presented reflect the correct order of magnitude for the social costs of electricity generation. Special mention has to be made of the study commissioned by the Union of West German Electricity Producers (VDEW) undertaken by the Institute for Nuclear Physics and Energy Technology at the University of Stuttgart in West Germany (Voss et al., 1989), the study by the Pace University School of Law for the New York State Energy, Research and Development Administration (Ottinger et al., 1990), the research by the Center for Energy and Environmental Studies at Newcastle in the UK undertaken for the EC Commission and the British Department of Energy (Hill et al., 1990) and the work at the Dutch Center for the Rational Use of Energy and Environmental Technology at Delft. Beyond this it should be mentioned that in July 1990 the Federal Ministry of Economic Affairs in West Germany has commissioned a rather extensive study on the identification and internalization of the external costs of the West German energy supply system. The results of this study undertaken by the Prognos AG in Basel should be available by early 1992. The state of the international discussion on the problem is mirrored quite well by a German-American workshop held at Ladenburg, West Germany, October 23-25, 1990 (see Ottinger and Hohmeyer, 1991). Due to the fact that the majority of the research projects in this field have not been concluded to date, the following remarks can only be looked upon as a snapshot picture of the results documented so far.

Focuses of the Discussion

In the following, the international discussion on the social or external costs of energy is summarized according to a few main focuses.

Environmental and Health Damages Due to Fossil Fuel Based Electricity Generation

Due to the fact that environmental and health damages contribute substantially to the social costs of fossil electricity generation, there is a lively debate on the real extent of the different damage costs and on the question which damage areas have to be considered.

The Role of Smoke Gas Desulphurization and Denitrification: It has been criticized that the our research (Hohmeyer, 1988) was based on an emission situation of power stations in the Federal Republic of Germany before these had been retrofitted with smoke gas desulphurization and denitrification equipment. For a new coal power plant built to the best available state of technology, Voss et al. (1989: 105) calculated 0.44 - 0.48 Pf/kWh damage costs, whereas we calculated damage costs between 1.1 - 5.85 Pf/kWh based on the 1982 emission situation of fossil electricity. The specific emissions considered in the two studies deviate by a factor of four. The assumption of a linear emission to damage relationship would explain the difference of the lower values of these estimates. For the upper estimate Voss et al. based their calculations on assumed health damages which are almost the same as in the lower estimate. Although these numbers cannot be (re-)calculated in detail on the basis of the publication by Voss et al. (1989), it is amazing that despite substantial uncertainties in the health damage research, the calculated range for health damages due to emissions from coal power plants varies only very slightly (0.1813 - 0.1835 Pf/kWh). This is equivalent to a variation of only 1 percent.

The results of recent U.S. studies on this matter are discussed below. The only study quoting health damages separately (Shuman and Cavanagh, 1984) gives health damage costs of 1.2 cents/ kWh for new coal power stations.

The attempt to extend the damage costs measured in past years at high levels of air pollution to later years with considerably reduced emissions is faced by the problem that the cause-effect relationships are not linear and that past damages can not easily be reversed. Due to the fact that many biological systems will only show signs of damages after reaching certain thresholds, and due to the ongoing accumulation of pollutants in ecosystems and living organisms, a reduction of the pollutant emissions will only lead to relief of the damaged systems with a considerable time delay and at a subproportionate decrease in the actual damages. Such considerations have not been taken into account in the analysis by Voss et al. (1989) with the exception of forest damages. Due to this fact the calculated environmental and health costs given in this study probably underestimate the real costs of new coal power plants substantially. Nevertheless, this very complex problem needs further intensive research if we want to arrive at reliable cost figures.

Results of Recent U.S. Studies on the Environmental and Health Costs of Fossil Electricity Generation: In an overview of the results of recent U.S. studies on the external costs of fossil-fired power stations, Koomey (1990) concludes that not considering CO_2 costs, new coal power plants cause external damages in the range of 0.83 - 1.53 cents/kWh (see Koomey, 1990, Table 4a). The quoted range does not take into account the estimates by the Electric Power Research Institute (EPRI) of 1987 which are quoted at 0.14 - 0.67 cents/kWh (see Koomey, 1990, Table 4a) and the special estimates for California given by Shilberg and the California Energy Commission (CEC) which are quoted at 7.09 cents/kWh (California Energy Commission, 1989) and 6.03 cents/kWh (Shilberg, 1989).

For existing coal power plants, Koomey gives a damage range of 1.93 - 3.54 cents/kWh based on the cited studies, again not considering the results of EPRI, the California Energy Commission and Shilberg as atypical values (see Koomey, 1990, Table 6). EPRI calculates a damage range of 0.5 - 2.19 cents/kWh for existing coal power plants while the estimates specifically for California range from 10.03 cents/kWh (calculated by Shilberg) to 18.52 cents/kWh (calculated by the California Energy Commission). The values calculated by Shilberg for the Los Angeles region even go up to 30.66 cents/kWh for the damage cost of existing coal fired power plants in that area.

It can be stated that the latest U.S. estimates for the environmental damage costs (including health damages) of coal-fired power plants show an average figure of 1.18 cents/kWh for new power stations and 2.75 cents/kWh for existing power plants. This seems to point to the fact that our results put forward in 1988 (1.1 - 5.85 Pf/kWh for existing power plants) seem to be closer to reality than the figures put forward by Voss et al. (0.44 - 0.48 Pf/kWh) for new coal power plants. Considering the results published so far it may be concluded that the costs not included in the energy prices of conventionally generated electricity are of the same order of magnitude as the results put forward in our first study (Hohmeyer, 1988).

Concerning SO_2 and NO_x emissions, our first results have to be updated according to the retrofitting of the existing power plants in the Federal Republic of Germany with smoke gas desulphurization and denitrification equipment. This needs to be done with the help of a non-linear model taking into account the complexity of the underlying cause-effect relationships. In Table 5.8, the cost figures calculated in our first study (Hohmeyer, 1988) for old power plants are cut by 50 percent to adjust these estimates roughly to the emission situation of new fossil-fired power plants in the FRG.

Possible Damages Due to CO_2 Emissions: In our publication (Hohmeyer, 1988) the possible damages due to CO_2 emissions

Table 5.8
Comparison of Social Costs for 1988 and 1990 Studies (1982 prices - pf/k Wh)

	Hohmeyer 1988, p. 8		New calculations incl. CO_2	
			Emissions 82	New power plants 90
a) Gross social costs of electricity fossil fuels (all figures are estimated minimal social costs)				
1. Environmental effects	1.14 -	6.09	2.6 - 10.67 Pf	2.05 - 7.93
2. Depletion surcharge (1985)		2.29		0.67 - 4.71
3. Goods and services publicly supplied		0.07		0.06
4. Monetary subsidies (including accelerated depreciation)		0.32		0.30
5. Public R&D transfers		0.04		0.02
Total	3.86 -	8.81	3.65 - 15.96	3.11 - 13.03
b) Gross social costs of electricity generated in nuclear reactors, excluding breeder reactors (all figures are estimate minimal social costs)				
1. Environmental effects (human health)	1.20 -	12.00		3.48 - 21.0
2. Depletion surcharge (1985)	5.91 -	6.23		4.88 - 47.42
3. Goods and services publicly supplied		0.11		0.11
4. Monetary subsidies		0.14		0.14
5. Public R&D transfers		2.35		1.46
Total	9.71 -	20.83		10.06 - 70.13
c) Average gross social costs of the electricity generated in the FRG in 1984			Fossil power plants 1982	New fossil power plants 90
1. Costs due to electricity from fossil fuels (weighting factor 0.705[1])	2.87 -	6.56	2.58 - 11.25	2.19 - 9.19
2. Costs due to electricity from nuclear energy (weighting factor 0.237[2])	2.48 -	5.32		2.38 - 16.62
Total (conventional electricity)	5.35 -	11.88	4.96 - 27.87	4.57 - 25.81
d) Net social costs of wind energy				
1. Environmental effects (noise)	(-)0.01		(-) 0.01	
2. Public R&D transfers (estimate)	-0.26 -	(-)0.55	-0.16 -	(-) 0.33
3. Economic net effects	+0.53 -	(+0.94)	+0.47 -	(+) 0.78
4. Avoided social cost of present electricity generation	+5.35 -	(+11.88)	+4.96-(+)27.87 (+4.57-(+)25.81	
Total social benefits rounded to three digits	+5.6 -	(+)12.3	5.26 - 28.32	4.87 - 26.25
mean		(+)8.9	16.8	15.6
e) Net social costs of solar energy (photovoltaics)				
1. Environmental effects (noise)	(-)0.44		(-) 0.44	
2. Public R&D transfers (estimate)	-0.52 -	(-)1.04	-0.33 - (-) 0.65	
3. Economic net effects (not including 1982 figures)	+2.40 -	(+)6.65	+2.35 - (+) 8.35	
4. Avoided social cost of present electricity generation	+5.35 -	(+)11.88	+4.96 -(+)27.87 (+)4.57-(+)25.81	
Total social benefits rounded to three digits	+6.8 -	(+)17.1	+6.54-(+)35.13	(+)6.16 -(+)33.07
mean		(+)11.9	20.8	19.6

[1] Old weighting factor 0.7444
[2] Old weighting factor 0.2556

and resulting climatic changes have only been included very insufficiently. The publication by Voss et al. (1989) did not take these costs into account at all. Meanwhile a number of research teams have addressed the CO_2 costs in the United States (see the overview presented by Koomey, 1990) and in the United Kingdom (see Hill at al., 1990). According to Koomey (1990, Table 4a), the latest research reports published in the United States show external costs of CO_2 emissions for coal-fired power plants in the range of 0.76 - 2.6 cents/kWh. These estimates are mostly based on control costs and not on actual damage costs. The published estimates show almost no difference between new and existing coal power plants. In a first rough estimate based on expected additional deaths due to climatic changes, Hill et al. (1990) give a possible damage range of 0.1 - 10 pound sterling/kWh. The figures are taken from an interim report by Hill et al. to the British Department of Energy (see Hill et al., 1990: 1). These rough estimates point to the fact that the cited U.S. figures based on control costs have to be looked upon as rather conservative estimates of the real damage costs due to CO_2 and resulting climatic changes. Our cost figures presented in 1988 (Hohmeyer, 1988) have to be corrected due to these latest estimates on the social costs of fossil electricity generation due to CO_2 emissions by adding at least 1.5 - 5 Pf/kWh. This does not take into account the far higher estimates presented by Hill.

Damages Due to Intermediate Production: The only study taking into account the damages due to intermediate production is the study by Voss et al. (1989). But the damages actually considered in this study only include a few central process chains. The results given show amazingly low damage costs for the processes included. The conclusions seem to be specially negative for photovoltaic electricity generation. Unfortunately, it is not possible to understand and recalculate these results because the calculations are not given at a sufficient level of detail and because the indirect effects are not given separately. The necessary broader analysis of this problem cannot be conducted at the moment because the analytical instrument (an enlarged input-output model including emission factors) is not yet available. Such a tool is being developed right now by the German Environmental Protection Agency (Umweltbundesamt), the German National Statistical Office (Statistisches Bundesamt) and the Fraunhofer-Institute for Systems and Innovation Research (see Hohmeyer, 1990).

Damages Due to the Use of Nuclear Energy

One heavily debated field in the present discussion are the social costs of nuclear energy as a result of major reactor failures. In our publication (Hohmeyer, 1988), the first results of the reactor catastrophe of Chernobyl have been used to make very rough projections for such reactor failures in the Federal Republic of Germany. These projections assume the same release rate for the nuclear inventory of the reactors in the Federal Republic of Germany as the rate documented for Chernobyl. Due to the fact that these calculations had to be based on the relatively few documented data on the Chernobyl accident back in 1987 and due to the fact that the German Reactor Safety Study Phase B on such accidents in nuclear power stations of the prevailing German type was not available, these results necessarily had to be rather provisional. This has led to harsh criticism, especially in the Federal Republic of Germany. As this criticism is mostly based on the calculations and results of the study conducted by Voss et al. (1989), this study needs some further consideration.

Based on the results of the German Reactor Safety Study Phase A, Voss et al. (1989) calculated a lower boundary for the damage costs of a nuclear reactor failure. Assuming a low temperature core melt-down and a controlled release of radioactivity without a containment rupture, a biological dose of 10 million person rem was assumed. This is based on the assumption of a fast evacuation of all areas possibly effected by the released radioactive inventory. Taking a probability of 9×10^{-5} for such core melt-downs per year of reactor operation and a mortality factor of 260 cancer incidents per 1 million person rem this results in a damage estimate of 0.0025 Pf per kWh. To derive the lower boundary estimate, additional onsite costs for damages of the reactor of 0.005 Pf/kWh were added (see Voss et al., 1989: 66). The upper limit of the estimated damage range was not calculated on the basis of the results of the German Reactor Safety Study (GRS, 1989) which had been published by the middle of 1989 and was available by the time Voss et al. prepared their study. Although the same research institute (of which Voss had been one of the directors) was involved in both of these studies, the research team chose to base their upper limit estimate on relatively old American nuclear safety studies conducted in conjunction with the so-called Rasmussen Report (U.S. NRC, 1975). The calculations conducted by Voss et al. on this basis cannot be reproduced based on the fragmentary information published. Nevertheless, it is quite astounding that the results of the American studies used by Voss et al. (1989) are only factor 9 higher than the lower boundary estimate based on a very moderate accident scenario, even though the original American figures had been multiplied by factor 100 by the German research team. The resulting upper limit estimate is just 0.07 Pf/kWh nuclear electricity.

A short glance at the summary of the German Reactor Safety Study Phase B shows that such an estimate can hardly be the upper limit for the most severe possible nuclear reactor core melt-down accident of a German nuclear reactor. On page 84 of the summary of the German Reactor Safety Study (GRS, 1989) the excursion terms of different reactor accidents possible in West German nuclear reactors are given. They show a difference of factor one million between the worst case (F1-SBV) of a high-pressure core melt-down with containment rupture and the best case of a low-pressure core melt-down similar to the core melt-down taken by Voss et al. from the German Reactor Safety Study Phase A (1989). As the probability of a high-pressure core melt-down is given in the study with 2.9×10^{-5} per year of reactor operation, which is somewhat lower as the probability assumed for the low-pressure melt-down in the Reactor Safety Study Phase A, the difference between the lower and upper boundary for the estimated damages should be about factor 300,000 not factor 9. Should it be possible to prevent 98.45 percent of all such high-pressure core melt-downs by so-called 'accident management actions,' as assumed in the Reactor Safety Study Phase B, the factor still would be about 4,500. If we take this figure multiplied by the lower damage estimate given by Voss, we get an upper estimate of about 11.6 Pf/kWh. If we don't take into account such accident management measures, because it has been internationally agreed so far that such measures should not be included in calculations of the probability of nuclear reactor accidents, about 7.73 DM/kWh result as the upper estimate for the off-site damage costs due to nuclear reactor accidents.

One important argument of Voss et al. (1989: 57) against the calculations put forward by my team (Hohmeyer, 1988) said that the potential radiological excursion terms which were analyzed in the German Reactor Safety Study Phase B would show that, with the exception of the noble gases, which are of little importance radiologically, all radioactive nuclides would be emitted at a rate at least one order of magnitude below the estimated excursion terms of Chernobyl. A short glance at the summary of the German Reactor Safety Study Phase B shows that the excursion term of the F1-SBV accident (GRS, 1989: 84) shows that iodine, caesium, tellurium, strontium and barium have excursion rates of 30-90 percent. As no reactor accident can have excursion terms with rates of more than 100 percent for each of these nuclides it is simply impossible that Chernobyl has had an excursion term lying at least one order of magnitude above any such term for a West German nuclear reactor. A comparison of the excursion terms for Chernobyl and the excursion terms according to the German Reactor Safety Study Phase B for the high-pressure core melt-down case F1-SBV and the F5 low-pressure core melt-down case shows that the term for the high-pressure core melt-down is factor 1.25 to factor 10 greater than the actual radioactive release term for Chernobyl. On average the release in the high-pressure core melt-down case (F1-SBV) in a German nuclear reactor is about 5.2 times higher than the term for the Chernobyl accident.

The argument put forward by Voss et al. (1989) that the German excursion terms would be very low in any case of an accident and that the upper damage costs for such nuclear accident would be negligible (0.07 Pf/kWh) has to be rejected as outright false. A rough estimate on the basis of the lower value given by Voss and the figures drawn from the German Reactor Safety Study Phase B gives cost figures between 11.6 Pf and 7.75 DM/kWh.

Taking the results of the German Reactor Safety Study Phase B into account in our calculations presented in 1988 (Hohmeyer, 1988), an excursion term results which is 5 times higher than the term assumed for Chernobyl. At the same time a lower accident probability (2.9×10^{-5}) has to be considered. This correction of the original calculations leads to damage costs of 3.48 Pf/kWh.

The latest calculations for the U.S. (see Ottinger et al. 1990) performed for the New York State Energy Research and Development Authority, based on the figures known for the Chernobyl accident, give damage costs of nuclear accidents of 2.43 cents/kWh for pressurized-water reactors and 2.56 cents for boiling-water reactors. It has to be taken into account that the United States has a population density of just about 25 persons per square kilometer whereas the population density in the Federal Republic of Germany is about 250 persons per square kilometer. Therefore, US\$ estimates would have to be raised by factor 10 to extrapolate them for an accident in Germany. Thus, the corresponding figure would be about 25 cents/kWh.

In the U.S. as well as in the United Kingdom, considerably higher costs per human life are assumed than in the our calculations (Hohmeyer, 1988). Based on contingency valuation methods, Hill (see Hill et al., 1990: 3) derives cost figures of 0.5 - 10 million pounds sterling per death case for the U.K. and Buchanan (1988) derives cost figures of about 3 million dollars for the U.S. These results point to the fact that the costs assumed by us (Hohmeyer, 1988) of 1 million DM per case underestimate the real costs by about factor 3 to 6. Taking this fact and the improved calculations on the basis of the German Reactor Safety Study Phase B (see GRS, 1989) into account results in a damage range for major reactor accidents based on high pressure core melt-downs of 10.5 - 21

Pf/kWh. This points out that our original estimates (Hohmeyer, 1988) probably give damage estimates in the right order of magnitude. The estimated 1.2 - 12 Pf/kWh nuclear electricity are most likely too low.

Recalculated Social Costs on the Basis of the Corrections Discussed Above

National and international discussions of the social costs of electricity generation have led me to correct my original figures (Hohmeyer, 1988) in the following areas:

- better representation of the CO_2 damages (additional costs of at least 1.5 - 5 Pf/kWh electricity based on fossil fuels);

- consideration of smoke gas desulphurization and denitrification for new and retrofitted power plants (this cuts the environmental and health damages for new fossil power plants approximately by half);

- consideration of the results of the German Reactor Safety Study Phase B and the latest international estimates on the costs of a human life (3.48 - 21 Pf/kWh instead of 1.2 - 12 Pf/kWh so far);

- examination of a national scarcity or reinvestment surcharge scenario;

    1. with a surcharge for fossil power stations of 0.47 - 3.32 Pf/kWh (instead of 2.29 Pf/kWh, as originally considered);

    2. for nuclear power stations a new surcharge of 4.88 - 47.42 Pf/kWh (instead of the original 5.91 - 9.88 Pf/kWh);

- reduction in annual R&D subsidies due to a lower assumed interest rate (5 percent instead of 8 percent).

Taking these considerations into account gives a minimum value of the social costs of conventional electricity generation of 4.36 Pf/kWh even in the case of the latest emission standards of new fossil power stations (see Table 5.8). This results in a net social benefit of 4.72 Pf/kWh for wind energy. The upper value estimated on the basis of the latest emission standards gives social costs of 22.74 Pf/kWh for conventionally generated electricity. Accordingly, net social benefits of 23.34 Pf/kWh for wind energy result. Based on the emission standards of 1982 (the original basis of the calculations we put forward in 1988), the estimates of the lower cost figures rise by 0.38 Pf/kWh and by 2.07 Pf/kWh for the upper estimates. The average values of the calculated net social benefits of the renewable energy technologies under analysis rise considerably. In the case of wind energy this is a rise from 8.4 to 14.0 Pf/kWh for new power plants or to 15.3 Pf/kWh for old power plants. Nevertheless, these calculations do not take into account the damage estimates put forward by Hill et al. (1990) for the costs induced by CO_2 emissions as these figures (0.1 - 10 pound sterling/kWh) go far beyond the 1.5 - 5 Pf/kWh considered in the calculations above.

In the case of photovoltaics a similar correction of the first results is necessary. The lower value of the estimated difference in the social costs of conventional electricity generation and photovoltaics drops from 6.8 Pf/kWh (1988 results) to 6.16 Pf/kWh as compared to new power plants (6.54 Pf/kWh for old plants). At the same time the estimated upper limit rises from 17.1 Pf/kWh to 33.07 Pf/kWh (compared to new conventional power plants) or 35.13 Pf/kWh as compared to the old plants. The average difference for the social costs (the net social benefits of photovoltaics) goes up from 11.9 Pf/kWh to 19.6 Pf/kWh (new plants) or 20.8 Pf/kWh (old plants). It can be stated that a systematic recalculation of our figures published in 1988 (Hohmeyer, 1988) leads to even greater differences in the cost elements not reflected in market prices of conventional electricity generation and the use of wind energy. Not considering these cost elements puts renewable energy sources like wind energy and photovoltaics at an even greater disadvantage than we have assumed so far.

Taking Social Costs into Account in Energy Policy

In spite of the fact that the recent discussion on the social or external costs of electricity generation originated from the Federal Republic of Germany, the U.S. seems to take an important role in the consideration of the results of this research in practical energy policy.

Least Cost Planning and Social Costs in the United States of America

Right now there is no activity at the level of the Federal Regulatory Commission (FERC) to take external or social costs into account in the setting of electricity prices. Under these circumstances it is remarkable that 29 states have started considering external environmental costs of electricity generation in the planning process for electricity generating capacity. The way these costs are considered reaches from an explicit quantitative inclusion in the process of least cost planning in cents/kWh through improved conditions for depreciation of less polluting energy sources to the simple ranking of generating technologies according to their relative environmental damages (see Ottinger, 1991: 364 ff.). The majority of these procedures attempting to take environmental costs into account are at the stage of drafting or enacting laws and regulations. Some states are already working out elaborate calculation methods. A very good overview is given by Ottinger et al. (1990).

Improved Buy-Back Rates and Subsidies for Wind Energy Converters Given by the German Ministry for Research and Technology

In the Federal Republic of Germany, a law has been passed by the German parliament (Bundestag and Bundesrat) forcing the utility companies to pay 90 percent of the electricity rates charged to consumers for electricity supplied to the grid from wind energy generators and photovoltaic installations starting at January 1, 1991. This is justified explicitly by the existence of substantial differences in the external costs of renewable energy sources and conventional electricity generation. The new law has led to a doubling of the rates paid until 1990 (from about 8 Pf/kWh to 16 - 17 Pf/kWh). Furthermore, it may be assumed that our preliminary results published in 1988 (Hohmeyer, 1988) have played a certain role in the fixing of a wind energy subsidy of 8 Pf/kWh given according to the new 200 MW demonstration program of the Federal Ministry for Research and Technology. The average figure for the difference in the social costs of conventional electricity and wind energy calculated in 1988 was 8.9 Pf/kWh (see Table 5.7 above).

Conclusion from the Recent International Discussion on the Social Costs of Electricity Generation

It is fair to say that the importance of the cost elements not represented in the market prices of electricity generation is even greater than our first calculations published in 1988 have shown. The opinion raised mainly by the German electric utilities that the external costs of conventional electricity generation are at least one order of magnitude lower than the internal costs can not be substantiated. The study on which this opinion is based (Voss et al., 1989) has been shown wrong in the vast majority of the points raised and the calculations performed.

Trends in Future Research and Practical Political Implementation

It is quite clear that the future focuses of research in this field will be the further analysis of the CO_2 and global warming problem on the one side and the improved assignment of damages to different causes and to emissions over time on the other. Beyond this it is quite obvious that the demonstrated analytical methodology will be extended beyond the field of electricity generation to many other areas where substantial social or external costs can be expected. The consideration of the rational use of energy as compared to supply technologies of heat and electricity or the comparison of competing transportation systems can be mentioned as high priority items on the agenda of such research. In practical politics there are sincere discussions in the U.K. and in the EC Commission on the introduction of a tax reform taking better account of the costs not included in the prices. Such a tax reform could certainly improve the general allocation situation in the national economies.

References

Buchanan, Shepard. 1988. "Methodology for Determining 'External Costs' of Environmental and Health Risks." Paper delivered at a Workshop conducted by the Department of Energy, State of Massachusetts, October 12, Billerica, Massachusetts.

California Energy Commission, Energy Facility Siting and Environmental Protection Division. 1989. "Valuing Emission Reductions for Electricity: Report 90." California Energy Commission. Staff Issue Paper No. 3R, Docket No. 88-ER-8.

Chernik, Paul and Emily Caverhill. 1989. "The Valuation of Externalities From Energy Production, Delivery, and Use" (Fall 1989 Update). A report by PLC Inc. to Boston Gas Company. Boston, Massachusetts.

Fischer, B. and L. Hahn. 1989. "Erste Beurteilung der Ergebnisse der Deutschen Risikostudie Kernkraftwerke" [First Assessment of the 'German Risk Analysis Nuclear Power Plants' Study]. Study for Gesellschaft für Reaktorsicherheit mbH. Darmstadt, FRG.

GRS (Gesellschaft für Reaktorsicherheit mbH). 1989. "Deutsche Risikostudie Kernkraftwerke Phase B. Eine zusammenfassende Darstellung" [German Reactor Safety Study Phase B: A Summary]. Report No. 72 (October) (second edition). Cologne, FRG.

Hill, Bob et al. 1990. "Environmental Costs of Energy Technologies." Draft report to the U.K. Department of Energy. Newcastle upon Tyne.

Hohmeyer, Olav. 1990. "The Analysis of Indirect Environmental Impacts of Economic Activities." Paper presented at the International Conference on 'Environmental Cooperation and Policy in a Single European Market,' Venice, April 17-20.

_____. 1989. *Soziale Kosten des Energieverbrauchs* [Social Costs of Energy Consumption] (2nd edition). Berlin: Springer-Verlag.

_____. 1988. *Social Costs of Energy*. Berlin: Springer-Verlag.

Kapp, William S. 1979. *Soziale Kosten der Marktwirtschaft* [Social Costs of Market Economies]. Frankfurt, FRG: Fischer Taschenbuchverlag.

Koomey, Jonathan. 1990. "Comparative Analysis of Monetary Estimates of External Costs Associated with Combustion of Fossil Fuels." Paper presented at New England Conference of Public Utilities Commissioners: Environmental Externalities Workshop. Portsmouth, New Hampshire.

New York State Energy Office, Division of Policy Analysis and Planning. 1989. "Environmental Externality Issue Report." Albany, New York.

Ottinger, Richard L. 1991. "Incorporation of Environmental Externalities in the United States of America." Pp. 353-374 in Richard L. Ottinger and Olav Hohmeyer (eds.), *External Environmental Costs of Electric Power: Analysis and Internalization*. Berlin, FRG: Springer-Verlag.

Ottinger, Richard L. et al. 1990. *Environmental Externality Costs of Electricity*. New York, NY: Oceana Publications.

Pigou, A. C. 1912. *Wealth and Welfare*. London: MacMillan and Company, Ltd.

Schneider, Hans K. 1980. "Implikationen der Theorie erschöpfbarer natürlicher Ressourcen für wirtschaftspolitisches Handeln" [Implications of the Theory of Non Renewable Resources for Political Action]. Pp. 815-844 in Horst Siebert (ed.), *Erschöpfbare Ressourcen* [Non Renewable Resources]. Berlin: Duncker und Humblot.

Schuman, Michael and Ralph Cavanagh. 1984. A Model Electric Power and Conservation Plan for the Pacific Northwest. Appendix 2: Environmental Costs. Portland: Bonneville Power Administration.

Shilberg, G. M., J. A. Nahigian and W. B. Marcus. 1989. "Valuing Reductions in Air Emissions and Incorporation into Electric Resource Planning: Theoretical and Quantitative Aspects." JBS Energy Inc. for the Independent Energy Producers.

Solow, Robert M. 1982. "Umweltverschmutzung and Umweltschutz aus der Sicht des Ökonomen" [An Economist's Perspective on Environmental Pollution and Protection]. Pp. 30-42 in Möller, Hans et al., *Umweltökonomik* [Environmental Economics]. Beiträge zur Theorie and Politik [Studies in Theory and Politics]. Königstein, FRG: Verlag Anton Hain Meisenheim GmbH.

U.S. NRC (Nuclear Regulatory Commission). 1975. "Reactor Safety Study: An Assessment of Accident Risks in U.S. Commercial Nuclear Power Plants" (WASH-1400). Washington, D.C.

Voss, A., R. Friedrich, E. Kallenbach, A. Thöne, H. H. Rogner and H. D. Karl. 1989. *Externe Kosten der Stromerzeugung* [External Costs of Electricity Generation]. Study for Verband Deutscher Elektrizitätswerke (VDEW). Frankfurt, FRG: VWEW Verlag.

Wicke, L. 1986. *Die ökologischen Milliarden: Das kostet die zerstörte Umwelt - so können wir sie retten* [The Ecological Billions: This is How Much Environmental Destruction Costs and This is How We Can Save the Environment]. Munich, FRG: Kösel-Verlag.

Chapter 6

Light Vehicles:
Policies for Reducing Their Energy Use and Environmental Impacts

Marc Ledbetter and
Marc Ross

Introduction

The transportation sector in the United States is an important focus of both energy and environmental policy because it is a large consumer of energy, primarily oil, and a large source of air pollution emissions linked with both urban smog and global warming. About a quarter of all energy and 70 percent of all oil consumed in the United States is consumed in the transportation sector. Some 96 percent of the energy consumed in the transportation sector is from oil, 61 percent of which is attributable to automobiles and light trucks.[1]

Furthermore, transportation fuel use is responsible for about 35 percent of U.S. carbon dioxide emissions. Automobiles and light trucks alone account for about 22 percent (280 million metric

---

[1]The usual fraction of oil used by transportation cited from the *Monthly Energy Review,* Energy Information Administration, U.S. Department of Energy, is 63 percent. Our calculation, however, excludes secondary petroleum-based fuel burned at oil refineries and in other industries from total U.S. oil consumption, because it would not be used if the primary uses of petroleum did not exist. We believe this approach better reflects the extent to which the transportation sector is responsible for oil consumption in the United States.

tons of carbon) of these emissions, making them, among final users of energy, the single largest contributor of carbon dioxide emissions in the United States.[2] Cars and light trucks also emit about 40 percent of U.S. carbon monoxide emissions and large fractions of other important urban air pollutants (Gordon, 1991).[3] Given their dominance in both energy and environmental problems in the transportation sector, this chapter focuses on light vehicles.

Since 1973, new car fuel economy has doubled, from 14 to 28 miles per gallon, and light truck fuel economy increased 60 percent from 13 to 21 mpg (Heavenrich and Murrell, 1990). Had this improvement not occurred, cars and light trucks (which now consume 6.5 million barrels of oil per day) would be consuming an additional 4 million barrels per day, more than twice as much as is being produced in Alaska, and over half our current level of imports. Avoiding 4 million barrels per day of oil consumption means the United States lowered its retail fuel bill by at least $60 billion per year, lowered its trade imbalance by at least $25 billion, and is emitting about 170 million less metric tons of carbon in the form of carbon dioxide. (About 1,300 million metric tons of carbon are emitted annually as a result of fossil fuel combustion in the United States.)

Unfortunately, the fifteen-year trend of rising new vehicle fuel economy that has almost held fuel consumption by light vehicles in check has come to a halt. Low gasoline prices, a cessation in the rise of fuel economy standards, and a cessation in the rise of the threshold for gas guzzler taxes have taken the pressure off automobile manufacturers to improve fuel economy. (Due to the 1990 Gulf Crisis, the average price of gasoline rose to about $1.35 per gallon at the time of this writing. In 1990 dollars, the average

---

[2]This calculation includes the carbon emissions resulting directly from combustion and indirectly from production and transportation (20.2 kg $C/10^9$ J) (MacDonald, 1990).

[3]Carbon monoxide also plays an important role in global warming because it destroys hydroxyl radical (OH), which oxidizes methane, another important greenhouse gas. So, a lower atmospheric concentration of OH results in a longer life for methane (MacDonald, 1990).

price of gasoline in the 1960s was about the same.) In the last few years, average new car and light truck fuel economy fell about 3 percent (Heavenrich and Murrell, 1990).

Making matters worse, the number of highway vehicle miles traveled (VMT) in the United States continues to grow rapidly, seemingly inexorably. Since World War II, VMT has risen steadily and rapidly, with the two major oil crises of the 1970s represented by small, temporary shifts in the upward trend (Figure 6.1). Recent analysis of the factors driving the growth in VMT indicates that VMT should continue to grow about 2.5 percent per year through the year 2000 (Ross, 1989).

Figure 6.1
U.S. Annual Vehicle Miles Traveled 1936-1989
(All Road Vehicles)

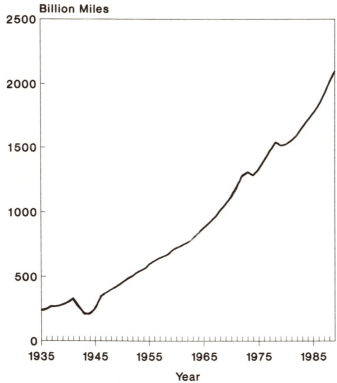

Source: Federal Highway Administration

Yet another factor contributing to increased oil use is the growing number of light trucks in the U.S. light vehicle fleet. On average, new light trucks achieve 21 mpg, 24 percent below the new car average of 27.8 mpg (test values). In 1970, they only represented 15 percent of new light vehicle sales, but they now represent about one third of those sales.

The large majority of light trucks are being used as passenger cars. A 1987 survey by the Bureau of the Census found that 81 percent of light trucks do not carry any freight (Bureau of the Census, 1990: Table 4). (As defined by the Bureau, freight even includes craftsman's tools.) Thus, for most people, a truck serves the same purpose as a car, but achieves much lower fuel economy.

Vehicles are also becoming much more powerful than they were in the early 1980s. Since 1982, average automobile 0-60 acceleration times have fallen from 14.4 seconds to 12.1 seconds, a 16 percent drop (Heavenrich and Murrell, 1990). Using an EPA-developed estimation procedure, we find that the move toward powerful cars has reduced average new car fuel economy by almost 10 percent (Heavenrich and Murrell, 1990).

Furthermore, the on-road fuel economy of new cars and light trucks is falling further behind their EPA-rated fuel economy. The on-road fuel economy is estimated to have been 15 percent lower than the EPA laboratory test value in 1982 (Hellman and Murrell, 1984). Analysts project that due to changes in driving patterns, primarily increasing traffic congestion, on-road fuel economy will fall 30 percent below test by the year 2010 (Westbrook and Patterson, 1989).

Taken together, stalled fuel economy improvements, rapidly growing VMT, increasingly powerful vehicles, traffic congestion and substitution of trucks for cars are putting strong pressure on oil demand. Only the final stages of the replacement of inefficient cars of the 1970s with today's more efficient cars is temporarily keeping oil consumption in check. At stake are national economic health, energy security, and the earth's climate. Among the many actions that can be taken to improve the situation, increasing the fuel economy of light vehicles should have a high priority.

Major changes will be required to reduce light vehicle energy use, or to even check its growth. Substantially improving light vehicle fuel efficiency will have the single largest effect on fuel consumption. As will be discussed below, it is within the range of technological and economic feasibility to improve the new car fuel economy to over 40 mpg within about ten years. Similar improvements could be achieved in light trucks. Although highly important, these major improvements, if achieved, will be largely offset by fuel consumption increases caused by growing traffic congestion and vehicle miles of travel. To achieve deep reductions in fuel use, the United States must not only improve fuel economies but slow the growth in vehicle miles of travel and provide attractive alternatives to single-occupancy vehicles.

The effect of future fuel economy improvements on global warming will of course depend on the degree of those improvements. If U.S. new light vehicle fuel economy is improved 40 percent by 2001, as is being proposed in Congress, carbon emissions will be 120 million metric tons per year lower by the year 2005 than they would be if new light vehicle fuel economy remains at today's levels. Although this is only 9 percent of current U.S. carbon emissions, no other single improvement in end-use energy efficiency, or plausible switch to low-carbon, nuclear, or renewable fuel, will yield reductions as large by the year 2005.

If other countries were to also substantially increase their new vehicle fuel economy, much larger reductions in CO_2 emissions would be possible. A recent EPA report to Congress estimates that increasing the world's fleet fuel economy to 50 mpg by the year 2025 would reduce projected global warming by 5 percent in a future scenario that assumes rapid technological change and economic growth (Lashof and Tirpak, 1989). (Note that this is not a 5 percent reduction in CO_2, but a 5 percent reduction in the projected average world temperature rise.) Again, although this may not seem large at first, one must consider the many greenhouse gases and their large number of sources. For perspective, EPA estimates that the 5 percent reduction is larger than the reduction in global warming that could be achieved through a near complete phaseout of CFCs by 2003, or through a rapid development of low-cost solar technology.

The Scope for Policy

We address policies in this chapter that improve energy efficiency and reduce greenhouse gas emissions, while providing daily "access" for people, and maintaining or improving values such as safety and environmental quality. By daily access we mean being able to reach places to work, shop, or engage in other activities. We do not, strictly speaking, mean mobility with its implication of expanded vehicle miles or passenger miles. In a given situation, improving access may involve enabling people to travel further, but it may instead involve reconfiguring land use patterns so that less travel is needed.

Policy areas which bear directly on improved access are:

- land use;
- public transport;
- substitutes for transportation;
- traffic and parking management, road controls, and road design;
- driver behavior, including vehicle maintenance and driving style; and,
- improvements in light vehicles.

Land use and public transportation policies are a major focus of those interested in improved access (Pushkarev and Zupan, 1977; Burchell and Listokin, 1982; and Holtzclaw, 1990). Their potential impact is suggested by the fact that per capita gasoline use in the Toronto metropolitan area is roughly half that in Houston, Phoenix, Denver, or Detroit (Newman and Kenworthy, 1988). Yet Toronto is not that different. It is a relatively affluent, high quality of life North American metropolis. The key characteristics of Toronto that appear to be responsible for Toronto's low gasoline use are regional control of land use and a well-developed, widely used public transportation system.

A major insight on provision of access is that while almost all passenger miles traveled (87 percent) are due to autos and light trucks, a relatively small increase in the use of public transport appears to be associated with a major decline in driving. Recent research indicates that one new mass transit passenger mile is associated with a reduction of 5 to 10 personal vehicle miles (Holtzclaw, 1990). This large leverage is argued to be a consequence of the synergism of mass transit and higher density housing, work sites, shopping, etc. With that kind of leverage, mass transit and appropriate land-use policies should eventually offer far more potential for reducing VMT than suggested by the small share of passenger miles provided by transit.

Substitutes for transportation, such as telecommunications, which enable some people to work and shop at home, and satellite places of work, which rely heavily on telecommunications, also have major potential. These are not primarily issues for public policy, but technology policies and regulation of communication systems are important to their success.

Traffic management in the form of high occupancy vehicle lanes, and car pooling assistance have had some success in reducing travel demand and fuel consumption (Burke, 1990). A key to the success of many of these programs is charging full cost for parking privileges (Replogle, 1990). Road charges in congested areas have long been considered in Europe and Asia and have been successful in Singapore, where they have been combined with provision of extensive modern public transport (Ang, 1991).

Highway controls, such as sophisticated signal management to encourage smooth traffic flow in congested areas, have been successfully developed, especially in Australia where resulting fuel savings of up to 20 percent were estimated (Watson, 1990). In addition, roads can be designed to mitigate stop and go driving, and the rate of vehicles entering expressways can be controlled to successfully limit congestion (Institute for Transportation Engineers, 1989). Enforcement of speed limits also contributes to efficiency.

Driving behavior is also important, but very difficult to influence. Proper vehicle maintenance, such as regular engine tuning and maintaining correct tire pressure, can contribute perhaps 10 percent to the fuel economy of the average car. Driving style, i.e., smooth flow as contrasted with rapid starts and rapid stops, significantly affects efficiency. Public education may be somewhat useful in this area.

While all these areas are highly important to efforts to reduce the environmental impacts and energy consumption of light vehicles, we chose in this paper to focus on policies that encourage technological improvements in light vehicles. Improving light vehicle technology will not, by any stretch of the imagination, be a sufficient means of resolving the enormous environmental and energy problems created by light vehicle use, but it may be the most important.

Some specialists have stated that the average fuel economy can be doubled again without radical changes in vehicle technology or substantial loss in the amenity provided (Bleviss, 1988; Horton and Compton, 1984). If much lighter, less powerful vehicles were acceptable, or if more radical technology were successfully developed, a much greater increase in efficiency could be achieved.

Several aspects of improving vehicle fuel economy are of interest to policy makers:

- modest modifications to conventional vehicles;
- alternative fuels;
- radical vehicle technology, such as the fuel cell vehicle, or the very light, small commuter car;
- interactions with vehicle safety; and,
- interactions with emissions of regulated pollutants.

Our emphasis will be on the first topic in the above list and its associated issues, i.e, near-term technological changes. We will also discuss some issues in the other areas.

Market Weaknesses

Fuel prices will clearly play an important role in spurring fuel economy improvements, as they have in the past, but we cannot assume that fuel prices alone are a strong enough motivator to improve fuel economy to levels that are cost-effective from a societal perspective. We conclude this for two reasons.

First, the cost of fuel is a relatively small part of the cost of driving a new car. At the price of gasoline that prevailed during the late 1980s, about $1.00 per gallon, annual fuel costs were only about 10 percent of the cost of driving for the average new car driver (see Figure 6.2). If fuel prices were twice as high, and the amount of driving remained the same, fuel costs would still only be about 20 percent of the cost of driving.

Second, buying a more fuel efficient car only has a small effect on annual driving costs. For example, purchasing a 35 mpg car instead of a 30 mpg car will reduce annual fuel costs only $50 per year. If the two cars are identical in every respect except fuel economy, the more fuel-efficient car will be more expensive because of additional manufacturing cost. We estimate the extra up-front cost, converted into an annual cost, is about $25 per year, making the net savings to the buyer of the 35 mpg car only $25 per year. With fuel costing twice as much, the net annual saving would still only be $75. We are not suggesting that most new car buyers do such calculations, but they are probably aware that for most cars, fuel economy performance does not greatly affect the economics of buying and owning a new car.

It is not surprising that new car buyers find fuel economy to be a secondary consideration. Many other attributes have higher priority: brand, safety, interior volume, trunk size, handling, price, reliability, etc. (McCarthy and Tay, 1989). Indeed, manufacturers have decided that fuel economy is of so little interest to buyers that

Figure 6.2
Costs of Owning and Operating a New Car

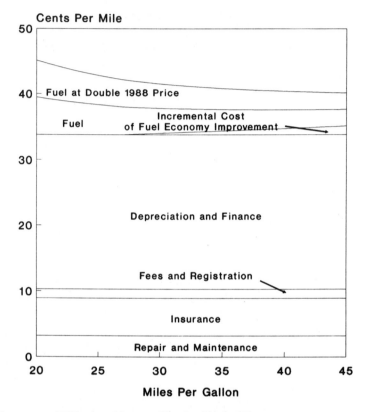

Cents Per Mile

Fuel at Double 1988 Price

Fuel

Incremental Cost
of Fuel Economy Improvement

Depreciation and Finance

Fees and Registration

Insurance

Repair and Maintenance

Miles Per Gallon

Source: ACEEE, adapted from von Hippel and Levi, 1983

they only offer it as part of a package in bottom-of-the-market
vehicles (such as the Geo Metro), making it impossible for buyers
to simply choose added fuel economy at extra cost while preserving
the other vehicle attributes in which they are interested.

A different way of expressing these observations is that the
value new-car buyers appear to place on future fuel savings is
low. That is, their implicit discount rate is high, perhaps 30 to
50 percent (as with other household energy conservation invest-

Table 6.1
A Comparison of 1988 New Car Vehicle Fuel Economies
and Gasoline Prices

	New Vehicle Fuel Economy (MPG)	Gas Price (U.S. $)
United States	28.3	0.95
West Germany	30.9	2.18
France	35.8	3.04
Japan	27.3	3.47
Norway	31.8	3.09
Italy	34.1	3.90

Sources: World Resources Institute and Lawrence Berkeley Laboratory

ments), rather that the 5 to 10 percent real interest on most new car loans.[4]   This implicit undervaluing of future fuel costs will probably continue to characterize new vehicle purchases, except perhaps in times of fuel crises.

Other evidence that higher fuel prices won't push passenger car fuel economy into the high 30s or 40s mpg is found in industrialized countries with gasoline prices that are two to four times higher than U.S. prices. Table 6.1 compares fuel economies and gasoline prices in selected countries. Of course, vehicle ownership and use are different in these countries than in the United States, so quantitative comparisons may be misleading. Nevertheless, it is impressive that much higher fuel prices are associated with new vehicle mpg values at most in the mid-30s.

---

[4]There is little quantitative information on this from automotive markets because, as mentioned above, buyers are not offered an opportunity to spend more to get higher fuel economy. High implicit discount rates have been determined in other areas, like household appliances and industrial equipment. Auto manufacturers behave as if their marketing surveys show buyer indifference to fuel economy.

Policy Mechanisms

Fuel Pricing

The market price of gasoline does not reflect its real cost to the U.S. economy. Some studies estimate that the national security cost of importing oil amounts to at least 30 cents per gallon (Broadman and Hogan, 1986). The costs of air pollution and the risks of climate change make the cost even higher.

Logically, these costs should be internalized through a tax on oil regardless of where it is used in the economy. A tax on transportation fuels, however, would be more practical. The potential for cost effectively increasing energy efficiency and reducing oil use in the transportation sector is large and would allow oil users the opportunity to reduce their tax bill. And taxes on transportation fuels would cause fewer problems for competitiveness than taxes in the industrial sector.

Evidence of the last few decades shows that higher gasoline prices have had a significant effect on gasoline consumption. A recent review of studies on consumer responsiveness to higher gasoline prices found a long run price elasticity of demand for gasoline of $-.78$ to be the most reliable (Khazzoom, 1988). The sample period from which the estimate is drawn is 1957-77.

Even though this estimate reflects relatively strong changes in demand for gasoline in response to price changes, it does not contradict the preceding discussion on why higher fuel prices won't push new car fuel economy to levels substantially higher than today's. First, new car fuel economy was much lower during 1957-77 than at present, and consequently, fuel costs as a fraction of total owning and operating costs were about 20 percent, twice today's level (Motor Vehicle Manufacturers Association, 1990). There is thus reason to believe that new car fuel economy today would not be nearly so responsive to changes in gasoline prices.

Second, in addition to reflecting changes in new car fuel economy, these price elasticities reflect changes in miles of travel. A

1984 review of gasoline demand segregated the mpg and travel demand responses to changes in gasoline prices (Bohi and Zimmerman, 1984). That review referenced several 1982 cross-country comparisons that found long run gasoline price elasticities of demand for mpg to congregate around 0.3. (When added to the reported long-run price elasticities for travel from the same studies [about 0.5], these results are consistent with the price elasticities of demand for gasoline cited by Khazzoom.)

Even though gasoline prices have historically had a small but significant effect on fuel economy, now that the fraction of total operating costs due to fuel is much lower, we shouldn't expect new car fuel economy to be as responsive to gasoline price changes as it was in the past (Greene, 1991). Nonetheless, when combined with other public policy measures to improve fuel economy, tax-induced higher fuel prices can help improve new vehicle fuel efficiency. Furthermore, as suggested by the relatively high price elasticities for travel referred to above, fuel taxes can be important in helping slow the growth in vehicle miles of travel.

While small federal and state gas tax increases have been adopted lately, large increases, especially those not earmarked for highway improvements, are strongly opposed. Some of this opposition, particularly from consumer and low-income interests, is driven by questions of fairness. Imposing large, immediate new fuel costs on people who earn their living driving cars and trucks, or those who have made living arrangements that require long-distance driving could unfairly shoulder a disproportionate share of the tax burden. And low-income individuals, whose fuel expenses represent a higher fraction of their incomes than higher income persons, could be unfairly burdened. Any efforts to substantially raise fuel taxes needs to address these issues.

However, there is at least one way to substantially increase the apparent price of gasoline without imposing new taxes or increasing the cost of driving: by restructuring the way we pay for automotive insurance. Instead of paying for all of our automobile insurance in independently arranged contracts with insurance companies, we could pay for a large fraction of our insurance needs at the gasoline pump. The price of gasoline at the pump could include a charge for basic, driving-related, automobile insurance that would be organized by state governments and auctioned in blocks to private insurance companies. All registered drivers in the state could automatically belong. Supplementary insurance above that provided by the base insurance purchased at the pump could be independently arranged, as we presently do for all of our insurance. For example, owners of expensive cars, or people who desire higher levels of liability coverage could purchase supplemental insurance. Drivers with especially bad driving records could be required to purchase supplemental liability insurance (El-Gasseir, 1990).

Such an arrangement has several advantages:

1. Insurance costs become much more closely tied to the amount of driving done. The more miles a person drives, the more insurance he pays. Since accident exposure is closely correlated with miles driven, the proposed system would be fairer than the present system in which people who drive substantially less than the average miles per year are given only small discounts, and people who drive substantially more than the average don't pay any additional premium.

2. Uninsured motorists would be brought into the system. By making insurance part of the cost of gasoline, a person could not drive without paying for insurance. In California, for example, uninsured motorists increase premiums for insured motorists by about $150 per year. Bringing uninsured motorists into the system would substantially lower the cost of driving for insured motorists.

3. The apparent cost of gasoline at the pump would rise substantially, roughly between 50 cents to a dollar per gallon. Such a price rise would encourage the purchase of more fuel efficient vehicles and help slow the growth in vehicle miles of travel. The increase in the price of fuel would be offset by a

decrease in the annual insurance premium motorists would pay directly to insurance companies, resulting in no net increase in driving costs. At least one financial analyst argues this system would result in a net decrease in driving cost because of the substantial savings in insurance brokerage and other insurance industry expenses (Tobias, 1982).

4. Unlike a gasoline tax, this system would not be regressive. Many low-income persons drive substantially less miles per year than their higher income counterparts. They would, consequently, see a substantial drop in the money they pay for auto insurance.

Another way to reform automobile insurance that would achieve similar results and would require a much simpler change in the insurance industry would be to have motorists pay for a part of their auto insurance on the basis of how many miles per year they drive, according to annual odometer readings reported to insurance companies. The National Organization for Women, which believes the current auto insurance system is biased against women, supports this approach. Pointing out that women, on average, drive about half as many miles per year as men, they argue that women are overcharged for auto insurance, and that insurance payments based on miles driven would more fairly allocate insurance costs (Butler et al., 1988). Although this approach would avoid the difficulty and political problems of setting up a state organized insurance pool, it would not encourage the purchase and use of more efficient autos.

Performance Standards

Fuel Economy. The Motor Vehicle Information and Cost Savings Act of 1975 set corporate average fuel economy (CAFE) standards that required the fuel economy of new cars to increase from about 14 mpg in the early 1970s to 27.5 mpg by 1985 (see Figure 6.3). The Act provided flexibility to manufacturers by applying the standard to the sales-weighted average for each corpo-

Figure 6.3
Trends In Fuel Price and Domestic New Car MPG

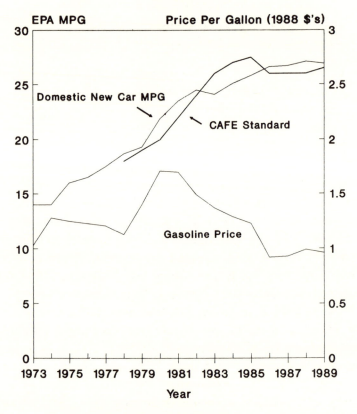

Source: ACEEE, adapted from U.S. EPA and U.S. DOE.

ration, instead of each individual vehicle. Further flexibility was provided by allowing manufacturers to earn credits for exceeding the standard in any year, and then allowing those credits to offset penalties in years when a manufacturer may fall short of the standard. Moreover, the Secretary of Transportation was given the discretion to set a lower standard, as was done for 1986 through 1989 on appeal from manufacturers (especially General Motors and Ford). The discretion to set standards for light trucks was also left to the Secretary of Transportation.

In hearings on the 1975 Act, the manufacturers stated that the technology to achieve 27.5 mpg was not available on the proposed time scale, and that the only way to achieve the standard would be by making the average car much smaller. They said it would "outlaw full-size sedans and station wagons" (Chrysler), "require all sub-compact vehicles" (Ford), and "restrict availability of 5 and 6 passenger cars regardless of consumer needs" (General Motors) (Energy Conservation Coalition, 1989). Indeed, there was some reduction in the ratio of maximum-power to weight, although almost none in interior volume, in the early 1980s (Heavenrich and Murrell, 1990). By the mid- and late-1980s, however, the manufacturers were achieving the mandated standards with vehicles of interior volume and maximum-power equal to and higher than those of the early 1970s. The CAFE standards were thus an important example of successful "technology forcing" by regulation.

Some have claimed that the CAFE regulations were unnecessary, and that the increased price of gasoline in the late 1970s and early 1980s was responsible for the fuel economy improvements (Mayo and Mathis, 1988; Crandall et al., 1986: Chapter 6). This argument is unconvincing on two related grounds:

- The estimated fuel price elasticities for vehicle purchase are moderate (Bohi and Zimmerman, 1984), whereas the increase in fuel economy in that period was more rapid than that for fuel price (see Figure 6.3).

- Statistical analysis of separate manufacturer's CAFE achievements show that "the CAFE standards were a significant constraint for many manufacturers and were perhaps twice as important an influence as gasoline prices" during that period (Greene, 1990).

General Motors and Ford have argued that the CAFE formulation placed them at a disadvantage because their mix of vehicles includes large cars while the Asian manufacturers' doesn't. As a consequence, they argue, it is much easier and less expensive for the Asian manufacturers to meet the standards, and the domestic, full-line manufacturers are forced to compete with new Asian large car introductions with one hand tied behind their back. Some evidence for bias against full-line manufacturers in the CAFE standards can be found in individual manufacturer CAFE trends. In recent years, with the regulated CAFE floor essentially fixed, the CAFEs achieved by domestic manufacturers have declined somewhat from 1988 to 1990 models (3 percent for both General Motors and Ford), while the CAFEs achieved by Asian manufacturers declined substantially more (6 percent on average, 9 percent for Toyota) as they introduced larger, less fuel-efficient cars (Murrell and Heavenrich, 1990). Of the major manufacturers, all now have CAFEs below 30 mpg except Honda.

Most recent fuel economy legislation introduced in the U.S. Congress seeks to address this problem by changing the basis of the standards so that each manufacturer is required to improve its fuel economy by the same percentage above its base year fuel economy.

Other industrialized countries have also adopted programs to improve fuel economy. Most have adopted voluntary programs, but some, including Sweden and Japan, have adopted mandatory programs like that of the United States (see Tables 6.2 and 6.3). Even though Japan has a mandatory fuel economy program, the average fuel economy of their new cars has slipped from 30.5 mpg in 1982 to 27.3 in 1988 as they have moved to progressively larger cars (MacKenzie and Walsh, 1990). The inability of Japan's fuel economy program to prevent this slippage is apparently a result of their fuel economy standards being based on weight classes.

Emissions. Early Clean Air Act (CAA) provisions required emissions reductions in the late 1960s and early 1970s which could be accomplished by improved control of engine operations. While Europe continued with a policy similar to the early CAA approach, subsequent U.S. regulations required reductions of tailpipe emissions to much lower levels. By 1981, emissions of hydrocarbons (HC) and carbon monoxide (CO) were limited to 10 percent

Table 6.2
European Agreements for Improved New Car Fuel Economy

Country	Requirements
U.K.	Compulsory reporting of fuel consumption data. 10 percent increase in mpg (9.1 percent reduction in fuel consumption) from 1978 levels, by 1985, for passenger cars only (diesels excluded).
France	Compulsory reporting of fuel consumption data. Mean fuel consumption in new automobiles to be less than 7.5 liters/100 km (greater than 31 mpg) by 1985.
West Germany	Ten to twenty percent reduction in fuel consumption in new autos, relative to 1978, by 1985.
Italy	Ten percent lower consumption in new autos, from 1978 levels, by 1985.
Sweden	New Car Fleet Averages: 8.5 l/100 km (28 mpg) by 1985 7.5 l/100 km (31 mpg) by 1990 Voluntary, but will be made mandatory in the event of noncompliance.
Notes:	All above fuel consumption targets are voluntary, except Sweden, as noted.

Table 6.3
Japanese New Car Fuel Efficiency Standards
Liters/100 km (mpg)

	Inertia Weight (kg)			
	625	750-875	1000-1250	1500-2000
1978 Actual	5.38	6.94	9.01	13.16
	(44)	(34)	(26)	(18)
1985 Mandated	5.05	6.25	8.00	11.76
	(46)	(38)	(29)	(20)
% Improvement	6.1	9.9	11.2	10.6

of the levels of 1970 and nitrogen oxides (NO_x) to 25 percent of those levels (Table 6.4). This became another example of successful technology forcing. Catalytic converters and supporting control systems were rapidly developed and have proved highly effective. (See below, however, on failures of emission control systems.) The present 3-way catalyst, which oxidizes HC and CO and deoxidizes NO_x, is a major accomplishment. The system requires that the exhaust contain very little oxygen or unburnt fuel, or specifically, that the initial quantities of fuel and air be correct to within 1 percent (or better) of the chemically correct combustion ratio. This is achieved with a closed-loop control system, in which catalytic converter operation parameters are fed back to engine controls to change the mixture of gases entering the converter.

The Overall Results: Mixed. Depending on one's perspective, the fuel economy and emissions programs could be viewed as ineffective or as remarkable successes. If one were to take a static perspective, in which we compare the absolute level of emissions and fuel consumption today with the levels that existed when the regulatory programs were begun, one wouldn't declare success. Despite the fact that a new car today has approximately twice the fuel economy and 10 percent of the emissions of cars built 10 to 15 years ago, the overall use of gasoline has actually grown somewhat and air quality has improved only slightly. But from a dynamic perspective, where one asks oneself what fuel consumption would have been without fuel economy improvements or emission reductions, the programs have been very successful. As pointed out earlier, had average light vehicle fuel economy not risen since 1973, the United States would be consuming an additional four million barrels of oil per day. Nonetheless, it is important to explore reasons for why such large improvements in fuel economy and emissions control have not produced large, absolute reductions in emissions and fuel use.

The fuel economy picture is relatively clear. Vehicle miles traveled on highways increased 59 percent from 1973 to 1989 (see Figure 6.1). In the same period, the average fuel economy of all

Table 6.4
Federal Tailpipe Emission Control Standards for Automobiles and Light Trucks[a]

Model Year	Automobiles			Light Trucks[b]		
	HC[c]	CO	NO$_x$	HC[c]	CO	NO$_x$
pre-control[d]	10.6	84.0	4.1	8.0	102.0	3.6
1972– 1974	3.0	28.0	3.1	–	–	–
1975– 1976	1.5	15.0	3.1	2.0	20.0	3.1
1984– 1987	0.41	3.4	1.0	0.8	10.0	2.3
1988– 1993	0.41	3.4	1.0	0.8	10.0	1.2
1994[e]	0.25	3.4	0.4	0.25	3.4	0.4

Keys: HC: Hydrocarbons
CO: Carbon Monoxide
NO$_x$: Nitrogen Oxides

Notes: [a]Standards for non-diesel fuel engines, certified for five years or 50,000 miles.

[b]Before 1984, trucks include all less than 8500 gross vehicle weight. After 1984, above standards apply to trucks from 0 to 3750 loaded vehicle weight (curb weight + 300 lbs.). HC, CO, and NO$_x$ standards for light trucks with LVW from 3751–5750 must meet 0.32, 4.4, and 0.7, respectively. Standards for light trucks with LVW greater than 5750 are 0.39, 5.0, 1.1, respectively.

[c]Before 1994, listed standards apply to all hydrocarbon emissions. After 1994 the listed standard applies to non- methane hydrocarbons (the pre-1994 standard continues to apply to total hydrocarbons in 1994 and afterwards).

[d]Estimate by Motor Vehicle Manufacturers Association.

[e]1994 and later standards from 1990 Clean Air Act Amendments. Standards listed here are Tier 1, 50,000 mile/5 year, non- diesel standards. Many changes in emissions standards are not reflected here. Refer to law for more detail.

cars on the road also improved, but not quite enough to compensate for the higher VMT. Average fuel economy grew about 45 percent, much less than the 100 percent improvement in the new-car test value. This discrepancy is primarily due to three factors: the long time required for retirement of old, inefficient vehicles; the increasing share of light trucks with their poorer fuel economy; and the increasing gap between EPA-rated fuel economy and actual, on-road fuel economy.

The on-road fuel economy of new cars and light trucks is falling further behind their EPA-rated fuel economy. The on-road fuel economy is estimated to have been 15 percent lower than the EPA laboratory test value in 1982 (Hellman and Murrell, 1984). Analysts project that due to changes in driving patterns, the on-road fuel economy will fall 30 percent below test by the year 2010 (Westbrook and Patterson, 1989). The reasons for the growth in this gap are increasing congestion with its stop-and-go driving, the increasing share of urban driving, and increased speed on open highways. In other words, the driving cycles (and their weighting) established for the federal fuel economy test procedure do not accurately reflect new driving patterns. A part of the problem is that very powerful vehicles are becoming commonplace and many are driven in high velocity/acceleration patterns different from those on the test.

The disappointment as seen from a static perspective is not that fuel economy regulation has been unsuccessful, it is that new vehicle fuel economy is only one aspect of the problem. As discussed, increased vehicle miles of travel and changes in driving patterns also have important effects on fuel use. The conclusion for policy making is the need for a package of policies that address all these problems, so that the gains in one aspect of the problem are not cancelled by losses in another.

The record on air quality regulations is more complex. Part of the story is the increase in vehicle miles traveled just mentioned, but the discrepancy between test tailpipe emissions and total emissions is much greater than the fuel economy discrepancy. Average emissions are estimated to be larger by as much as a factor of 10 than they would be if total emissions equaled the allowed tailpipe level (U.S. EPA Motor Vehicle Emissions Laboratory, 1988). As Table 6.5 shows, much of the HC emissions are not from the tailpipe but from evaporation from the vehicle and from vehicle fueling. In addition, a small fraction of vehicles are probably responsible for average tailpipe emissions far in excess of the limit for new cars. These are vehicles: 1) whose emissions control systems have severely deteriorated or failed; or 2) which are old enough to have had legal high emissions when new. As suggested by Table 6.4, if the catalytic converter system fails, emissions will increase by a factor of 5 or more. The average CO and NO_x emissions are also much higher in practice than the limits even though there is no evaporative component.

Table 6.5
Typical Light Duty Vehicle Emission Rates[a]
(grams/mile)

	from vehicle tailpipe	evaporation from fueling facilities[b]	evaporation from vehicle	total	tailpipe standard for cars
HC[c]	1.9[d]	0.5[e]	0.6[f]	3.0	0.41
CO	20.0[d]	–	–	20.0	3.4
NO$_x$	1.6[g]	–	–	1.6	1.0

Notes: [a]Light-duty gasoline fueled vehicles.

[b]Refinery and distribution system losses not included.

[c]Non-methane.

[d]Fleet estimate from MOBILE4 (U.S. EPA Motor Vehicle Emissions Laboratory). Emissions vary strongly with model year, tampering, maintenance.

[e]Emissions are strongly dependent on season and region. Estimates adapted from Argonne National Laboratory.

[f]During both running and parking. Emissions vary strongly with season and region. Crude estimate based on preliminary MOBIL4 analyses.

[g]Author's estimate.

There are EPA-mandated programs to address evaporative emissions and failure of vehicle emissions control systems. Recently, powerful steps have been taken to reduce evaporation into the air, but it is too soon to evaluate the effort. With respect to emissions control systems, inspection and maintenance programs have been in place many years in metropolitan areas with serious ambient pollution. Many of these programs have been disappointing. The test used in most regions measures emissions while the engine idles. Many vehicles will pass an idle test but emit heavily under load. Moreover, the inspection is carried out in many regions at individual garages. Often the mechanic and the vehicle owner have a mutual interest in avoiding the cost of repairing the emissions control system.

A fundamental complication is that the ambient pollutant of most concern, ozone, is the result of atmospheric chemistry involving two precursors, HCs and NO_x. It is believed that, for most high-ozone events, one or the other precursor is critical, i.e., reducing it would reduce ozone while reducing the other may even increase ozone levels. There is not a consensus on which, HC or NO_x, is typically the more important target.

In summary, emissions are much more sensitive to things going wrong than is fuel economy. Where fuel economy can be cut 10-20 percent by an engine going out of tune, emissions can increase an order of magnitude when something goes wrong, e.g., when an oxygen sensor fails. Moreover, the fuel economy problem may be noticeable in terms of poor performance, which often induces corrective action. The same can't be said for degradation in emissions performance. The apparent failure of emissions regulations to be effective over the life of many vehicles, such that actual emissions are much higher than envisioned by the regulations' authors, is a major deficiency of present policies.

The Next Generation of Regulatory Standards. Regulatory performance standards are an important policy option for bringing motor vehicle fuel use under control. They have worked in the past, and market conditions and technological opportunities are such that they will likely work well again. The near-term technological opportunities for improving fuel economy fall into three categories:

- technological changes which add moderately to the new vehicle cost but do not affect the performance or size of the vehicle;

- technological changes with slight impacts on driving, such as electronic transmission management and continuously variable transmission for small cars; and,

- reduced performance (acceleration) and/or size (interior volume).

We will address the first two because they are the most relevant to today's policy debates. The third is less relevant because few policy makers are currently willing to consider policies that would make a car any less comfortable, drivable, or powerful than today's average car. As discussed earlier, however, there is a strong association between acceleration capability and fuel economy. Thus, a decrease in average acceleration performance would be a technically easy and effective way to improve new car fuel economy.

We have created a conservation supply curve (Figure 6.4) for automobile fuel economy improvement based on technologies already in some production models or well-demonstrated in prototypes (Ledbetter and Ross, 1990). These are all modifications to the standard gasoline-fueled vehicle which preserve performance and size. The supply curve shows how much fuel savings are cost-effective (x-axis) at a given gasoline price (y-axis). For example, at a gasoline price of $1.32/gal (1989 US$) we find that an average 44 mpg (test value) would be cost effective, and, perhaps, practical to achieve by year 2000, compared with 28 mpg in 1989. The cost of these fuel economy improvements corresponds to a retail price increase of about $750 per car. When this cost is spread over the gasoline saved over the vehicle's lifetime and discounted

Figure 6.4
Conservation Supply Curve
Auto Fuel Efficiency, Year 2000

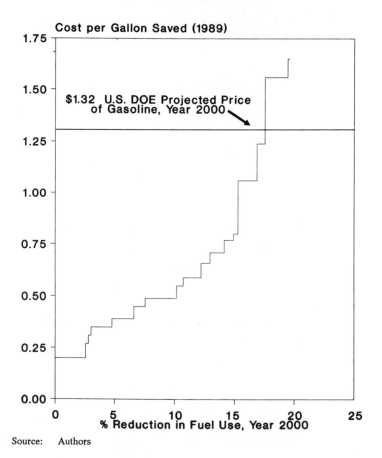

Source: Authors

to present value, the cost amounts to 53 cents per gallon saved, less than half the projected price of gasoline in 2000.

Conservation supply curves usually reflect that up-front costs are incurred in making more efficient equipment. This is somewhat paradoxical for cars, since the high fuel economy cars on the market are cheaper, not more expensive. The market does not, in fact, offer the kind of choice illustrated by Figure 6.4. The reason is that manufacturers have made the marketing decision that high fuel economy should be offered at the low end of the market, associated with lower-powered and smaller vehicles rather than with technological improvements of types (1) and (2). (Some technologies of the types considered in Figure 6.4 are incorporated in many cars, but usually in forms that increase power rather than improve fuel economy.)

Another important feature of Figure 6.4 is that the added up-front expenditure for fuel economy improvement is justified by savings on gasoline. That is, money would be saved by regulatory forcing of these improvements. The analyst takes a critical step, however, in making this determination: choice of the discount rate that enables the up-front cost to be re-expressed as an ongoing cost, which can be compared with the cost of fuel. For Figure 6.4 we chose a 7 percent per year real discount rate, roughly consistent with real loan rates. (This discount rate does not, however, reflect the new car buyer's behavior. As discussed above, the individual new car buyer has a much higher implicit discount rate for fuel economy improvements.)

Since substantially higher fuel economies are practical and cost-effective, and since society has a major interest in reducing petroleum demand, it is not surprising that stronger regulatory standards for fuel economy are actively being considered in Congress. Senator Bryan sponsored a bill that would have required each manufacturer to increase its average fuel economy 40 percent above its 1988 level by 2001. On average, the bill would require new cars to reach 40 mpg. It was supported by a majority of the Senate, but failed to overcome a filibuster in late 1990. The bill was re-introduced in early 1991.

Automobile manufacturers strongly oppose the legislation and claim, as they did in 1975 before the first CAFE standards were passed, that it is not practical to substantially improve fuel economy except by moving, on the average, to much smaller cars.

Manufacturers are stonewalling on this point. Other, more compelling reasons for their opposition are:

- major tooling investments would be needed to make the changes, especially if a moderately rapid timetable is required as proposed;

- the required rate of improvement in fuel economy would prevent manufacturers from fully exploiting sales opportunities for low fuel economy models already in production; and,

- high fuel economy standards would somewhat restrict designers' options in developing new vehicles and markets, e.g., there would be a premium on streamlining and on certain kinds of transmission shift management.

It is important to address such concerns by creating a schedule of strengthened standards allowing adequate time for manufacturers to adjust, and by enacting policy packages (with components discussed elsewhere in this chapter) such that the burden of compliance would not fall entirely on the manufacturer. Policies should be enacted that motivate buyers to select high fuel economy vehicles. The underlying concept in these suggestions is that we recognize the difficulties of substantially raising vehicle fuel economy, and that an increase in the standards by itself is not a sufficient policy for boosting average fuel economy to 40 mpg or higher.

Fees and Rebates on Vehicle Purchases

The Gas Guzzler Tax. The gas guzzler tax, enacted as part of the Energy Tax Act of 1978, has been overlooked as an effective policy tool for improving fuel economy (see Table 6.6). However, there is strong evidence that the gas guzzler tax played an important role in improving fuel economy, especially between 1983 and 1986.

Table 6.6
Gas Guzzler Tax, Energy Tax Act of 1989[a]

MPG	1980	1981	1982	1983	1984	1985	1986 & After
0–12.5	$550	$650	$1,200	$1,550	$2,150	$2,650	$3,850
12.5–13.0	550	650	950	1,550	1,750	2,650	3,850
13.0–13.5	300	550	950	1,250	1,750	2,200	3,200
13.5–14.0	300	550	750	1,250	1,450	2,200	2,700
14.0–14.5	200	450	600	1,000	1,150	1,800	2,250
15.0–15.5	0	350	600	800	1,150	1,500	2,250
15.5–16.0	0	350	450	800	950	1,500	1,850
16.0–16.5	0	200	450	650	950	1,200	1,850
16.5–17.0	0	200	350	650	750	1,200	1,500
17.0–17.5	0	0	350	500	750	1,000	1,500
17.5–18.0	0	0	200	500	600	1,000	1,300
18.0–18.5	0	0	200	350	600	800	1,300
18.5–19.0	0	0	0	350	450	800	1,050
19.0–19.5	0	0	0	0	450	600	1,050
19.5–20.0	0	0	0	0	0	600	850
20.0–20.5	0	0	0	0	0	500	850
20.5–21.0	0	0	0	0	0	500	650
21.0–21.5	0	0	0	0	0	0	650
21.5–22.0	0	0	0	0	0	0	500
22.0–22.5	0	0	0	0	0	0	0

Note: [a]The tax rate doubled in January 1991.

Figure 6.5 shows a plot of the average fuel economy of cars whose average fuel economy was below 21 mpg in 1980, the year before the gas guzzler tax took effect. Also plotted on the graph are the gas guzzler tax threshold and the real price of gasoline for the years 1980 through 1987. As can be seen, the fuel economy of low-mpg cars rose after the guzzler tax threshold was raised high enough to pose a tax threat. Manufacturers clearly decided it was more economic to improve fuel economy than to even pay a small gas guzzler tax. This improvement in fuel economy occurred during a period of sustained decreases in the price of gasoline. As can be seen in Figure 6.6, this improvement in low mpg cars occurred when the fuel economy of the remainder of the new car

Figure 6.5
Change in the Fuel Economy of Low MPG
Cars and the Gas Guzzler Tax

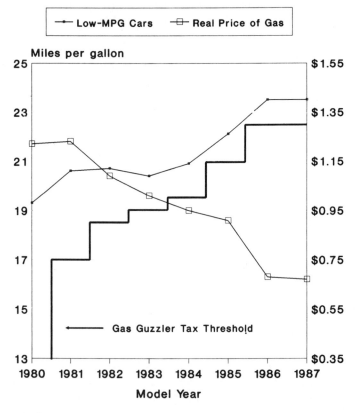

Source: Authors

fleet hardly improved, suggesting that the gas guzzler tax played a major role in post-1983 fuel economy improvements.

Gas guzzler taxes have a number of desirable features. Since the tax only applies to new cars, low-income persons will be largely unaffected by the tax. And since the tax is a large penalty imposed at the point of automobile purchase, instead of very small sums

Figure 6.6
Change in the Fuel Economy of
Low-MPG Cars vs. All Other Cars

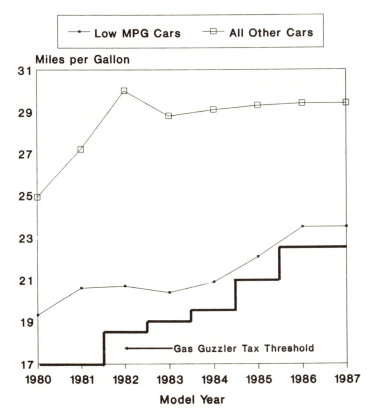

Source: Authors

stretched out over many years (as caused by a gasoline tax), it is likely to have a strong effect on the willingness of car buyers to seek higher mileage cars.

We also recommend that a gas guzzler tax be established for light trucks, and as for passenger cars, the guzzler tax threshold should be increased by the same percentage as the light truck fuel economy standard.

Drive +. An extension of the concept of the gas-guzzler tax is a system of fees and rebates that would be levied on new cars according to whether they were above or below an average level of fuel economy. Such an approach has been introduced in legislation in California, and has been dubbed "Drive+" (Gordon and Levenson, 1990). As proposed there, fees and rebates would also be set according to whether a car's emissions were above or below an average level. Drive+ would thus encourage cars to be produced that are certified for emissions at levels below the legal limits. There is good evidence, from cars made by Volkswagen, Suzuki and others, that such low emissions can be achieved at modest cost, at least by high fuel economy vehicles. The program is designed to be revenue neutral, so that total rebates roughly equal total fees. The concept is just as appropriate at the federal level as it is at the state level. The Drive+ program was passed overwhelmingly by the California state legislature in 1990, but was vetoed by the Governor. Given the new governor's expressed support, it may become law in 1991.

Fees and rebates at the point of purchase of a new vehicle are an important tool to improve fuel economy and emissions (Geller, 1989). Given our society's sensitivity to first cost, it is easier and more effective to adjust for market imperfections and influence new car fuel economy and emission levels at the point of capital equipment purchase than it is to adjust for imperfections in the course of operations as, for example, with a gasoline tax.

Technology Policy

The policies discussed above indirectly encourage the creation of new technology to meet the changed economic conditions or regulatory constraints. Experience shows, however, that a more direct policy focus on new technology can be highly effective. Before considering such policies, let us briefly suggest the possibilities for new technology to meet our goals.

By new technology we mean vehicles and their energy supply systems which could radically reduce energy requirements and emissions, but which are not close to being in mass production. There are three potential types of vehicles:

1. vehicles with much higher fuel economy, but still based on gasoline or diesel fuel and still serving four or more passengers with, roughly, today's driving capabilities;

2. special-purpose vehicles requiring much less energy at the drive wheels, such as a small commuter car; and,

3. alternative-fuel vehicles including those which could flexibly operate on both gasoline and an alternative fuel.

In Group 1 the engine could be an advanced, direct-injection diesel, now entering production in Europe, which is about one-third more efficient than corresponding conventional gasoline-powered engines. High fuel economy prototype vehicles incorporating advanced diesels have been built or partially developed by Volvo, Volkswagen, Renault, Peugeot, and Toyota, with in-use fuel economies estimated to be almost 70 mpg and higher (Bleviss, 1988).

In Group 2, there are vehicles such as the proposed Lean Machine and the demonstration electric vehicle called Impact, both developed by General Motors. The Lean Machine is a two seater with one passenger behind the driver. Both the Lean Machine and the Impact are small, have little air and tire drag, and require very little power to be delivered to the wheels in typical driving. (The fact that the Impact is an electric vehicle is incidental to this discussion.) Both of these prototype vehicles happen to have rather high acceleration performance. It is not clear if that is an important attribute for marketing such a vehicle. Safety is a critical issue for such vehicles. It may be important to consider separate lanes on high speed roadways.

In Group 3 there is an enormous range of possibilities. We mention only two of the most exciting: hybrid electric and fuel-cell vehicles. The hybrid electric is powered by both batteries and an internal combustion engine. A common configuration is for the car to use the batteries (and electric motor) on short day trips, and to use the internal combustion engine for longer trips. The batteries would be expected to be recharged overnight, when electric demand is low and there is substantial unused electricity generating capacity. The hybrid overcomes the severe disability of electric vehicles: their short daily range and long battery recharge period.

The fuel cell, essentially a large battery, has the advantage of relying on a stored fluid fuel like methanol. The fuel cell converts the chemical energy of the fuel to electricity without combustion. Extremely little, if any, emissions are associated with fuel cell operation, with the exception of carbon dioxide. Much higher efficiencies of conversion are possible than with the present kind of engine.

Emissions regulations and control is another area where new technology could have a revolutionary impact. Inexpensive equipment to measure, record, and communicate information about emissions into the air may be able to alter the strategy for regulation of emissions from its focus on design criteria and isolated tests to a focus on actual performance. To illustrate, it is now becoming possible to measure emissions from the tailpipe of a car driving down a road, using a source of light and a receiver on opposite sides of the road (Stedman, 1990). When this technology is developed, it will be possible, first, to determine quantitatively how important the most polluting cars are to overall emissions from the automobiles in a particular airshed. And second, if the problem is indeed dominated by a small number of serious offenders, it may be that identifying these offenders will become a particularly cost-effective approach to clean-up. A competing, or perhaps complementary, approach for vehicles may be to measure and record emissions performance with on-board technology that is beginning to be developed.

Technology Push and Pull Policies. The U.S. government has been highly effective in encouraging new technology in some sectors like agriculture, commercial aircraft, and semiconductors. The tools used are, broadly, technology push and technology pull.

Technology push concerns the creation of technology: research, invention, development, and demonstration. This is not a linear sequence of activities, in which one follows the next, but a complex interaction in which new technologies are created. Technology push policies involve government support for research, development and demonstration (RD&D) and government encouragement of private sector RD&D through tax incentives, patent law, etc.

Technology pull concerns the demand for new technology, i.e., demand for it after it reaches initial commercial status. It cannot be over emphasized that the existence of a likely market for a new or improved process or product strongly motivates development and production of new technologies, and the apparent absence of a market strongly inhibits them. Government policies can provide technology pull through government purchases and by encouraging the private sector's propensity to purchase new technology (Ross and Socolow, 1990).

A major example of a technology push policy is government-supported research and development on generic technologies that could form the basis for many new product developments. Modest government involvement is proving very beneficial in electrochemistry (new and improved batteries), combustion (understanding of knock and soot formation), and ceramic insulation (for the combustion chamber). It would be valuable to continue support in these areas and greatly expand the government's efforts in, e.g., engine friction and control approaches for hybrid-electric vehicles.

It may seem that it is the private sector's responsibility to conduct research on generic technologies such as those just mentioned. It is well known and well documented, however, that the private sector under invests in research (Young, 1986). The roots of this under investment lie in a firm's inability to prevent its competitors from capturing many of the benefits of its research. Other contributing factors are the short time horizons and the heavily cyclical earnings patterns experienced by many firms. The private sector cannot support research leading to innovation in many socially useful areas of technology, at least not nearly at a level consonant with today's needs.

An attractive example of a technology pull policy is providing extra fuel economy credits to manufacturers that produce automobiles or light trucks that attain exceptionally high levels of fuel economy. Such a provision would reward manufacturers for aggressively introducing new technology, providing an incentive for manufacturers to take a significant leap forward with fuel economy technologies, as opposed to taking more conservative, incremental steps. The incentive could be made especially strong for improving the fuel economy of mid-size and large cars.[5]

A schedule of fuel economy thresholds for the major EPA automobile size classes could be established as part of a strengthened fuel economy standards law. The schedule could define, for each size class and for specified years, which level of fuel economy would have to be exceeded for a manufacturer to qualify for the credits. A schedule that would be consistent with fuel economy standards requiring a 40 percent increase in fuel economy might be as shown in Table 6.7. If a manufacturer produced a car that exceeded the above specified levels, it could count the fuel economy of that car (for purposes of complying with CAFE standards) as being, for example, 50 percent higher than its test fuel economy. Present fuel economy regulations already include similar CAFE credits for alternate fuel vehicles.

Fuel Economy and Safety

Opponents of efforts to improve automobile fuel economy have recently argued that the standards increase highway fatalities. Fuel-efficient cars are commonly equated with small, light cars.

---

[5] As pointed out above, high fuel economy has been associated with bottom-of-the-market vehicles. One of the major policy challenges is to inspire and encourage manufacturers to create "green" cars in the middle of the market.

Table 6.7
Proposed Schedule: Minimum Fuel Economies
to Earn Extra Fuel Economy Credits[a]
(MPG)

	1996	1997	1998	1999	2000	2001
Subcompact	43.0	44.5	46.0	47.5	49.0	50.5
Compact	41.0	42.5	44.0	45.0	46.5	48.0
Mid-size	37.5	39.0	40.0	41.0	42.5	44.0
Large	33.0	34.0	35.0	36.5	37.5	39.0

Note: [a]Minicompacts and two seaters are left out of this schedule because the kinds of cars that fall under these classes are very diverse, and their fuel economies are widely divergent.

However, the record shows that fuel economy can be substantially increased without reducing vehicle weight. The average new car fuel economy began to improve sharply after 1974. Initially, much of this fuel economy improvement was due to reducing average vehicle weight. It was the easiest and cheapest way for manufacturers to improve fuel economy. But since 1980, the average vehicle weight has remained almost constant, while the fuel economy increased by about 20 percent (see Figure 6.7). Manufacturers were able to improve fuel economy without reducing vehicle weight by relying on technological improvements in engines, transmissions, aerodynamics and other means. The potential for making further fuel economy improvements without reducing vehicle weight remains large (Ledbetter and Ross, 1990).

Points in Figure 6.8 represent the weight and safety performance of 1984 to 1988 model year cars crash tested by the U.S. Department of Transportation's National Highway Traffic Safety Administration. These cars were crashed into a fixed barrier at 35 mph. The measure of safety performance is the driver head injury criterion (HIC), which reflects the potential for injury to a driver's brain. The higher the number, the higher the potential for injury. As shown here, there is no relationship between automobile weight and head injury criteria. In fact, there are some heavy

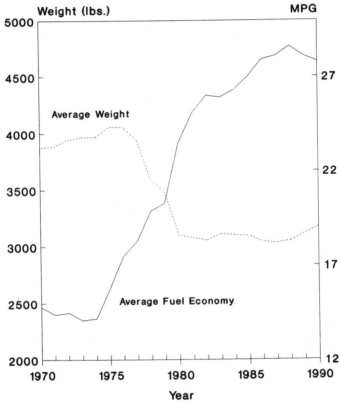

Figure 6.7
U.S. Automobile Weight and Fuel Economy 1970-1990

Source: ACEEE, adapted from U.S. EPA

vehicles that perform poorly (upper right portion of the figure) and some light vehicles that perform very well (lower left portion of the figure). A plot of the passenger side HIC yields very similar results.

Crashing a car into a fixed barrier does not necessarily measure how weight affects a car's performance in a crash. Nonetheless, Figure 6.8 illustrates that there are large differences in the crash worthiness of automobiles, independent of weight. A 1982

Figure 6.8
Auto Weight vs. Driver Head Injury Criterion

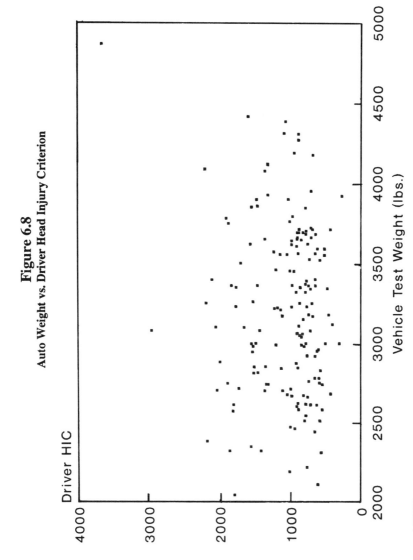

Source: ACEEE

study pointed out that the differences in crash performance within weight classes were greater than the differences among weight classes (Office of Technology Assessment, 1982).

There are many existing light-weight cars that perform well in crash tests. But much safer and more fuel-efficient cars are possible. The Volvo LCP 2000, a prototype high-efficiency car, was designed with both safety and fuel economy in mind. The car weighs 1500 pounds (less than half today's average new auto weight of about 3200 pounds), achieves 63 mpg in the city and 81 on the highway, and can withstand frontal and side impacts of 35 mph, and a rear impact of 30 mph (Bleviss, 1988). U.S. regulations require only that vehicles can withstand a frontal impact of 30 mph.

The U.S. Department of Transportation's Research Safety Vehicle Program, which existed from 1977 to 1980, developed an experimental car that was both safe and fuel efficient (U.S. Department of Transportation, 1980). The program concluded that a car using then-current technology (ten years old now) could carry five passengers; achieve 43 mpg; and withstand 80 mph frontal impacts, 50 mph side impacts, and 45 mph rear impacts.

Evidence that fuel economy and automobile safety can be improved simultaneously is also found in the statistical record established in the United States. Since 1973, the average fuel economy for all cars on the road rose from 13 mpg to 20 mpg. During the same period, traffic fatalities fell from 3.5 per 100 million vehicle miles traveled to 2.4. Safer cars and highways, increased use of seatbelts, and anti-drunk driving campaigns are widely recognized as major reasons for the improvement.

Despite the evidence that improving fuel economy and automobile safety are compatible goals, adherents to the view that improved fuel economy means higher traffic fatalities cite studies of actual automobile crash data that demonstrate a relationship between car size and fatalities, or between car weight and fatalities. A common problem, however, with studies based on actual accident data is that it is difficult to separate the effects of driver behavior from vehicle characteristics when estimating the propensity of certain cars to be involved in fatal accidents. For example, the bad fatality record of a few high-performance sports cars may lead one to conclude that these cars are inherently unsafe. But dangerous driving practices of people who most commonly own and drive these cars may be partly or fully responsible for their bad safety record. Similarly, the worse-than-average safety record of a few small, inexpensive, and fuel-efficient cars may be due to the atypical driving behavior of people who tend to buy these cars, e.g., drivers of small cars tend to be young.

In summary, research has shown that with careful design, cars can be both fuel efficient and safe. Nonetheless, the results of some recent studies justify a close look at the effect of car size and weight on crash performance. If new research indicates that as vehicles evolve weight or size will be a primary consideration in designing vehicles to achieve lower fatality rates, then future fuel economy improvements should be based on approaches other than weight or size reduction. With either approach, current and future technologies provide a broad range of ways to substantially improve auto fuel economy while simultaneously improving auto safety.

Conclusions

Federal policies made a major contribution toward the fuel economy improvements achieved since 1975. But because they require no further improvements, and because real gasoline prices have fallen for years, the long upward trend in fuel economy has stalled. This cessation in fuel economy improvement puts our nation's economy and security at risk. Among the options for reducing our oil imports and carbon dioxide emissions within the next ten to twenty years, none will have greater effect than substantially improving light vehicle fuel economy (see Figures 6.9 and 6.10).[6] The market could be of great assistance in pushing

---

[6]The 40/30 mpg standard referred to in Figure 6.9 is for cars and light trucks, respectively.

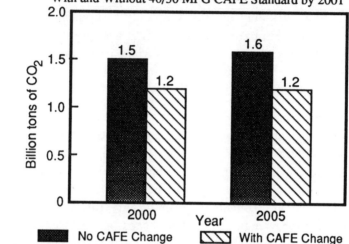

Figure 6.9
Projected U.S. Light Vehicle Carbon Emissions
With and Without 40/30 MPG CAFE Standard by 2001

No CAFE change scenario assumes new vehicle fuel economy does
not rise above current levels.
Source: ACEEE.

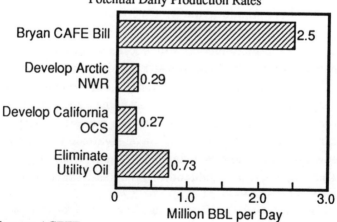

Figure 6.10
Selected New U.S. Oil Resources
Potential Daily Production Rates

Source: ACEEE.

fuel economy levels higher, but because of large externalities and other barriers, it will not be sufficient.

In addition to fuel economy improvements, it is imperative that we slow growth in vehicle miles of travel, and offer attractive transportation alternatives to low-occupancy light vehicles. Otherwise, even with fuel economy improvement we could find ourselves looking back on the fifteen years that follow 1990 with the same sense of running in place that we get when looking back on the fifteen years since 1975.

Policies to reduce light vehicle fuel consumption will not only benefit the United States directly, but given the enormous influence U.S. policies and technologies could have on other countries, these policies could leverage large international reductions in transportation fuel use.

Acknowledgement

This research was supported by the Joyce Foundation, the Educational Foundation of America, John A. Harris, IV, the Alida Rockefeller Charitable Lead Trust, the John D. and Catherine T. MacArthur Foundation, and the Lawrence Berkeley Laboratory. We also thank Howard Geller for many useful comments.

References

Ang, B. W. 1991. "Traffic Management Systems and Energy Savings: The Case of Singapore." Pp. 41-51 in D. L. Bleviss and M. L. Birk (eds.), *Driving New Directions: Transportation Experiences and Options in Developing Countries*. Washington, DC: International Institute for Energy Conservation.

Bleviss, Deborah L. 1988. *The New Oil Crisis and Fuel Economy Technologies*. Westbury, CT: Quorum Books.

Bohi, Douglas and Mary Beth Zimmerman. 1984. "An Update on Econometric Studies of Energy Demand Behavior." *Annual Review of Energy* 9: 105-154.

Broadman, H.G. and W. W. Hogan. 1986. "Oil Tariff Policy in an Uncertain Market." Cambridge, MA: Energy and Environmental Policy Center, Harvard University.

Burchell, Robert W. and David Listokin (eds.). 1982. *Energy and Land Use.* Piscataway, NJ: Center for Urban Policy Research, Rutgers University.

Bureau of the Census. 1990. "Truck Inventory and Use Survey." *1987 Census of Transportation.* Washington, DC: U.S. Government Printing Office.

Burke, Monica. 1990. "High Occupancy Vehicle Facilities: General Characteristics and Potential Fuel Savings." Washington, DC: American Council for an Energy-Efficient Economy.

Butler, Patrick, et al. 1988. "Sex-Divided Mileage, Accident, and Insurance Cost Data Show That Auto Insurers Overcharge Most Women." *Journal of Insurance Regulation* 6/3 (Part 1), and 6/4 (Part 2).

Crandall, R. W. et al. 1986. *Regulating the Automobile.* Washington, DC: The Brookings Institution.

El-Gasseir, Mohamed. 1990. "The Potential Benefits of Pay-As-You-Drive Automobile Insurance." Submission to the California Energy Commission. Docket No. 89-CR-90. Sacramento, CA.

Energy Conservation Coalition. 1989. "The Auto Industry on Fuel Efficiency: Yesterday and Today." Fact Sheet. Washington D.C.

Geller, Howard. 1989. "Financial Incentives for Reducing Auto Emissions: A Proposal for Clean Air Act Amendments." Washington, DC: American Council for an Energy-Efficient Economy.

Gordon, Deborah. 1991. *Steering a New Course: Transportation, Energy and the Environment.* Boston, MA: Union of Concerned Scientists.

Gordon, Deborah and Leo Levenson. 1990. "Drive +: Promoting Cleaner and More Fuel-Efficient Motor Vehicles Through a Self-Financing System of State Sales Tax Incentives." *Journal of Policy Analysis and Management* 9/3: 409-415.

Greene, David L. 1991. "Vehicle Use and Fuel Economy: How Big is the Rebound Effect?" Oak Ridge, TN: Oak Ridge National Laboratory.

_____. 1990. "CAFE or Price?: An Analysis of the Effects of Federal Fuel Economy Regulations and Gasoline Price on New Car MPG, 1978-89." *The Energy Journal* 11/3: 37-57.

Heavenrich, Robert M. and J. Dillard Murrell. 1990. "Light-Duty Automotive Technology and Fuel Economy Trends Through 1990." Ann Arbor, MI: U.S. EPA Office of Mobile Sources.

Hellman, Karl and J. Dillard Murrell. 1984. "Development of Adjustment Factors for the EPA City and Highway MPG Values." Warrendale, PA: Society of Automotive Engineers, 8400496.

Holtzclaw, John. 1990. "Explaining Urban Density and Transit Impacts on Auto Use." Testimony before the California Energy Commission. Docket No. 89-CR-90, April 23. Sacramento, CA.

Horton, E. J. and W. D. Compton. 1984. "Technological Trends in Automobiles." *Science* 225: 587-593.

Institute of Transportation Engineers. 1989. "A Toolbox for Alleviating Traffic Congestion." Washington, DC.

Khazzoom, Daniel J. 1988. "Quantifying the Environmental Impact of a Gasoline Tax: A Study in the Use of Energy Conservation as a Strategy for Emission Abatement in the Transportation Sector." San Jose, CA: San Jose State University.

Lashof, Daniel A. and Dennis Tirpak. 1989. "Policy Options for Stabilizing Global Climate." Washington, DC: Office of Policy, Planning and Evaluation, U.S. Environmental Protection Agency.

Ledbetter, Marc and Marc Ross. 1990. "Supply Curves of Conserved Energy for Automobiles." *Proceedings of the 25th Intersociety Energy Conservation Engineering Conference.* New York, NY: American Institute of Chemical Engineers.

MacDonald, Gordon. 1990. "The Future of Methane as an Energy Source." *Annual Review of Energy* 15: 53-83.

MacKenzie, James and Michael Walsh. 1990. *Driving Forces: Motor Vehicle Trends and their Implications for Global Warming, Energy Strategies, and Transportation Planning.* Washington, DC: World Resources Institute.

Mayo, John, and John Mathis. 1988. "The Effectiveness of Mandatory Fuel Efficiency Standards in Reducing the Demand for Gasoline." *Applied Economics* 20: 211-219.

McCarthy, Patrick S., and Richard Tay. 1989. "Consumer Evaluation of New Car Attributes." *Transportation Research* 23A/5: 367-375.

Motor Vehicle Manufacturers Association. 1990. "MVMA Facts and Figures '90." Detroit, MI: Motor Vehicle Manufacturers Association.

Murrell, J. D. and R. M. Heavenrich. 1990. "Downward Trend in Passenger Car Fuel Economy — a View of Recent Data." Technical Report EPA/AA/CTAB/90-01. Ann Arbor, MI: U.S. EPA Office of Mobile Sources.

Newman, Peter G. and Jeffrey R. Kenworthy. 1988. *Cities and Automobile Dependence: A Sourcebook.* Aldershot, England: Gower Technical.

Office of Technology Assessment, U.S. Congress. 1982. "Increased Automobile Fuel Efficiency and Synthetic Fuels." Washington, DC: U.S. Government Printing Office.

Pushkarev, Boris S. and Jeffrey M. Zupan. 1977. *Public Transportation and Land Use Policy.* Bloomington, IN: Indiana University Press.

Replogle, Michael. 1990. "U.S. Transportation Policy: Let's Make it Sustainable." Washington, DC: Institute for Transportation and Development Policy.

Ross, Marc. 1989. "Energy and Transportation in the United States." *Annual Review of Energy* 14: 131-171.

Ross, Marc and Robert Socolow. 1990. "Technology Policy and the Environment." Presented at "Toward 2000: Environment, Technology and the New Century," a conference held at Annapolis, MD. Copies of presentations available from World Resources Institute, Washington, D.C.

Stedman, Donald. 1990. University of Denver. Private communication.

Tobias, Andrew. 1982. *The Invisible Bankers.* New York, NY: Pocket Books.

U.S. Department of Transportation. 1980. "The Safe, Fuel-Efficient Car: A Report on its Producibility and Marketing." Washington, DC: U.S. Government Printing Office.

U.S. EPA Motor Vehicle Emissions Laboratory. 1988. MOBILE4 Workshop held on November 30, Ann Arbor, MI.

Watson, H. C. 1990. University of Melbourne. Private communication.

Westbrook, F. and P. Patterson. 1989. "Changing Driving Patterns and Their Effect on Fuel Economy." Presented at the May SAE Government/Industry Meeting, Washington, D.C.

Young, J. A. 1986. "Global Competition — The New Reality: Results of the President's Commission on Industrial Competitiveness." In R. Landau and N. Rosenberg (eds.), *The Positive Sum Strategy.* Washington, DC: National Academy Press.

PART IV

The Policy Challenge

Chapter 7

Policy for Energy and Sustainable Development

Mohan Munasinghe

Introduction

Energy became a major international issue in the 1970s, following the oil crisis. More recently, global climate change induced by excessive greenhouse gas accumulation in the atmosphere has emerged as a potential problem that further complicates energy issues. In this paper, we will focus on energy related environmental issues in the developing countries. The development related energy needs of the Third World and their financial implications, the potential for better energy management, barriers to reducing greenhouse gas emissions, and financial mechanisms and policies that can improve the performance of developing countries in this respect, will be explored below.

The experience of the industrialized countries emphasizes that a reliable supply of energy is a vital prerequisite for economic growth and development. For example, the observed trends relating to electricity demand in developing countries (which indicate annual growth rates in the region of 6 to 12 percent) are consistent

Author's Note: The opinions expressed in this chapter are those of the author, and do not necessarily represent the views of any institution or government. Assistance provided by Chitru Fernando and Ken King is gratefully acknowledged.

with the development objectives that these countries all share. Up to the present time, many developing countries have been struggling with the formidable difficulties of meeting these demands for energy services at acceptable costs. If such needs cannot be met, economic growth is likely to slow down and the quality of life will fall.

Given these already existing handicaps, the growing additional concerns about the environmental consequences of energy use considerably complicate the policy dilemma facing the developing countries. In the past, industrial countries that faced a tradeoff between economic growth and environmental preservation invariably gave higher priority to the former. These richer countries have awakened only recently to the environmental consequences of their economic progress, and only after a broad spectrum of economic objectives have been reached. This model of economic and social development has been adopted by many Third World regions. Therefore, until both developed and developing countries find a less material intensive sustainable development path, environmental protection efforts will be hampered.

The developing countries (LDCs) share the deep worldwide concerns about environmental degradation, and some have taken steps already to improve their own natural resource management as an essential prerequisite for sustained economic development. However, they also face other urgent issues like poverty, hunger and disease, as well as rapid population growth and high expectations. The paucity of resources available to address all these problems constrains the ability of LDCs to undertake costly measures to protect the global commons.

The crucial dilemma for LDCs is how to reconcile development goals and the elimination of poverty — which will require increased use of energy and raw materials — with responsible stewardship of the environment, and without overburdening already weak economies. The per capita GNP of low income economies (with half the world population) averaged US$290 in 1987, or under one sixtieth of the U.S. value ($18,530). In the two largest developing countries, India and China, per capita GNP was $300 and 290 respectively. Correspondingly, the U.S. per capita energy consumption of 7265 kilograms of oil equivalent (kgoe) in 1987 was 35 and 15 times greater than the same statistic in India and China respectively.

The disparity in both per capita income and energy use among different countries also raises additional issues in the context of current global environmental concerns, and the heavy burden placed on mankind's natural resource base by past economic growth — fossil fuel related CO_2 accumulation in the atmosphere is a good example. The developed countries accounted for over 80 percent of such cumulative worldwide emissions during 1950-86 — North America contributed over 40 billion tons of carbon, Western and Eastern Europe emitted 25 and 32 billion tons respectively, and the developing countries share was was about 24 billion tons. On a per capita basis the contrasts are even more stark, with North America emitting over 20 times more and the developed countries as a whole being responsible for over eleven times as much total cumulative CO_2 emissions as the LDCs. The LDC share would be even smaller if emissions prior to 1950 were included. Clearly, any reasonable growth scenario for developing nations that followed the same material-intensive path as the industrialized world, would result in unacceptably high levels of future greenhouse gas accumulation as well as more general depletion of natural resources.

Up to now, scientific analysis has provided only broad and rather uncertain predictions about the degree and timing of potential global warming. However, it would be prudent for mankind to buy an "insurance policy" in the form of mitigatory actions to reduce greenhouse gas emissions. Ironically, both local and global environmental degradation might affect developing countries more severely, since they are more dependent on natural resources while lacking the economic strength to prevent or respond quickly to increases in the frequency, severity and persistence of flooding, drought, storms, and so on. Thus, from the LDC viewpoint, an attractive low cost insurance premium would be a set of inexpensive measures that could address a range of national and global environmental issues, without hampering development efforts.

The recent report of the Bruntland Commission (WCED, 1987), which has been widely circulated and accepted, has presented arguments along the theme of sustainable development, which consists of the interaction of two components: needs, especially those of the poor segments of the world's population and limitations, which are imposed by the ability of the environment to meet those needs. The development of the presently industrialized countries took place in a setting which emphasized needs and de-emphasized limitations. The development of these societies has effectively exhausted a disproportionately large share of global resources — broadly defined to include both the resources that are consumed in productive activity (such as oil, gas and minerals), as well as environmental assets that absorb the waste products of economic activity and those that provide irreplaceable life support functions (like the high altitude ozone layer). Indeed, some analysts argue that this development path has significantly indebted the developed countries to the larger global community.

The division of responsibility in this global effort is clear from the above arguments. The unbalanced use of common resources in the past, should be one important basis on which the developed and developing countries can work together to share and preserve what remains. The developed countries have already attained most reasonable goals of development and can afford to substitute environmental protection for further growth of material output. On the other hand, the developing countries can be expected to participate in the global effort only to the extent that this participation is fully consistent with and complementary to their immediate economic and social development objectives.

In the context of the foregoing, this paper identifies critical energy-environmental issues, using examples from the highly capital intensive and pivotal power sector to illustrate specific points. It also explores some policy implications, constraints and opportunities at the national and global level for both the developing countries as well as the wider international community, and examines the role of emerging mechanisms such as the global environmental fund and ozone defense fund, in the allocation of resources for addressing transnational environmental problems.

Electric Power Needs
of the Developing Countries

Despite some anomalies, the link between energy demand and GDP is well established. Electric power, in particular, has a vital role to play in the development process, with future prospects for economic growth being closely linked to the provision of adequate and reliable electricity supplies. Figure 7.1 indicates the relationship between electricity use and income for both developed and developing countries. A more systematic analysis of World Bank and UN data over the past two or three decades indicates that the ratio of percentage growth rates (or elasticity) of power system capacity to GDP is about 1.4 in the developing countries.

Assuming no drastic changes in past trends with respect to demand management and conservation, the World Bank's most recent projections indicate that the demand for electricity in LDCs will grow at an average annual rate of 6.6 percent during the period 1989-99 (World Bank, 1990). This compares with actual growth rates of 10 percent and 7 percent in the seventies and eighties, respectively. Such rates of growth indicate the need for total capacity additions of 384 GW during 1990-99 (see Figure 7.2), and annual energy consumption of 3844 TWh by 1999. As indicated in Figure 7.3, the Asia region, requirements dominate with almost two thirds of the total, and coal and hydro are the main primary sources — both of which have specific environmental problems associated with their use.

The investment needs corresponding to these indicative projections are also very large. Table 7.1 shows the projected breakdown of LDC power sector capital expenditure in the 1990s. Of a total of $745 billion (constant 1989 US$), Asia (which includes both India and China), again dominates, accounting for $455 billion or over $45 billion annually. In comparison with the total

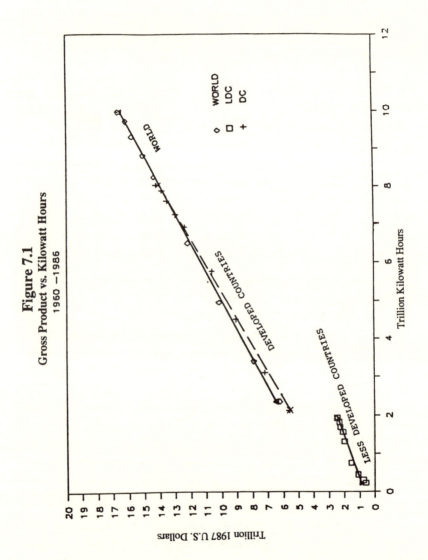

Figure 7.1
Gross Product vs. Kilowatt Hours
1960 —1986

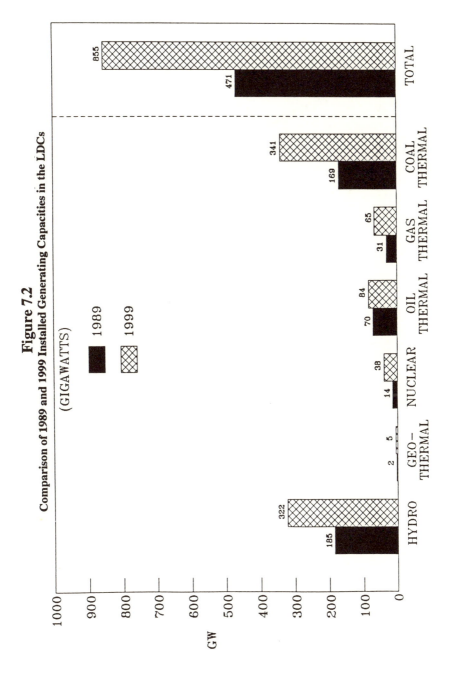

Figure 7.2

Comparison of 1989 and 1999 Installed Generating Capacities in the LDCs

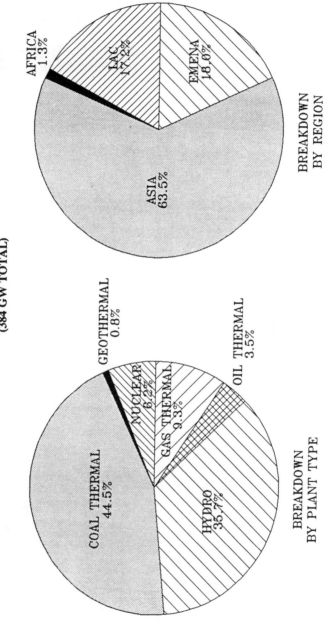

Figure 7.3

Breakdown by Plant Type and Region of Capacity Expected to Be Added in the LDCs in the 1990s

(384 GW TOTAL)

Table 7.1
Regional Breakdown
of LDC Power Capital Expenditures
in the 1990s

	Asia	EMENA[a]	LAC[b]	Africa	Total
Generation	277	82	83	6	448
Transmission	39	8	32	2	81
Distribution	100	23	27	2	152
General	39	11	13	1	64
TOTAL	455	124	155	11	745
Percent	61.1	16.6	20.8	1.5	100

Source: The World Bank.

Notes: [a]Europe, Middle East and North Africa (Meditarranean region).
[b]Latin America and the Caribbean.

projected annual requirement for LDCs of $75 billion, the present annual rate of investment in developing countries is only around $50 billion. Even this present rate is proving difficult to maintain. Developing country debt which averaged 23 percent of GNP in 1981, increased dramatically to 42 percent in 1987 and has not declined significantly since then. In low income Asian countries, outstanding debt doubled, from 8 percent in 1981 to 16 percent in 1987. Capital intensive power sector investments have played a significant role in this observed increase.

If the developing countries follow this projected expansion path, the environmental consequences are also likely to increase in a corresponding fashion. There is already a growing concern about the environmental consequences at the national level, of energy use in developing countries. At a recent workshop on acid rain in Asia, participants reported on a wide range of environmental effects of the growing use of fossil fuels, especially coal, in the region (Foell, 1989). For example, total 1985 sulphur dioxide emissions in Asia were estimated at around 22 million tons, and these levels, coupled with high local densities, have led to acid deposition in many parts of Asia.

The developing countries feel that any attempts to mitigate these environmental effects, however, cannot jeopardize the critical role played by electric power (and more generally, energy) in economic development. Similarly, the allocation of resources to environmental programs in developing countries cannot diminish the resources needed to fund projected expansion of supply. Energy and environmental policymakers in both developing countries and the global community are, indeed, confronted with a formidable dilemma.

The Economics of
Energy-Environmental Issues

The foregoing discussion has helped to establish a rational and equitable basis for addressing the problems of energy-environmental impact mitigation. In this section we present an economic efficiency framework which ties together the issue of environmental protection with the existing energy sector goals of energy efficiency and economic growth.

It is convenient to recall here that traditionally, the specific prerequisites for economic efficiency have included both (Munasinghe, 1990b):

(a) efficient consumption of energy, by providing efficient price signals that ensure optimal energy use and resource allocation; and

(b) efficient production of energy, by ensuring the least-cost supply mix through the optimization of investment planning and energy system operation.

A new issue which has emerged in recent decades as an area of particular concern, is the efficient and optimal use of our global natural resource base, including air, land and water. Since there has been much discussion also about the key role that energy efficiency and energy conservation might play in mitigating environmental costs, it is useful first to examine how these topics relate to economic efficiency. Specific issues dealing with the formulation and implementation of economically efficient energy policies are presented later in the chapter.

Major environmental issues vary widely, particularly in terms of scale or magnitude of impact, but most are linked to energy use. First, there are the truly global problems such as the potential worldwide warming due to increasing accumulation of greenhouse gases like carbon dioxide and methane in the atmosphere, high altitude ozone depletion because of release of chlorofluorocarbons, pollution of the oceanic and marine environment by oil spills and other wastes, and excessive use of certain animal and mineral resources. Second in scale are the transnational issues like acid rain or radioactive fallout in one european country due to fossil-fuel or nuclear emissions in a neighboring nation, and excessive downstream siltation of river water in Bangladesh due to deforestation of watersheds and soil erosion in nearby Nepal. Third, one might identify national and regional effects, for example those involving the Amazon basin in Brazil, or the Mahaweli basin in Sri Lanka. Finally, there are more localized and project specific problems like the complex environmental and social impacts of a specific hydroelectric or multipurpose dam.

While environmental and natural resource problems of any kind are a matter for serious concern, those that fall within the national boundaries of a given country are inherently easier to deal with from the viewpoint of policy implementation. Such issues that fall within the energy sector must be addressed within the national policymaking framework. Meanwhile, driven by strong pressures arising from far-reaching potential consequences of global issues like atmospheric greenhouse gas accumulation, significant efforts are being made in the areas of not only scientific analysis, but also international cooperation mechanisms to implement mitigatory measures.

Given this background, we discuss next some of the principal points concerning energy use and economic efficiency (Munasinghe, 1990a). In many countries, especially those in the developing world, inappropriate policies have encouraged wasteful and unproductive uses of some forms of energy. In such cases, better energy management could lead to improvements in economic efficiency (higher value of net output produced), energy efficiency (higher value of net output per unit of energy used), energy conservation (reduced absolute amount of energy used), and environmental protection (reduced energy related environmental costs). While such a result fortuitously satisfies all four goals, the latter are not always mutually consistent. For example, in some developing countries where the existing levels of per capita energy consumption are very low and certain types of energy use are uneconomically constrained, it may become necessary to promote more energy consumption in order to raise net output (thereby increasing economic efficiency). There are also instances where it may be possible to increase energy efficiency while decreasing energy conservation.

Despite the above complications, our basic conclusion remains valid — that the economic efficiency criterion which helps us maximize the value of net output from all available scarce resources in the economy (especially energy and the ecosystem in the present context), should effectively subsume purely energy oriented objectives such as energy efficiency and energy conservation. Furthermore, the costs arising from energy-related adverse environmental impacts may be included (to the extent possible) in the energy economics analytical framework, to determine how much energy use and net output that society should be willing to forego, in order to abate or mitigate environmental damage. The existence of the many other national policy objectives — including social goals that are particularly relevant in the case of low income populations — will complicate the decisionmaking process even further.

The foregoing discussion may be reinforced by the use of a simplified static analysis of the trade-off between resource use and net output of an economic activity (see Figure 7.4).

Figure 7.4
Trade-off Between Resource Use and Net Output (Illustration)

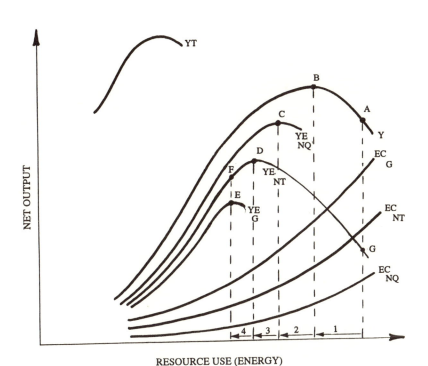

Net output, resource use and environmental cost.
$YE_{NQ} = Y - EC_{NQ}$; $YE_{NT} = Y - EC_{NT}$; $YE_G = Y - EC_G$.

Energy Efficiency

Y represents the usual measurement of the net output of productive economic activity in a country, as a function of some resource input (say energy) — considering only the conventional internalized costs, i.e., not accounting for environmental impacts.
Due to policy distortions (for example, subsidized prices), the
point of operation in many developing countries appears to be at
A, where the resource is being used wastefully. Therefore, without
invoking any environmental considerations, but merely by increas-

ing economic and resource use efficiency (i.e., energy efficiency), output as usually measured could be maximized by moving from A to B. A typical example might be improving energy end-use efficiency or reducing energy supply system losses (some practical examples of this will be presented later).

Quantifiable National
Environmental Costs

Now consider the curve ECNQ which represents economically quantifiable national environmental costs associated with energy use. The latter might include air pollution related health costs of coal power plant or the costs of environmental protection equipment (like scrubbers and electrostatic precipitators to reduce noxious gas and particulate emissions) installed at such a plant, or the costs of resettlement at a hydropower dam site. The corresponding corrected net output curve is: $Y_{NQ} = Y - EC_{NQ}$; which has a maximum at C that lies to the left of B, implying lower use of (more costly) energy.

Non-Quantifiable National
Environmental Costs

Next, consider the "real" national output Y_{NT}, which is net of total environmental costs, whether quantifiable or not. The additional costs to be considered include the unquantified yet very real human health and other unmonetized environmental costs. These total (quantifiable and non-quantifiable) costs are depicted as EC_{NT}; and once again $Y_{NT} = Y - EC_{NT}$. As shown, the real maximum of net output lies at D, to the left of C.

Transnational Environmental Costs

Finally, EC_G represents the globally adjusted costs, where the transnational environmental costs (to other countries) of energy use within the given country have been added to EC_{NT}. In this case, $YE_G = Y - EC_G$; is the correspondingly corrected net output which implies an even lower level of optimal energy use.

For example, consider the costs imposed on other countries (such as transborder impacts of a major dam or global climate impacts of carbon dioxide emissions). If it is decided to reduce resource use within this country further in order to achieve the internationally adjusted optimum at E, then a purely national analysis will show this up as a drop in net output, i.e., from D to E. As other countries benefit, this drop in net output may justify compensation in the form of a transfer of resources from the beneficiary countries. Note that the transnational costs imposed by other countries on the nation in question will be a function of regional or global resource use rather than the national resource use shown on the horizontal axis.

The additional curve Y_A shows net output for a technologically advanced future society that has achieved a much lower resource intensity of production.

Policy Measures for the LDCs

The foregoing analysis illustrates the crucial dilemma for developing countries. In Figure 7.4, all nations (including the poorest) would readily adopt measures that will lead to shift (1) which simultaneously and unambiguously provides both economic efficiency and environmental gains. Most developing countries are indicating increasing willingness to undertake shift (2). However, implementing shift (3) will definitely involve crossing a "pain threshold" for many Third World nations, as other pressing socioeconomic needs compete against the costs of mitigating nonquantifiable adverse environmental impacts.

We note that real economic output increases with each of the shifts (1), (2) and (3) — shown by the movement upward along the curve YE_{NT}; from G to D. However, these shifts are mistakenly perceived often as being upward only from A to B (energy efficiency improvements), followed by downward movements from B through C to D. It is therefore important to correct any misconceptions that environmental protection results in reduced net output — this can be achieved through institutional development, applied research, strengthening of planning capabilities etc. However, it is clear that shift (4) — would hardly appeal to resource constrained developing countries unless concessionary external financing was made available, since this movement would imply optimization of a global value function and costs that most often exceed in-country benefits. In the foregoing, we have neglected considerations involving reciprocal benefits to the given country due to energy use reductions in other countries.

Therefore, we may conclude briefly that, while the energy required for economic development will continue to grow in the developing countries, in the short to medium run there is generally considerable scope for most of them to practice better energy management, thereby increasing net output, using their energy resources more efficiently, and contributing to the effort to reduce global warming. In the medium to long run, it will become possible for the developing countries to adopt newer and more advanced (energy efficient) technologies that are now emerging in the industrialized world, thus enabling them to transform their economies and produce even more output using less energy.

In other words, the developing countries could be expected to cooperate in global environmental programs only to the extent that such cooperation is consistent with their national growth objectives. The role of the developed countries, on the other hand, is to incur the risks inherent in developing innovative technological measures which are the prerequisites for the next level in environmental protection and the mitigation of adverse consequences. These risks include the possibility that the more extreme measures may turn out to be unnecessary or inapplicable after all, given the prevailing uncertainty about the future impact of current environmental developments.

National Framework for
Energy-Environmental Policy Analysis

The previous section introduced a way of considering energy-environmental issues in terms of four shifts. In this section a rational framework for energy-environmental policy analysis within a country is presented in terms of these shifts. This coverage is expanded to the global level in a later section, focusing particularly on the interaction between developed and developing countries.

Developed countries generally differ from the developing countries in the extent to which the shifts have already been made. The LDCs are more likely to be characterized as being at point A in Figure 7.4, while the developed countries are somewhere between C and D. This means that for developing countries there is still considerable scope for environmental improvement by undertaking programs that are consistent with the national objective of increasing overall output. The challenge for national decisionmakers and the international community is to find as many areas as possible where such consistency and complimentarity exist, between growth and environmental protection goals.

Advantages of an Integrated Approach

Successful policy analysis requires an integrated approach, unified in an economic sense so that all feasible options can be balanced and traded off if necessary in the search for an overall optimal strategy. It is within such a comprehensive framework that barriers to and opportunities for making various choices will become apparent. For successful energy policy analysis, a better understanding of economywide linkages is useful, whatever the prevailing political system. It will help decisionmakers in formulating policies and providing market signals and information to economic agents that encourage more efficient energy production and use, as well as better protection of the environment. We summarize in Figure 7.5, a hierarchical framework for integrated national energy planning (INEP), policy analysis and supply-demand management to achieve these goals (Munasinghe, 1990a).

Although the INEP framework is primarily country focussed, we begin by recognizing that many energy-environmental issues have global linkages. Thus individual countries are embedded in an international matrix, while economic and environmental conditions at this global level will impose a set of exogeneous inputs or constraints on decisionmakers within countries. The next hierarchical level in Figure 7.5 treats the energy sector as a part of the whole economy. Therefore, energy planning requires analysis of the links between the energy sector and the rest of the economy. Such links include the energy needs of user sectors, input requirements of the energy sector, and impact on the economy of policies concerning energy prices and availability.

The next level of the integrated approach treats the energy sector as a separate entity composed of sub-sectors such as electricity, petroleum products and so on. This permits detailed analysis, with special emphasis on interactions among the different energy sub-sectors, substitution possibilities, and the resolution of any resulting policy conflicts. The final and most disaggregate level pertains to analysis within each of the energy subsectors. It is at this lowest hierarchical level that most of the detailed energy resource evaluation, planning and implementation of projects is carried out by line institutions (both public and private). In practice, however, the three levels of INEP merge and overlap considerably. Thus the interactions of electric power problems and linkages at all three levels need to be carefully examined.

Energy-environmental interactions (represented by the vertical bar) tend to cut across all levels and need to be incorporated into the analysis. Finally, spatial disaggregation may be required also, especially in larger countries. Such an integrated framework facilitates policymaking and does not imply rigid centralized planning. Thus, such a process should result in the development of a flexible and constantly updated energy strategy designed to meet the national goals mentioned earlier. This national energy

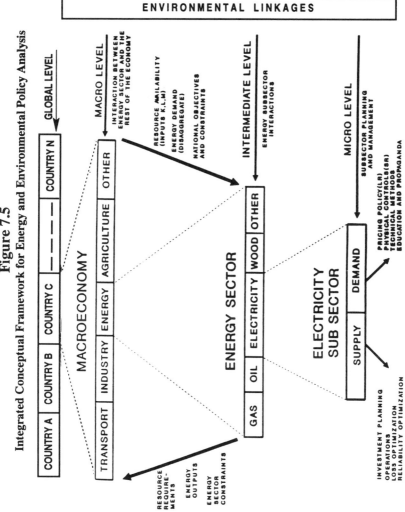

Figure 7.5
Integrated Conceptual Framework for Energy and Environmental Policy Analysis

strategy (of which the investment program and pricing policy are important elements), may be implemented through a set of energy supply and demand management policies and programs that make effective use of decentralized market forces and incentives.

Policy Tools and Constraints

To achieve the desired national goals the policy instruments available to Third World governments, for optimal and energy management include; (a) physical controls; (b) technical methods; (c) direct investments or investment-inducing policies; (d) education and promotion; and (e) pricing, taxes, subsidies and other financial incentives. Since these tools are interrelated, their use should be closely coordinated for maximum effect.

The chief constraints that limit effective policy formulation and implementation are: (a) poor institutional framework and inadequate incentives for efficient management; (b) insufficient manpower and other resources; (c) weak analytical tools; (d) inadequate policy instruments; and (e) other constraints such as low incomes and market distortions.

Technological Options

The INEP framework is particularly appropriate for considering shift (1) in Figure 7.4, which implies improvement in overall economic efficiency but without any explicit consideration of the external (environmental) costs. Such efficiency improvements require better energy supply and demand management. More specifically, the former category includes more accurate demand forecasting, improved least cost investment planning, and the optimal operation of energy systems — implying that plant performance, operating and maintenance procedures, loss levels, etc. are optimized. The latter comprises efficient electricity end use, load management and pricing (described in the next section). All the above options constitute an attractive policy package for most power utilities in both the developing and developed countries.

There is a spectrum of technological options which the developing countries could potentially utilize in order to improve energy efficiency and thereby reduce environmental effects arising from energy sector activity. These range from simple infrastructural retrofits to the use of advanced energy supply technologies. Among the short term technological options for the developing country power sector, reducing transmission and distribution losses, and improving generation plant efficiencies appear to be the most attractive. Recent studies show that up to a certain point, these supply efficiency enhancing measures yield net economic savings or benefits that are several times the corresponding costs incurred (Munasinghe, 1990b). While estimates of such power system losses vary, they all point to levels which are far in excess of accepted norms. Table 7.2 presents estimates for some Asian countries in comparison with industrialized countries. While acceptable loss levels may be about 6-8 percent in transmission and distribution as a percentage of gross generation, these losses in Third World power systems are estimated to average in the 16-18 percent range (of which about one third could be theft).

The consequences of reducing these losses can be quite important. On the basis of our previous estimates of capacity requirements, a one percentage point reduction in losses per year would reduce required capacity by about 5 GW annually in the developing countries. The estimated saving in capital investment would be around 10 billion dollars per year. Meanwhile, the Agency for International Development (USAID, 1988) has estimated that the average heat rate of LDC power plants is around 13,000 Btu/kWh, compared to 9,000-11,000 Btu/kWh if these plants were operated efficiently. The energy savings (and positive environmental consequences) implied in these figures are quite significant also.

Similar gains are possible by conservation on the demand side. Johansson et al. (1989) provide an insightful review of the developments that have been taking place in end-use technologies

Table 7.2
Electrical Transmission and Distribution Losses
(% of gross generation)[a]

Pakistan	28%
India	22%
Bangladesh	31%
Sri Lanka	18%
Thailand	18%
Philippines	18%
South Korea	12%
Japan	7%
US	8%

Sources: The World Bank and USAID

Note: [a]These loss estimates include non-technical losses (i.e. due to deficient metering and theft).

which can have a major impact on energy efficiency. These technologies (which developed in the industrialized countries as a response to the oil price escalation in the seventies) can be easily applied towards more efficient lighting, heating, refrigeration and air conditioning around the developing world, as described below.

Substitution of primary energy sources in power generation is another potential means of achieving dual benefits. In the developing world, natural gas is the most likely candidate for coal or oil substitution. The economic benefit of natural gas substitution comes from either import substitution for petroleum products or releasing these products for export. On the environmental front, natural gas firing typically achieves reduction in carbon emissions of 30-50 percent. Many Asian countries are endowed with significant resources of natural gas, including Malaysia, Indonesia and Thailand.

In the longer term, the developing countries will need to rely on more advanced technological options which are currently being developed in the industrialized countries. As we have discussed above, power generation capacity in developing countries is expected to nearly double by the turn of the century, and will increase further thereafter. This provides opportunities to add state-of-the-art technologies which have been designed with regard to both economic and environmental criteria. Clean coal technologies, cogeneration, gas turbine combined cycles, steam-injected gas turbines etc. are all part of this menu of technologies which have important potential in developing countries. Similar applications will become available for emission control technologies. However, as we have argued previously, the developing countries will look to the industrialized nations to provide the leadership in refining and proving these technologies before they are implemented in the developing world.

As one indicative example of the state-of-the-art in supply planning and demand management possibilities, we summarize the results of a recent Swedish study (Johannson et al., 1989). The power sector in Sweden, currently supplied half by hydro and half by nuclear generation, faces the following severe restrictions: (a) hydro expansion limited by environmental constraints; (b) mandatory phasing out of all nuclear units by 2010; and (c) no increase permitted above present CO_2 emission levels. The demand for electricity derived services is projected to increase by 50 percent, from 1987 to 2010. If end use efficiency remained unchanged, then under this "frozen efficiency" scenario, the electrical load also would increase by 50 percent, from 129 TWh in 1987 to 195 TWh in 2010, at an average annual growth rate of 1.8 percent.

The same output of electrical services could be provided, but with steadily declining electricity input needs and load levels — based on the increasingly energy efficient scenarios A, B, C and D, shown in Figure 7.6. The corresponding loads in 2010 would be 140, 111, 96 and 88 TWh, respectively. Only options C and D permit the load to be met after all the nuclear plants are retired in 2010. Figure 7.7 indicates that the total costs of energy supply also fall progressively under the scenarios A through C (some of the costs are undefined for scenario D). In addition, there are three supply scenarios based on different selection rules for generation —

the supply costs rise steadily as we move through the economic despatch, natural gas/biomass, and environmental despatch options. These costs exclude taxes and subsidies, and are based on a 6 percent discount rate, 1987 world oil and coal prices, and coal equivalent gas prices for steam power generation.

Figure 7.6
Generation Capability and Load Under Various Scenarios

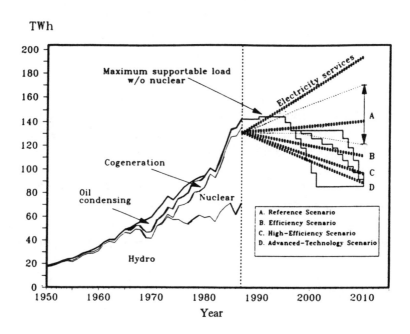

Source: Bodlund et al (1989)

Notes: [a]Electricity services = end use efficiency frozen at 1987 level
[b]Scenario A = normal penetration of energy efficient end use technologies (vertical arrows show range of uncertainty)
[c]Scenario B = high penetration of energy efficient end use technologies that are cost effective and commercialised
[d]Scenario C = same as scenario B, but includes uncommercialised newly developed technologies
[e]Scenario D = same as scenario C, but includes advanced technologies still in the R&D stage
[f]Downward stapped curves indicate generation capability with different options for phasing out 12 nuclear plants

Figure 7.7
Total Energy Supply Costs Under Various Scenarios

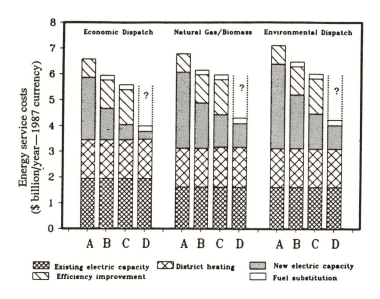

Source: Bodlund et al (1989)

Notes: [a]Scenarios A to D are the same as in Figure 1.6, but efficiency improvement
costs are unknown for scenario D
[b]Economic despatch = traditional least cost generation expansion and operation
[c]Natural gas/biomass = intensive use of gas and biomass, with coal use banned
(to limit CO_2 emissions)
[d]Environmental despatch = generation expansion and operation in order of
increasing CO_2 emissions per kWh produced

Economic Incentives and Related Options

Providing the correct economic signals, or more specifically
price rationalization, offers the most attractive demand-side option for improving energy sector efficiency, that also corresponds
to the shift (1) in Figure 7.4. While the economic principles of
energy pricing are now well understood, pricing policy in developing countries is guided by a tradeoff between economic efficiency

on the one hand and a series of financial and socio-economic considerations on the other. It is widely accepted that energy is fundamental to productivity and economic growth. However, the strong perception among decisionmakers that access to energy is a basic need that improves living standards of the people has driven a policy in which affordability competes with economic efficiency as the criterion for energy pricing. Furthermore, in practice it has been difficult to separate social and economic criteria within the same pricing structure, leading to poorly designed policies that may be both economically inefficient and socially regressive (or perverse).

A recent study of over 350 electric power utilities in developing countries (Munasinghe et al., 1988) indicates that electricity tariffs have not kept up with cost growth. The operating ratio(defined as the ratio of operating costs before debt service, depreciation and other financing charges, to operating revenue) for the extensive sample studied deteriorated from 0.68 in the 1966-73 period to 0.80 between 1980 and 1985. At the same time, the financial rate of return on fixed assets has decreased steadily from over 10 percent in the mid-1960s to around 5 percent in the mid-1980s. In some countries these declines are significantly greater.

This study and other available evidence indicates that a significant shift towards economic criteria in electricity pricing would be possible without creating undue hardship to the poorer segments of the population. While extensive information (in the form of price elasticities) is not available for most developing countries, several recent studies provide a reasonable basis for projections. Assuming the price elasticity for electric power to be -0.3, a 20 percent real increase in electricity prices (which would restore the above operating ratio to its 1960/70's level) would result in a 6 percent reduction in electricity demand.

Apart from price rationalization, there is also scope for applying a coordinated package of other measures aimed at improving the efficiency of energy use. These would include taxes and subsidies based on fuel type, technology, R&D, retrofits, conservation programs, etc. In most instances these programs are likely to achieve desirable effects on both energy use and environmental impacts. Fiscal instruments such as emission fees and carbon-based user fees can be used to control environmental impacts more directly. In many LDC applications, however, problems of implementing and monitoring such mechanisms are significant.

To conclude, generally the first priority is to improve the efficiency of energy supply and use, through technical means and pricing energy at marginal economic cost. Improvements in energy intensive industries could yield significant efficiency gains. In transport, considerable opportunities exist to reduce fuel consumption by improving traffic management methods, using less energy intensive travel modes, and phasing out inefficient vehicles. Substitution of fossil fuels with less polluting fuels (like natural gas, where available), and increasing the efficiency of fuelwood use, could also be environmentally and economically sound. Agriculture presently contributes about 14 percent of all CO_2 emissions, mainly due to forest clearing and burning of wastes. Strengthening property rights, protecting forest lands, and improving land use planning and management (e.g., through agro-ecological zoning), are some key actions in this sector.

Examples of more expensive options are non-conventional energy sources, large-scale reforestation, advanced energy technologies, and substitution of chlorofluorocarbons (CFCs). LDCs will need significant financial assistance to implement such measures, once the less costly options have been exhausted.

National Level Organizational/ Institutional Options

The energy sector in developing countries is typically owned and controlled by the government, and is characterized by large monolithic organizations. While there is some rationale for this centralization, it could be a critical barrier in the path of greater efficiency and improved flexibility. The desperate circumstances of many developing country energy supplying enterprises have generated pressures for new approaches to organizing the sector. In particular, there appears to be considerable interest in the scope for more decentralization and greater private participation. Developing countries power sector officials have been very active in studying this option, and some countries have already prepared the necessary legislative and institutional groundwork for this transition. India plans to install as much as 5,000 MW of private power capacity over the 1990-95 period, and similar plans are underway in Indonesia, Malaysia, Thailand, Philippines and Pakistan. In Sri Lanka, a private company has been distributing power since the early eighties and significant efficiency and service improvements have been observed during this period.

Despite these trends, enhanced private participation in the energy sector is likely to be more successful when it is one element in a broader economic package involving policy reforms in other parts of the economy. Market forces confined to the power sector in a highly distorted economy may not necessarily improve the power sector situation since private participants will try to maximize financial rather than economic costs. Thus, private sector participants would make full use of cheaper generation inputs such as coal even when this is potentially detrimental (both economically and environmentally). Even in a reasonably market oriented economy, the introduction of private participation in the energy sector is unlikely to lead to environmental benefits, unless the costs of pollutants can be fully captured (i.e., internalized) in the financial cost to the participant. Thus, while private participation is likely to bring significant gains by the infusion of new capital and innovative management methods, it is likely to remain one of several methods aimed at restructuring the sector.

Environmental Costs

With regard to environmental issues, the national framework in which the utility functions is likely to play an equally important role. Actions of the utility need to be backed up by a set of consistent national policies and legislative support. The development of environmental standards and regulations is likely to (and should) take place outside the utility, and the public needs to understand the importance of a commitment to a program of environmental mitigation.

Our integrated framework also provides an appropriate starting point for consideration of shift (2) in Figure 7.4, that seeks to incorporate the quantifiable environmental costs. A number of techniques exist for valuing environmental impacts of power projects, and these can be used for incorporating environmental costs into methodologies mentioned above for least-cost planning and estimating the long-run marginal cost of energy production. However one should be aware of the uncertainties in such estimates and be prepared to perform sensitivity tests where appropriate.

Going beyond the quantifiable environmental costs is of course problematical, but to the extent that these costs are significant an attempt must be made rather than implicitly assuming that these costs are negligible. Non-quantifiable environmental costs can be incorporated in various ways, such as adding new constraints on the optimization that reflect social concerns or absolute environmental standards, or even by using an entirely different methodology than least-cost planning, e.g., a type of multi-attribute assessment. This is still within the tradition of INEP, although the various trade- offs would be made explicitly on social-environmental criteria rather than implicitly in economic terms.

Global Environmental Issues in the LDC Context

The developed and the developing countries are at different points in resolving domestic energy-environmental interactions and this is an important difference which must be taken into account when devising forms of cooperation for solving transnational and global energy-environment problems. Developing countries still have considerable scope for environment-improving activities that are economically attractive for them, e.g., energy conservation and ameliorating the domestic environmental consequences of energy use. These actions will, of course, have positive global environmental benefits also. While no country can be said to have exhausted the potential for shifts (1), (2), and (3), the developed countries are generally closer to D in Figure 7.4, at which point they need to explicitly consider trade-offs in domestic policy options to improve the global commons.

The foregoing sets the context within which the developing countries are capable of participating in environmental mitigation efforts at the global level. It is quite obvious that LDCs do not have the ability to contribute financially for global environmental cleanup efforts where the measurable benefits to the national economy are too low to trigger investment. Indeed, this paper has argued that many LDC projects which do have positive measurable benefits at the national level are being bypassed on account of capital constraints.

The principle of assistance to developing countries for environmental mitigation efforts, in terms of technology transfer, financial support and other means, is already well established. The Montreal Protocol, which was adopted in 1987 as a framework within which reduction in the consumption and production of certain types of chlorofluorocarbons (CFCs) is to be achieved, recognized the need for global cooperation and assistance to the developing countries. Subsequent Ministerial Conferences on various aspects of global environmental issues have reinforced the idea of protecting the global commons.

Currently, discussions are underway among world bodies and governments to define effective criteria and mechanisms for both generating and disbursing funds to address global environmental issues. While a broad workable agreement will not be easy to reach, global financing issues might be analyzed and resolved through a tradeoff involving several criteria: affordability/additionality, fairness/equity and economic efficiency (Munasinghe, 1990c).

First, since LDCs cannot afford to finance even their present energy supply development, to address global environmental concerns they will need financial assistance on concessionary terms that is additional to existing conventional aid. The latter will have to be increased also, to assist developing countries in dealing with local environmental degradation. Second, as noted in the recent Brundtland Commission report, past growth in the industrialized countries has exhausted a disproportionately high share of global resources, suggesting that the developed countries owe an "environmental debt" to the larger global community. This approach could help to determine how the remaining finite global resources may be shared more fairly and used sustainably. Finally, the economic efficiency criterion indicates that the "polluter pays" principle may be applied to generate revenues, to the extent which global environmental costs of human activity can be quantified. If total emission limits are established (eg., for CO_2), then trading in emission permits among nations and other market mechanisms could be harnessed to increase efficiency.

One specific mechanism that has recently been implemented includes a core multilateral fund of about US\$1.5 billion — the Global Environment Facility (GEF) — to be implemented as a pilot over the next three years. This fund would finance investment, technical assistance and institutional development activities in four areas: global climate change, ozone depletion, protection of biodiversity, and water resource degradation. A more narrowly focussed Ozone Fund of about US\$160 - 240 million has been set up also, to help implement measures to reduce CFC emissions under the Montreal Protocol.

Both funds are being managed under a collaborative arrangement between the UNDP, UNEP and the World Bank. In particular, they would fund those investment activities that would provide cost-effective benefits to the global environment, but would not have been undertaken by individual countries without concessions. Thus, these funds are being specifically designed to fill the void which is created by the lack of individual national incentives for those activities which would, nonetheless, benefit us all.

Conclusions

International pressures to implement environmentally mitigatory measures place a severe burden on developing countries. The crucial dilemma this poses to LDCs is how to reconcile development goals and the elimination of poverty — which will require increased use of energy and raw materials — with responsible stewardship of the environment, and without overburdening economies that are already weak. This paper has argued that in view of the severe financial constraints that developing countries already face, the response of these countries in relation to environmental preservation cannot extend beyond the realm of measures that are consistent with near-term economic development goals. More specifically, the environmental policy response of LDC's in the coming decade will be limited to conventional technologies in efficiency improvement, conservation and resource development.

The developed countries are ready to substitute environmental preservation for further economic expansion and should, therefore, be ready to cross the threshold, providing the financial resources that the LDC's need today and developing the technological innovations and knowledge-base to be used in the 21st century by all nations. The Global Environmental Fund (GEF) and Montreal Protocol Ozone Fund (MPOF), recently established, will facilitate the participation of LDCs in addressing issues at the global level.

Clearly, both the GEF and MPOF are pilot facilities to explore the relative effectiveness of different mechanisms for international cooperation, as well as technology and policy options aimed at solving global environmental problems. The total sums initially pledged to both funds (about US$1 - 2 billion) are several orders of magnitude smaller than the amounts ultimately required to address issues like global climate change. However, the experience gained in the 2 to 3 year operating period of these funds will be invaluable in facilitating the successful launching of more ambitious international environmental financing efforts — perhaps after the 1992 U.N. Conference on Environment and Development in Brazil.

While global environmental issues will have to be addressed in the developing world, through concessionary or grant funds, more conventional aid will also be needed to reverse local environmental degradation and eliminate poverty worldwide. These resource flows, as well as the associated development, transfer and adaptation of technology and policy options will require new modalities of cooperation in the international community.

References

Asian Development Bank. 1988. "Private Sector Participation in Power Development" (November). Manila, Philippines.

Economic and Social Commission for Asia and the Pacific (ESCAP). 1987. "Structural Change and Energy Policy" (May). United Nations.

Flavin, C. 1989. "Slowing Global Warming: A Worldwide Strategy." World Watch Institute Paper No. 91 (October), Washington, DC.

Foell, W. 1989. "Report on the Workshop on Acid Rain in Asia" (November). Asian Institute of Technology, Bangkok, Thailand.

Johansson, T. et al. 1989. *Electricity.* Sweden: Lund University Press.

Krause, F., W. Bach and J. Koomey. *Energy Policy in the Greenhouse* Vol. 1. International Project for Sustainable Energy Paths (IPSEP), El Cerrito, CA 94530.

Munasinghe M. 1990a. *Energy Analysis and Policy.* London: Butterworths Press.

_____. 1990b. *Electric Power Economics.* London: Butterworths Press.

_____. 1990c. "The Challenge Facing the Developing World." *EPA Journal* March/April.

Munasinghe, M., J. Gilling and M. Mason. 1988. "A Review of World Bank Lending for Electric Power." Industry and Energy Department, Energy Series Paper No. 2 (March), The World Bank, Washington, DC.

Starr, C. and M. Searl. 1989. "Global Projections of Energy and Electricity." Paper presented at American Power Conference Annual Meeting (April), Chicago, IL.

USAID. 1988. "Power Shortages in Developing Countries" (March). Washington, DC.

Wilbanks. T. and D. Butcher. 1990. "Implementing Environmentally Sound Power Sector Strategies in Developing Countries." *Annual Review of Energy* (January).

World Bank. 1990. "Capital Expenditures for Electric Power in the Developing Countries in the 1990s." Industry and Energy Department Working Paper No. 21 (February), Washington DC.

World Bank. 1989. *World Development Report 1989.* Oxford University Press.

World Commission on Environment and Development (WCED). 1987. *Our Common Future.* London: Oxford University Press.

Chapter 8

Toward a Political Economy of Global Change:
Energy, Environment and Development in the Greenhouse

John Byrne and
Daniel Rich

The use of energy for industrial production and consumption over the last 200 years has altered the natural environment to an extent unparalleled in human history. Since the late 1700s, carbon dioxide (CO_2) in the earth's atmosphere has increased 26 percent. In the same period, concentrations of nitrous oxide (N_2O) rose by 9 percent, methane (CH_4) by 20 percent, and tropospheric ozone (O_3) by 133 percent (Cicerone, 1989). Currently, 7 billion tons of CO_2, 85 million tons of nitrogen oxides (NO_x), 350 million tons of carbon monoxide (CO), 90 million tons of CH_4, and 100 million tons of sulfur oxides (SO_x) are annually released into the atmosphere from fossil fuel combustion (OECD/IEA, 1991; French, 1990; World Resources, 1990). The magnitude of this emission stream and its impact on atmospheric chemistry have triggered phenomena that, in the words of climatologist Nicholas Shackleton, have taken us "outside what nature has experienced in the recent past 500,000 years" (*New York Times*, January 16, 1990).

The thinning of stratospheric ozone, the increasing acidification of rain, snow and even large bodies of water, and the prospect of global climate change have all been linked to industrial development generally, and to industrial energy production and use specifically. Nonetheless, the conventional view remains that industrial society has hitherto exercised little, if any, determinative role in the natural order (Schneider, 1990). Instead, "nonliving forces" such as volcanic eruptions, storms, droughts and continental plate tectonics are considered the predominant causes of natural change on a global scale. Social science has done little to examine, much less challenge, this view of an environment subject largely, if not entirely, to "nonliving forces." For the most part, social scientists have either ignored the environmental implications of social development, or normatively assumed that human society should seek dominion over nature (Redclift, 1987; Merchant, 1980; Wolin, 1960). Recently, some social scientists (see, e.g., Schelling, 1990) have maintained that the social causes of environmental degradation are irrelevant to addressing issues of the environment. The view has been expressed that societies should seek to adapt to, rather than prevent, pending environmental threats. Adherents portray such a view as realistic, practical and even public-minded. A recent *New York Times* article (November 19, 1989), based on interviews with several prominent American economists, captures the spirit of this style of thinking. Citing a U.S. Environmental Protection Agency estimate that it will cost $73 to $111 billion to build sea walls to protect American coastal cities from a three-foot sea rise triggered by global warming, the writer concedes that this is "a lot of money but not so much compared with the likely cost of prevention." The article concludes that "it may be cheapest to deal with the effects of global warming rather than the causes."

What is striking about the current treatment of energy-environment-development linkages is the active resistance manifested to peaceful, environmentally benign change. This resistance is especially evident in the international energy system where non- or low-polluting options have been available for some time. Yet, industrial societies have preferred to subsidize fossil fuel and nuclear energy. These societies are not now, and were not throughout the industrial era, without energy choices that would have avoided high levels of pollution, attendant worldwide economic inequality and frequent reliance on military force to maintain energy security. To arrive at the present predicament, it was necessary for industrial societies to *actively* disregard the environmental costs and health and safety risks of the world energy economy and, at the same time, to support energy technologies that create a permanent threat of human extinction and environmental catastrophe. At this point, these societies even appear ready to risk altering atmospheric chemistry in order *not* to change the industrial energy system.

The most serious policy challenge now facing the world community is the recognition that global development, energy and environmental problems are systemic in nature. Our analysis begins with an identification of the systemic problems that arise from the persistence and dominance of a worldwide energy and development orientation that, with few exceptions, values economic growth over all else. Described as the *politics of commodification,*[1] this orientation obstructs the transition to a sustainable system of energy, environment and development relations. A *politics of sustainability* is proposed that would reconstruct energy-environment-development relations. The policy and institutional requirements necessary to foster a transition to sustainability are examined and the resistance they will engender is discussed.

Systemic Certainties

Few would dispute that the international energy, environmental and development situations are fraught with *uncertainties* and *risks.* World energy prices and fuel supplies are among the least predictable phenomena in the world today. Similarly, we are unsure of the scope or magnitude of the environmental, health and

---

[1] Commodification is defined as a development orientation pursued by societies in which progress is determined by increased social capacities to produce and purchase goods and services. Under this orientation, the physical environment is valued either directly as a commodity in the form of energy, raw materials and resources extracted for social use; or indirectly as a "least-cost" means of disposing of wastes (thereby improving the "efficiency" of commodity production and use).

safety impacts of our existing energy practices. And the development problems and extremes of inequality in the world order appear intractable, threatening international peace and stability. These uncertainties and the risks they engender are emblematic of our time. Yet, as important as these are, we would do well to focus less on these uncertainties and risks, and instead concentrate our attention on the energy, environmental and development *certainties* that have become apparent over the last two decades.

First among these certainties is that the present global energy system is inadequate to the task of meeting the needs of most of the world's people. Although global in organization, the energy production and distribution system serves the needs of only, roughly, one-third of the world's population. Figure 8.1 depicts the international movement of oil and coal, fuels which account for nearly seventy percent of world commercial energy consumption. Yet, less than one-fifth of this consumption is dedicated to the needs of the poorest two-thirds of the human community. Projections of oil availability at current consumption rates suggest that in 40-50 years, this system will not be able to meet the needs of even the wealthy one-third of the human community who currently can afford to consume its products (Flavin and Lenssen, 1990: 11).

When we consider the energy required to meet the development aspirations of Asia, Africa and Latin America, it is certain that the current energy system is not up to the task. According to the Institute for Applied Systems Analysis (1981) energy needs of developing countries will more than triple (on a 1990 base) by 2020. If we use a demand projection model (e.g., Goldemberg et al., 1987: 293-303) that assumes aggressive adoption by developing countries of end-use efficiency strategies, energy needs are still forecasted to double by 2020. Altogether, world energy use is likely to increase by roughly 40 percent over the next three decades, but neither the resource nor the technology base exists to support these energy requirements for development (Wang et al., 1988). If we consider the trillions of dollars invested in the present world energy system, the need to multiply this investment three-

Figure 8.1
International Movement of Oil and Coal: 1984

Oil (million tons)

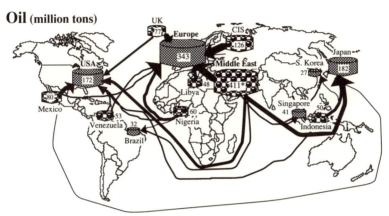

Major Exporters

Major Importers

* Sum of Iraq, Kuwait, Iran, United Arab Emirates and Saudi Arabia

** Two countries, Japan and the USA, use more than a quarter of world oil production; and two countries, the CIS (the USSR) and Saudi Arabia, provide just under a quarter of world oil exports.

Coal (million tons)

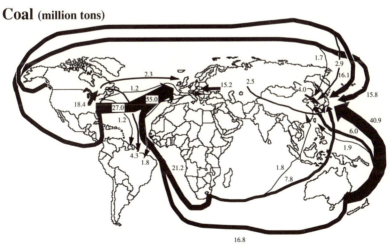

Sources: UN, *Yearbook of World Energy Statistics* ; *BP* ; CIA, *World Oil Market*   (as produced in *The New State of the World Atlas,* 1987).

fold to promote a more equitable development pattern worldwide, and the declining availability of key energy resources (especially oil), there is little doubt that systemic energy failure looms in the future unless steps are taken to change our course and pursue a new development path.

Our systemic energy problem is matched by an equivalent scale environmental dilemma. We can be certain that continued energy-intensive social development along the lines of the last 200 years will result in increased pollution; that this pollution will occur on an expanding geographic scale; and that it will entail more complex threats than we presently face. World pollution levels will continue to increase so long as societies depend upon fossil fuel combustion for most of their energy needs. From oil spills to the depletion of stratospheric ozone and the build-up of greenhouse gases, the current path of development will continue to expand our pollution dilemmas and complicate their resolution. There is no compelling reason to expect markedly different environmental results so long as we remain on our current path.

The principal source of world environmental pollution is, and will continue to be, industrial development. As illustrated by Figure 8.2, the industrialized countries are the largest contributors of global CO_2 production. The industrialized countries also emit most of the air-borne sulphur oxides, nitrogen oxides, carbon monoxide and hydrocarbons (see Figure 8.3). Developing countries will increase their pollution contributions, and perhaps their share of world environmental degradation, so long as they follow the development path of the already industrialized nations. Choice in this matter for developing countries is greatly restricted by the entrenched political, economic and technological power of the industrialized countries. However, the certainty of continued and more complex environmental problems need not be self-fulfilling. Avoiding tomorrow's systemic environmental problems, though, will require basic change in the development path of the already industrialized nations, and a restructuring of the development options available to meet the needs of the currently non-industrialized world.

Figure 8.2
Carbon Emissions from Fossil Fuels: 1955-88

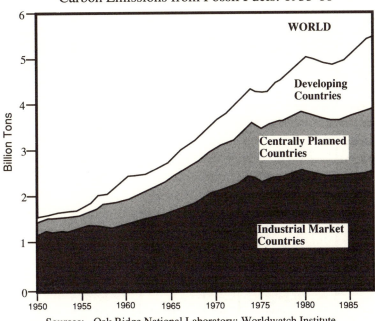

Sources: Oak Ridge National Laboratory; Worldwatch Institute.

The final certainty concerns the social implications of the existing pattern of industrial growth, encompassing continually increasing energy requirements and pollution. Simply stated, it is unworkable at the global level; it does not and will not provide acceptable outcomes for most of the world's population. While there remains debate about the particulars, it should be clear that the existing path of development is problematic and that its viability, if not its longevity, is in doubt. Indeed, the present distribution of energy, financial and industrial power is at the center of world

Figure 8.3

Total World Emissions of Common Air Pollutants from Human Activities in 1980

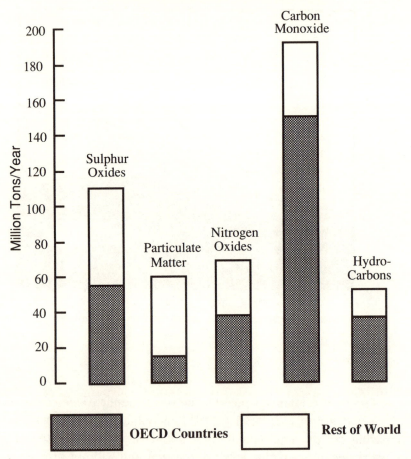

Source: United Nations Environment Programme. 1987. *The State of the World Environment.*

problems of unsustainability. Figures 8.4, 8.5, and 8.6, illustrate the extent to which the productive and reproductive capacities of the world economy perpetuate pervasive global inequality. For example, all of the nations of South America and Africa together do not have manufacturing output equal in value to that of the United Kingdom (Figure 8.4). Sub-Saharan Africa, from the point of view of commercial capital, does not exist (Figure 8.5). Two-thirds of the 33 countries in this region lack national capital reserves equivalent to the 500th largest bank in the world, the Commerce Union Bank of Nashville, Tennessee. And, the combined purchasing power of South America and Africa is about half that of Japan (Figure 8.6).

Such inequality, as the World Commission on Environment and Development has observed, forces the poor to become partners in environmental degradation (1987: 67-68):

International economic relationships pose a particular problem for poor countries trying to manage their environments, since the export of natural resources remains a large factor in their economies, especially those of the least developed nations. The instability and adverse price trends faced by most of these countries make it impossible for them to manage their natural resource bases for sustained production. The rising burden of debt servicing and the decline in new capital flows intensify those forces that lead to environmental deterioration and resource depletion occurring at the expense of long-term development.

Avoiding the systemic failures that loom at the close of the 20th century will require the creation of conditions for equitable and sustainable social development. But the achievement of a sustainable future, in turn, will require a rethinking of the definition of social progress itself.

Figure 8.4
International Distribution of Industrial Power: 1981 - 83
(Value of Gross Manufacturing Output)

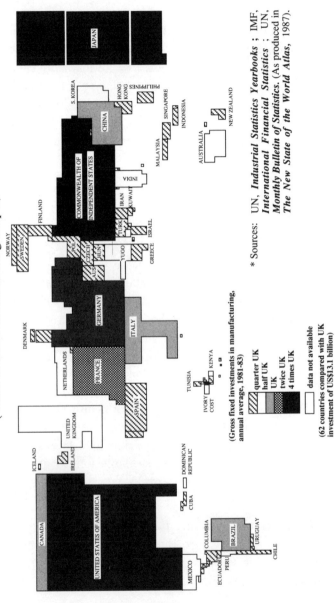

(Gross fixed investments in manufacturing, annual average, 1981-83)

quarter UK
half UK
UK
twice UK
4 times UK

data not available

(62 countries compared with UK investment of US$13.1 billion)

* Sources: UN, *Industrial Statistics Yearbooks* ; IMF, *International Financial Statistics* ; UN, *Monthly Bulletin of Statistics*. (As produced in *The New State of the World Atlas*, 1987).

Figure 8.5
International Distribution of Commercial Capital: 1985

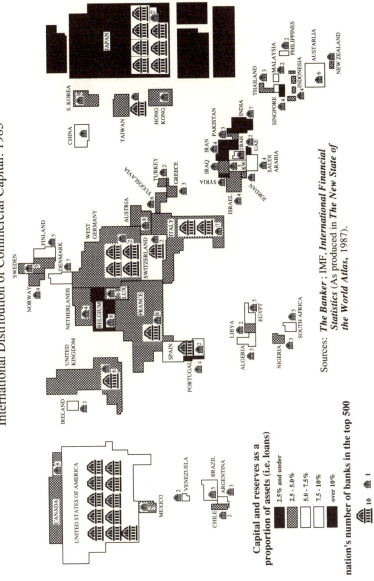

Sources: *The Banker*; IMF, *International Financial Statistics* (As produced in *The New State of the World Atlas*, 1987).

Capital and reserves as a proportion of assets (i.e. loans)

■	2.5% and under
▨	2.5 - 5.0%
□	5.0 - 7.5%
▢	7.5 - 10%
■	over 10%

nation's number of banks in the top 500

🏛 10   🏛 1

Figure 8.6

International Distribution of Purchasing Power: 1984 - 85
(National Shares of Total World GNP)

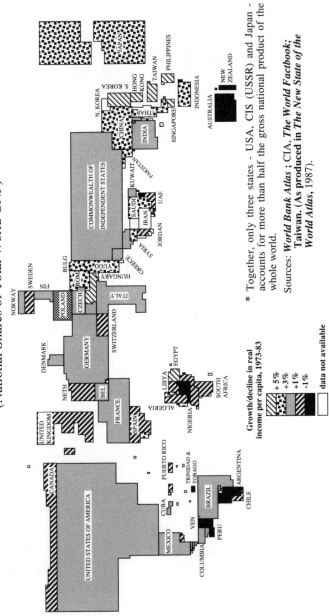

* Together, only three states - USA, CIS (USSR) and Japan - accounts for more than half the gross national product of the whole world.

Sources: *World Bank Atlas* ; CIA, *The World Factbook; Taiwan.* (As produced in *The New State of the World Atlas*, 1987).

The Politics of Commodification

The underlying source of our systemic problems is the persistence of a worldwide development orientation that values economic growth over sustainability and rationalizes the growing and pervasive costs of prevailing energy, environmental and development policies and practices. This development orientation has its roots in the idea of progress that historically has propelled Western industrial order.

Since the industrial revolution, the West has depended upon a basic formula for progress — improve the technology of material production so that wealth and economic opportunity expand. With more of both technology and economic growth, it was reasoned, the human condition would be bettered. This formula of "more is better" has steadily attracted adherents throughout the industrial era, and in the final decade of this century, this formula is poised to become a worldwide ideal.

While improvements in many social areas, from health to general welfare, have accompanied Western commitments to a technological formula for progress, we are now confronted with environmental problems that are uniquely the result of our technological success. The very capacity to produce and consume more, and to depend upon technology to clean up the mess, has blinded the prophets of Western industrial progress to the basic flaw in the formula — that the path of development to which they are committed is unsustainable. It is exceedingly difficult, however, for the leaders of the industrial tier to recognize, much less accept, that their optimism about technology and economic growth may actually be a source of our present systemic energy, environmental and development problems. Indeed, the more common and more comfortable approach, at least for the wealthy, is to see the relationship in reverse; that is, to view systemic problems as testifying to the need for redoubled technological efforts to produce "green paths" of economic growth.

The equation of technologically driven economic growth with progress presumes a certain autonomy between the social and natural spheres which we are learning is no longer accurate. Our systemic problems reflect the fact that the natural order[2] is reacting to the activities of modern society in structural[3] ways. In effect, the physical environment is undergoing a process of social capture. Its capture derives from the dominance of a path to social progress which treats the environment as a commodity subject to prevailing economic priorities and technological capacities. In so far as human progress is defined in terms of enhanced technical and economic capacities to produce and consume things, environmental consequences are, at best, a residual concern. Nature is incidental to the human drama; the quality of life and the experience of life are regarded as essentially technological and economic in nature.

Prevailing industrial ideology presumes that structural transformation of the environment is beyond the reach of social influence. Mainstream ideas in natural and social science support this view in promoting an understanding of the laws of nature and the laws of social motion as operating in autonomous spheres. The architectures of social and natural order are presented as maintained by relations and rules which are distinct to each sphere. In this respect, the natural and social worlds are purported to operate as dual and basically separate realities — one social and one natural.

---

[2]By natural order we mean the chemical, biological and other physical relations that constitute and sustain physical existence. Natural laws represent scientific efforts to generalize certain of these relations. Similarly, social order refers to political, economic, cultural, psychological and other social relations that constitute and sustain societies, with social laws stating in general form certain of these social relations. We are not aware of any case in which theories of the physical and natural sciences conceive natural laws as contingent upon social order and social laws.

[3]Structure is used in this paper to refer to physical or social relations which provide regularity and continuity to certain phenomena. Thus, physical relations which regulate continuously the surface temperature of the earth are a natural structure; and social relations which underpin a development orientation that routinely treats the physical environment as a commodity are a social structure.

Implicit in the dual-realities premise is the assumption of the permanent availability of nature as a reservoir for social activities. It is presumed that virtually anything can be socially practiced and repeated without long-lasting, structural environmental consequences. To speak about environmental "spillover effects," "externalities" and "social costs," it is essential to believe that the natural reservoir is, in effect, bottomless; that the problems of environmental disruption or degradation, eventually, can be internalized within the social structure. This understanding does not deny periodic social catastrophes — the starvation of large populations, the spread of epidemics, the demise of entire societies — but, ultimately, it depicts such disasters as exclusively affecting the structure of the social sphere. The structure of nature is assumed to be independent and permanently apart from that of society.

Environmental Commodification in Technological Society

Historically considered, a process of commodification of the environment has been at work since industrialism achieved worldwide influence. This process has encompassed several overlapping phases reflecting levels of maturation in the energy-environment-development relations of industrialism. The reach and range of commodification embedded in these relations has successively expanded with each phase, and this cumulative expansion, deeply interconnected with the characteristics and demands of modern technological society, has compounded our systemic problems.

Normalized Pollution

The initial features of commodification were aptly described by Lewis Mumford who recognized that industrial societies, from their earliest periods of development, had surrendered all semblance of balance with the natural order and had reduced the focus of human life to the mere production of things (Mumford, 1961). An alliance of science, capitalism and carbon power reorganized social order on the pervasive principle of *quantification* (Mumford, 1961: 570; and 1938: 160):

> Quantitative production has become, for our mass-minded contemporaries, the only imperative goal: they value quantification without qualification. In physical energy, in industrial productivity, in invention, in knowledge, in population the same vacuous expansions and explosions prevail. As these activities increase in volume and in tempo, they move further and further away from any humanly desirable objectives...In short, numbers begot numbers; and concentration once well started, tended to pile up in ever-increasing ratios, claiming increase by inertia where it could no longer promise more effective economic performance.

As the new social order produced goods at an unparalleled rate and magnitude, pollution of a type and scale hitherto unknown was also manufactured (Mumford, 1934: 168-169):

> In this [industrial] world the realities were money, prices, capital, shares: the environment itself, like most of human existence, was treated as an abstraction. Air and sunlight, because of their deplorable lack of value in exchange, had no reality at all...the reek of coal was the very incense of the new industrialism. A clear sky in an industrial district was the sign of a strike or a lock-out or an industrial depression.

The nature and contents of what Mumford called the "atmospheric sewage" of modern industry changed in the 20th century, but the chain of energy combustion-to-environmental degradation was not altered. The alliance of science and technology, the energy complex, and the industrial economy ushered in a social order of environmental mining and pollution as a functional part of human progress. In effect, pollution was "normalized."

Continually throughout the 20th century, this phase of environmental commodification was distinguished by its rationalization of nature as alternately a resource mine and a bottomless sewer into which the residue of industrial production could be deposited. The industrial degradation of nature, of course, did not exempt human life from the damage. Indeed, industrial tolerance for pollution often meant that human suffering was accepted as part of the equation. As the air is fouled through technological and economic advance, 20th century cities, like their 19th century counterparts, were afflicted with the worst pollution. Circulated through an industrially-manufactured cloud of chemical waste (mostly energy-based), urban air worldwide exacted the price of modern existence — life threatened by the involuntary, heretofore life-giving, act of breathing. The World Health Organization (WHO) estimates that only 35 percent of the world's urban population currently breathe air with acceptable concentrations of sulfur dioxide (see Figure 8.7). For the other urban air pollutant monitored by WHO suspended particulate matter, the contemporary situation is even worse: concentrations of this pollutant exceed standards for healthy respiratory and heart function in seventy percent of the world's urban areas (WHO 1987: 7).

As the centers of industrialization, large cities serve as spatial networks of development and pollution. Urban success in industrial development now assumes a concurrent chemical change in air quality. Until recently, the environmental impacts of industrial urbanization, while recognized as regrettable, were nonetheless thought to be contained local problems. However, a number of climate simulations (e.g., Lashof and Tirpak, 1989) point to the structural involvement of urbanization in the CO_2 buildup. There is simply no known way of stabilizing global warming commitment without a massive reforestation campaign and an overhaul of urban transportation systems.

When industrial leaders have worried about industrial pollution or social health, for the most part it has been to assure that popular efforts to address these problems pose no threat to the basic pattern of development. In this objective they have been as-

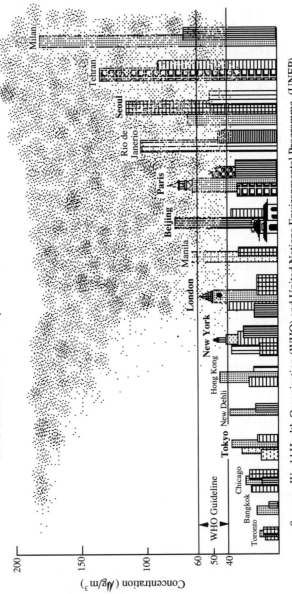

Figure 8.7

Summary of the Annual SO_2 Averages
in Selected GEMS/Air Cities: 1980-1984

Sources: World Health Organization (WHO) and United Nations Environmental Programme (UNEP) 1987. *Global Pollution and Health* ; Center for Energy and Urban Policy Research, University of Delaware.

sisted by the "rational thinking" of economics which abstracts environmental and social abuse from the workings of the production system, assigning them the residual status of "externalities." In this treatment, those who profit from pollution or threaten human health are exempted from responsibility for cleaning up; society as a whole is to bear the environmental burdens of progress. Policy and law have followed the "analytic" view of the economists, reflecting institutionalized acceptance of the environment as an industrial waste dump.

Technological Pollution

A second phase of commodification, encompassing additional environment implications of industrial progress, became visible as a series of pollution catastrophes beginning in the late 1960s disrupted the quantitative progress of industrialism. One of the most significant for the United States occurred in January 1969 when an oil well off the shores of Santa Barbara, California, drilling to a depth of nearly 3,500 feet suffered a "blowout, an uncontrolled eruption" of oil (Easton 1972: 8). The eruption lasted 12 days, creating an oil slick that covered an area of 800 square miles.

While politically important for the U.S., the Santa Barbara "spill" ranks as a mere 46th in the modern cavalcade of spectacular oil spills (Ware, 1989). A second environmental warning on March 23, 1989, suggests how rapidly the scale of damage escalated. The Exxon Valdez oil tanker, running into a reef in the Alaskan Prince William Sound, spilled 37,415 tons of crude. The oil spread to five National Wildlife Refuges and three National Park areas; the slick covered 900 square miles.

The Santa Barbara and Prince William Sound devastations point to an important change in energy-environment-development relations. No longer is the fuel source, its emissions or its wastes the principal agent of environmental violation. Both disasters are examples of "normal accidents" (Perrow, 1984) of the technological system. In such cases, industrial society degrades nature not only because of its commitment to a carbon economy, but also because of its allegiance to technological progress. Environmental catastrophes have become ordinary occurrences of the "normal" workings of technological society.

Oil spills are only one type of pollution experienced and accepted as part of the mundane operations of contemporary, technologically advanced political economy. Also threatened are the interior waterways of the industrialized territories into which are dumped the liquid and solid effluvia of technological civilization. This source is undeniably obnoxious, but dated in its sophistication. Like coal slag, the dumping of industrial wastes in streams, rivers and lakes is a product of old-fashioned technology. The manufacture of "acid rain," on the other hand, is a distinctively modern technique for fouling waters, resulting significantly from the power production needed to sustain a technologically advanced civilization. The important elements of acid deposition — sulfur dioxide and, to a lesser degree, nitrogen oxides — are transformed chemically in the atmosphere and fall to earth as acidic rain, snow, fog or dry particles. Damage to aquatic resources, estuaries and coastal waters, timber and recreational resources, buildings, monuments and statues, and public health are the result. A ubiquitous social tolerance for the rapid destruction of forests and lakes has accompanied this phase of commodification.

A third example of technological pollution is nuclear power. In this technology, societies create both the conditions for pollution spectaculars and long-term, transcontinental-scale threats to all forms of life and habitat. With the knowledge of nuclear fission, the human race acquired the permanent capacity to destroy the basis of life on earth (Schell, 1982). This capacity renders obsolete nature as we have traditionally known it. No society can escape the threat of nuclear annihilation, but must depend upon the mutual decisions of the community of nations to forego use of certain military applications of atomic knowledge. A parallel condition of dependency upon social decisions and actions exists for the natural order as well.

As was learned in the Chernobyl accident, civilian application of nuclear technology likewise threatens society and nature. While the catastrophic dimension of the accident cannot be overlooked, an even more serious question is raised in its aftermath. Traces of iodine 131 and cesium 137 in milk throughout Europe (Flavin, 1987: 15) underscore the enormously hazardous risks associated with the use of nuclear reactions to produce electricity. The gases, and their components, released in the accident are the same as those to be found in a safely operating reactor. The rubble at the Chernobyl site is dangerous to human health for tens of thousands of years; but so are the interior surfaces of the containment vessels of nuclear plants retired after decades of successful, accident-free operation. Indeed, the rubble is no different in the risk it poses to life than the waste products generated from the normal operation of a nuclear plant.

In this respect, nuclear technology and the accidents that can accompany its use are catastrophe-prone. Nuclear energy requires, as an inherent condition of its use, that protective social institutions be constructed outside the mainstream of society which are dominated by technical experts and the military. Further, these institutions must last longer than any in the human record. Indeed, management of the nuclear waste stream requires 1,000 year nuclear security zones and 100,000 year surveillance mechanisms (Weinberg, 1979: 94-95; Anderson et al., 1980: 30). Only successful technological management and innovation can prevent the natural order from destruction by a nuclear accident. Yet, continued spread of nuclear technology will only increase the frequency of accidents, and the stockpile of long-lived, toxic waste, bringing into sharp focus the hegemony of commodity values over life-affirming ones.

Only technologically advanced political economies can manufacture this order of pollution. Rather than being a product of technological failures, *Valdez*-scale oil spills, continental and transcontinental acid pollution and the threat of nuclear catastrophe are "normal," systemic outcomes of mature industrialism. They represent pollution regimes that derive directly from technological progress. Moreover, because these forms of pollution are remediable only by sophisticated technological means, our social and natural futures are increasingly contingent upon ever more intensive social commitments to technological progress. At the same time, however, the continued spread of modern technology will likely increase the frequency of accidents, and the stockpile of long-lived, toxic wastes. Notwithstanding the escalation of risk and destructive potential, industrial momentum simultaneously requires acceptance of environmental degradation and the authoritativeness of technology to maintain progress. In this respect, modern society increasingly struggles with itself: it is a captive of the environmental problems that it is uniquely capable of creating; and likewise a captive of the technological solutions which, once employed, invariably breed new, more difficult social and environmental problems.

Technological progress is paramount in advanced industrial economies. Human existence has been broken into endless acts of commodity production and consumption which in turn depend for their accomplishment upon networks of technology. In an explicit sense, society is governed by technological institutions which create and manage the conditions of human experience. Nature is reduced in this phase to a technical problem. An authoritarianism of technique prevails in the social and, increasingly, natural spheres.

Environmental Commodification in the Greenhouse

We are now on the threshold of a new and distinctive phase of commodification, a phase that embodies the full dimensions of the systemic problems we face. If this phase reaches fruition, nature will no longer simply be exploited for its particular "resource" attributes; rather, it will be transformed and reshaped in order to meet the needs of technological civilization. Whether this transformation is intentional is largely beside the point. Technological societies now, or in the near future will, possess the capacity to alter the very structure of nature regardless of intent. Global warming is both the threat and promise of this phase.

The principal "greenhouse" gases — CO_2, N_2O, O_3, CH_4 and CFCs (chlorofluorocarbons) — have continuously increased as concentrations in the atmosphere since the pre-industrial period. The primary source of these gases is fossil-fuel combustion, which accounts for nearly one-half of the CO_2 increase and is an important source of higher N_2O levels. If we sum across social activities, nearly 60 percent of worldwide greenhouse emissions are associated with energy production and use. Greenhouse theory hypothesizes that an atmosphere composed of high concentrations of these gases will result in higher surface temperatures. Certainly, data on global mean temperatures over the past 100 years of worldwide industrialization confirm that the planet is warming. Although the precise magnitude and physical dynamics of the greenhouse effect remain the subject of much debate, a scientific consensus appears to have formed on its existence (COSEPUP, 1991).

Indisputably structural in character, the greenhouse effect includes not only the prospect of higher temperatures, but changes in sea level and the distribution and location of dry and wet land areas, as well as the alteration of a host of other biological and climatological processes. The implications for human and natural existence of such changes are serious enough in their own right. But perhaps even more disturbing is the prospect that social capacities exist to instigate such radical alterations in nature. The most vivid means of illustrating this concern is to first consider the process by which global temperature change is effected in an exclusively natural structure. Recent climatic history is thought to have been determined by the confluence of three astronomical cycles which regulate the earth's orbital ellipse, axial tilt and wobble. The orbit cycle, which fixes the earth's travel within the solar system, takes approximately 100,000 years to complete the series of elliptical modifications involved; the tilt cycle lasts about 41,000 years to accomplish a series of axial corrections; and the elapse of the wobble cycle is nearly 23,000 years. Together, these cycles control the timing of global warming and cooling by altering the angles and distance from which solar energy reaches the earth (*New York Times*, January 16, 1990).

To appreciate the magnitude of the impact of recent social interference, these very long-lived cycles must be placed alongside the 200 years of industrialization (with the last 100 years representing, by far, the most carbon-intensive), which are cumulatively believed to have begun a social process of temperature change. The time disjuncture in these terms of reference points to the immense capacity assembling in the world political economy to impact nature. Even skeptics of the present status of the greenhouse effect should be awed by the potential for social engineering to change the natural structure, which, if not available presently, almost certainly will soon be.

The carbon buildup that has accompanied industrialization is a testament to the systemic imposition of commodity values on the society-nature relation. It is the environmental expression of energy-economic quantification. The extent to which commodified nature is presumed by the existing social order can be exemplified by considering how the carbon dependence of modern development might be slowed or reversed. In a remarkable series of scenario analyses, a U.S. Environmental Protection Agency (EPA) report on *Policy Options for Stabilizing Global Climate* (Lashof and Tirpak, 1989), gives some indication of the carbon dependency of the world political economy. Using a 110-year planning horizon, the EPA study first sought to identify a series of global carbon-reduction strategies which might stabilize atmospheric greenhouse gases at a concentration which assumes a 1.5 - 2.0°C increase in global average temperature. That is, the scenario *assumed* that global warming is inevitable, but that we can hope to place a ceiling on the magnitude of warming. Introducing policy options iteratively into the climate change model used for the project, the researchers discovered that single, or even limited numbers, of policy steps could not achieve chemical stability. Rather, *eleven* major initiatives would be needed which ranged from a phase-out of CFC use by the year 2003, to a major reforestation effort worldwide, adoption of a series of energy-efficiency improvements including the achievement of a global fleet-average auto fuel efficiency of 50 miles per gallon (mpg), and government-sponsored speedup of the commercialization of solar technologies. Even with these substantial responses implemented, the study relied upon increased nuclear power production[4] to meet the goal of a warming commitment of 1.5 - 2.0°C.

A second simulation defined the objective as no *additional* warming beyond the year 2000. Again, policy planning was stretched over the period from the present to the year 2100. The analysis began with the implementation of all strategies in the atmospheric chemical stabilization scenario, and found that eight additional policy responses would be required. High carbon emission fees would have to be imposed on the production of fossil fuels in proportion to CO_2 emissions potential, and an excise tax on fossil fuel use would need to be enacted for the industrialized countries. Separate fuel efficiency standards would be required that mandate 50 mpg fleet averages by 2000 and 65 mpg by 2025 for the U.S. auto fleet. Deforestation would have to be halted worldwide by 2000, and reforestation efforts doubled over the stability scenario.

These analyses demonstrate the results of 200 years of commodification of society and nature. Just to moderate the process (the stability scenario) requires extraordinary global cooperation. To begin to undo the commodification of the atmosphere (the rapid reduction scenario), global cooperation is not enough. Steps are also required toward the restructuring of industrial societies and of the development process associated with the modern idea of progress. Removing the prospect of transforming nature depends upon radical structural action in the social sphere.

Rationalizing Systemic Failures

The manufacture of acid rain and holes in the upper ozone, the extinction of plant and animal species (and the engineering of new

---

[4] Although, to rationalize the technology's promotion, it was necessary to assume annual 0.5 percent *decreases* in construction costs, something the world has yet to experience in the 40 years that the industry has operated.

ones), the reduction of the planet's capacity to breathe (due to deforestation, among other things), the production of highly toxic, long-lived radioactive poisons which are so dangerous that they require 1,000 year security zones, and the creation and satisfaction of consumptive appetites which in their aggregate portend a change in global climate — all have been rationalized as the necessary accompaniments of the efficient workings of modern technological society. Thomas Schelling (1990) illustrates the mindset that rationalizes the Greenhouse era of environmental commodification in his analysis of the "abatement-adaptation tradeoff" concerning global warming. Elsewhere (*New York Times*, November 19, 1989) he points out that, "both the will and technological ability to adapt to radically different weather [has changed rapidly]. In 1860 two percent of Americans lived outside temperate or subtropical zones. By 1980 the percentage had increased to 22 percent." Schelling further argues that:

> The appealing idea of bequeathing the biosphere intact seems arbitrary. The quality of life in 100 years... will depend as much or more on the endowment of technology and capital as on the percentage of carbon dioxide in the air. And if money to contain carbon emissions comes out of other investments, future civilizations could be the losers.

This logic presumes not only that advanced industrial life transpires outside the constraints of nature, but that nature is appropriately relegated to commodity status, to be purchased and sold in the world political economy along with other products and services. Sustainability is treated solely as a technological and economic matter. Although this presumption is typically manifested in economic terms and thus continues to be most concretely presented in discussions of trade-offs between environmental protection and material progress, its deeper implication is the demise of any idea of the inviolability of nature. There is *nothing* in advanced industrial logic that lies beyond the reach of technological manipulation.

In sum, technological civilization presently operates without normative constraint on its environmental impacts. The only limits on society's interaction with nature are instrumental: economy, efficiency and technological feasibility identify the boundaries of action. It is in this context that recent proposals by members of the policy and scientific communities to address global change need to be understood.

Initiatives ranging from the imposition of a global carbon tax and emissions trading systems, to worldwide programs of reforestation, recycling, energy efficiency, the development of renewable energy options and the establishment of technology transfer between rich and poor nations offer practical means to retard or halt industrial destruction of the environment. The urgency for action which gave rise to these proposals is not disputed, but such steps leave unexamined the underlying social relations of energy, environment and development that have produced and will continue to reproduce structural threats to the physical environment. Burden sharing, emissions trading and abatement-adaptation tradeoff schemes address only the effects of 200 years of commodification. Moreover, these schemes can all too easily become forms of industrial escape as well-to-do societies bargain with the poor to "share the burden" that the latter had little part in making.

The systemic problems that we now face point to the difficulty, indeed the self-destructiveness, of maintaining the assumption of dual realities — one natural and one social. The environmental impacts of commodification are no longer limited to sporadic acts of natural disturbance or degradation. Rather, the very structure of nature is being subjected to the design principles of social forces; commodification is now encroaching on the structural organization of nature itself.

The Politics of Sustainability

The impact of contemporary social relations on the natural environment reflects the worldwide dominance of a particular form of political economy. Degradation of the environment is not a "natural" process operating independently from social forces, but rather, an historical process that is the product of economic and political relations. In this respect, we agree with Michael Redclift's assertion (1987: 3) that the natural environment needs to be examined as a "social construction." Indeed, the systemic problems that we now face point to the self-destructiveness of maintaining the assumption of dual realities — one natural and one social.

Overcoming our systemic crises of energy, environment and development requires a reconstruction of economic and political relations with the natural order. At the core of this reconstruction is the need to create a pattern of social development that is no longer animated and rationalized by the politics of commodification, but instead, is consistent with a politics of sustainability. While recognizing that the concept of sustainable development has been subject to diverse definitions and may still be regarded as an idea in evolution, our meaning builds upon the propositions of the U.N. sponsored World Commission on Environment and Development. As the World Commission proposes (1987: 40, 9):

> Sustainable development seeks to meet the needs and aspirations of the present without compromising the ability to meet those of the future...it recognizes that the problems of poverty and underdevelopment cannot be solved unless we have a new era of growth in which developing countries play a large role and reap large benefits...

> Sustainable development is not a fixed state of harmony, but rather a process of change in which the exploitation of resources, the direction of investments, the orientation of technology development, and institutional change are made consistent with future as well as present needs.

The pursuit of sustainable development requires a reconstruction of the world political economy. In the broadest terms, this reconstruction embodies a shift away from the prevailing industrial model of economic growth that focuses on wealth-creating material expansion, and towards a new pattern of development that focuses on stable, long-term, and widely distributed improvements in the quality of life (Byrne et al., 1991: 43-50). Progress in sustainable development should be judged by the achievement of balanced, uninterrupted social and economic development of communities rather than short-term material improvements subject to cycles of growth and decline. In this context, the social value of equity in the distribution of wealth counterbalances the industrial value of additions to our wealth-creation capabilities.

The requirements for sustainable development are apparent in the changes needed in prevailing systems of energy-environmental relations. Progress towards sustainable development requires a shift away from reliance on energy-environmental systems that are commodity-oriented and that depend for their stability upon continual increases in supplies of resources to produce goods and services and to meet escalating growth in commodity demand. By contrast, sustainable development embodies a growing reliance on energy and environmental systems that are conservation-oriented, that select the most energy efficient and least environmentally disruptive means to achieve desired social outcomes.

As well, we need to abandon the conventional goals of prevailing energy systems which concentrate on production of abundant, low-cost energy supplies. Most often, this leads to a preoccupation with achieving a mix of fuel sources and attendant technological delivery systems that can alternately stimulate and satisfy economic growth. This type of energy system is inherently rigid and unstable, politically and economically. To maintain itself, it must protect against external disruptions, specifically by reducing its vulnerability to world fuel price changes. As a result, national energy policy institutions tend to focus on production incentives, reliability-focused regulation, and standardization of technologies and delivery systems. Under the conventional growth model of development, energy systems are characteristically supply-oriented, capital intensive and technology focused; prices reflect fuel competition among systems of production that tend toward monopoly or oligopoly; and technology innovation focuses on the development of large-scale, centralized and interconnected supply systems.

Sustainable development requires that energy system goals concentrate on achieving end-use efficiency in the delivery of energy services. The goal of energy efficiency should incorporate a concern for integrated resource planning that evaluates a wide array of supply and demand options for addressing energy needs. The energy system should seek to support stable long-term development, to respond to anticipated future energy needs as well as current energy demands. In the context of this longer-term perspective, energy system goals need to include a concern for enhancing social adaptability and maintaining environmental quality.

A new set of institutional relations is required to support the goals of sustainable energy systems. For example, national energy policy institutions need to concentrate on conservation (rather than production) incentives, and the creation of new, diversified institutions, technologies and delivery systems to promote a wide array of energy conservation options. Technology choice and innovation need to be guided by the criterion of long-term resource conservation. At the same time, energy markets must become innovation-oriented and responsive to competition among a diversity of capital projects for delivering energy conservation; prices need to reflect the social/environmental costs of service options and the competition among diverse service providers; and technology institutions need to focus on the development of numerous, moderate scale, decentralized systems that are responsive to user needs rather than the needs of conventional systems of production and delivery.

The requirements for change in energy systems include a shift in the prevailing premises guiding energy decision-making. In conventional energy systems, decision-makers act on the premise that increased energy consumption equals economic growth. Decision-makers also tend to emphasize the values of technical reliability and economic optimization; social and environmental impacts are treated as external to energy decisions. For the most part, energy choices are profit-oriented and technology-reliant with a focus on centralized, capital intensive systems of production and delivery capable of providing abundant fuel supplies to meet the requirements of industrial wealth-creation. By contrast, in an energy system that promotes sustainable development, energy decision-makers would act on the premise that conservation is central to development. The values of social flexibility, equity, and participation are emphasized, and social and environmental impacts are recognized as inherent in energy decisions.

Clearly, the pursuit of sustainable development requires institutional change on a global scale. Responsibility for change falls on both developed and developing countries. Because of their disproportionate consumption of the world's energy/environmental resources, however, industrialized countries need to act first to reverse the resource intensity of their development in order for developing countries to progress. At this juncture, the energy, environment and development paths of all nations depend on the path chosen by industrialized nations. To end this condition of social, political, and economic dependency, it is essential that the already industrialized shift their development orientation and abandon the politics of commodification.

Conclusion

The systemic problems we face have gestated for very long periods of time and will require long-term attention to solve or abate. Bruce Tonn (1986) has labeled them "500 year problems" and argues that unconventional methods of social intervention are needed to address their sources. It is easy to conclude that these systemic problems are unsolvable not only because of the scale of the dilemmas they present, but because their resolution poses basic challenges of political will and vision that, until now, no society has proved capable of meeting. Few would argue that national or international commitments now exist, or soon will, to confront the linked issues of uneven development, pervasive environmental destruction and energy unsustainability. Yet urgent action is needed if we are to penetrate the reproduction cycle of such problems in time to prevent more societies and more of the natural environment from being drawn into the crisis. Our actions should be guided by a recognition that existing economic, political and technology systems are transformable, however impervious to change they may appear from our present vantage point in history.

References

Anderson, Jane et al. 1980. "Decommissioning Commercial Nuclear Power Plants," University of Minnesota, Center for Urban and Regional Affairs, Minneapolis, MN.

Byrne, J. et al. 1991. *Toward Sustainable Energy, Environment and Development.* Report to ESMAP/World Bank. Report available from the Center for Energy and Urban Policy Research, University of Delaware.

Cicerone, Ralph. 1989. "Global Warming, Acid Rain and Ozone Depletion." Pp. 231-238 in D. E. Abrahamson, ed., *The Challenge of Global Warming.* Washington, DC: Island Press.

(COSEPUP) Committee on Science, Engineering and Public Policy. 1991. *Policy Implications of Greenhouse Warming.* Washington, DC: National Academy Press. COSEPUP is a joint committee of the National Academy of Sciences, the National Academy of Engineering and the Institute of Medicine (U.S.).

Easton, Robert O. 1972. *Black Tide: The Santa Barbara Oil Spill and Its Consequences.* New York, NY: Delacorte Press.

Flavin, Christopher. 1989. *Slowing Global Warming: A Worldwide Strategy.* Worldwatch Paper 91. Washington, DC: Worldwatch Institute.

_____. 1987. *Reassessing Nuclear Power: The Fallout from Chernobyl.* Worldwatch Paper 75. Washington, DC: Worldwatch Institute.

Flavin, C. and N. Lenssen. 1990. *Beyond the Petroleum Age: Designing a Solar Economy.* Worldwatch Paper 100. Washington, DC: Worldwatch Institute.

French, H. F. 1990. *Clearing the Air: A Global Agenda*. World-watch Paper 94. Washington D.C.: Worldwatch Institute.

Goldemberg, Jose et al. 1987. *Energy for a Sustainable World*. New York, NY: John Wiley & Sons.

International Institute for Applied Systems Analysis. 1981. *Energy in a Finite World: Paths to a Sustainable Future*. Cambridge, MA: Ballinger.

Kerr, R. A. 1990. "New Greenhouse Report Puts Down Dissenters." *Science*, 242 (April 3): 481-482.

Kidron, M. and R. Segal. 1987. *The New State of the World Atlas*. New York: Simon and Schuster.

Lashof, D. A. and D. A. Tirpak, eds. 1989. *Policy Options for Stabilizing Global Climate*. Draft report to the U.S. Congress. Washington, DC: U.S. Environmental Protection Agency.

Merchant, Carolyn. 1980. *The Death of Nature*. San Francisco, CA: Harper & Row.

Mumford, Lewis. 1961. *The City in History*. New York, NY: Harcourt, Brace and World.

_____. 1938. *The Culture of Cities*. New York, NY: Harcourt, Brace.

_____. 1934. *Technics and Civilization*. New York, NY: Harcourt, Brace and Jovanovich.

New York Times. 1990. "In the Ebb and Flow of Ancient Glaciers" (January 16): C1, C5.

_____. 1989. "Curing the Greenhouse Effect Could Run into the Trillions" (November 19): 1, 18.

OECD/IEA. 1991. *Greenhouse Gas Emissions: The Energy Dimension*. Paris: OECD Publications Services.

Perrow, Charles. 1984. *Normal Accidents: Living With High-Risk Technologies*. New York, NY: Basic Books.

Redclift, Michael. 1987. *Sustainable Development: Exploring the Contradictions*. New York, NY: Methuen.

Schell, Jonathan. 1982. *The Fate of the Earth*. New York, NY: Knopf.

Schelling, Thomas C. 1990. "International Burden Sharing and Coordination: Prospects for Cooperative Approaches to Global Warming." Presented at the Conference on Economic

Responses to Global Warming. University of Maryland, October 19.

Schneider, Stephen H. 1990. "Debating Gaia." *Environment* 32/4 (May): 5-9 and 29-32.

Tonn, B. E. 1986. "500-Year Planning: A Speculative Provocation." *American Planning Association Journal* (Spring): 185-193.

Wang, Y., et al. 1988. "Energy Needs for Economic Expansion in the Developing World: Trends in the Energy-Development Relationship." In Heinonen, J., et al. eds., *Proceedings of the International Symposium on Energy Options for the Year 2000*, Vol. 4, pp. 4.109-4.116. Newark, DE: Center for Energy and Urban Policy Research, University of Delaware.

Ware, Leslie. 1989. "Oil in the Sea: The Big Spills and Blowouts." *Audubon* 91 (September): 109.

Weinberg, Alvin. 1979. "Nuclear Energy: Salvaging the Atomic Age." *The Wilson Quarterly* (Summer): 88-115.

Wolin, Sheldon. 1960. *Politics and Vision: Continuity and Innovation in Western Political Thought*. Boston, MA: Little, Brown.

World Commission on Environment and Development (Brundtland Report). 1987. *Our Common Future*. New York, NY: Oxford University Press.

WHO (World Health Organization) and the United Nations Environment Program (UNEP). 1987. *Global Pollution and Health*. London: Yale Press.

World Resources Institute. 1990. *World Resources 1990-91*. With the International Institute for Environment and Development, in collaboration with the United Nations Environment Programme. New York, NY: Oxford University Press.

Contributors

Dean Abrahamson is professor of public affairs at the Hubert H. Humphrey Institute of Public Affairs, University of Minnesota. He has been employed as a nuclear reactor physicist with Babcock and Wilcox Co. and as a senior research scientist with Honeywell, Inc. He has held visiting appointments at the Swedish Royal Institute of Technology and, recently, Lund University's Department of Environmental and Energy Systems. He is a Trustee of the Natural Resources Defense Council and a Fellow of the American Association for the Advancement of Science. His research interest is the intersection of energy and environmental policies.

John Byrne is professor of urban affairs and public policy and Director of the Center for Energy and Urban Policy Research, University of Delaware. He has served as an advisor to the Finnish Department of Energy and the Korea Energy Economics Institute. He is co-editor of *The Politics of Energy Research and Development* and *Energy, Environment and Sustainable World Development* (a special issue of *Energy Sources*); and the principal author of *Toward Sustainable Energy, Environment and Development*, a 1991 report prepared for the World Bank. His current research is on the political economy of sustainable development.

Dolores Greenberg is professor at Hunter College and the Graduate of University Center, City University of New York. She is Director of the interdisciplinary Energy Policy Studies Program at Hunter College. She has been the recipient of a Rockefeller Foundation Fellowship, an Exxon Educational Foundation Award, a Mellon Grant and the Berkshire Prize for best article published by a woman historian. She has published extensively on energy and industrial issues and is the author of *Financiers and Railroads.* Her current project is a study of energy and social change in the Anglo-American experience.

Olav Hohmeyer is Deputy Head of the Technical Change Department of the Fraunhofer Institute on Systems and Innovation Research in Karlsruhe, Germany. His research on the social costs of energy has been supported by the European Community Commission. His book *Social Costs of Energy Consumption* provides a path-breaking analysis of environmental and societal costs and risks of energy systems. Much of the recent debate on the presence and magnitude of cost elements associated with energy consumption that are not reflected in market prices draws from Dr. Hohmeyer's highly original work. His current research is focused on technology assessment and technology forecasting.

Marc Ledbetter is Deputy Director of the American Council for an Energy-Efficient Economy. He has worked for fifteen years with non-profit, public-interest organizations on energy and environmental policy, including analysis of energy conservation, solar energy, coal strip mining, power plant siting and air quality issues. He frequently testifies before the U.S. Congress on energy and environmental issues and is a recognized authority on energy efficiency technologies and economics. He is co-author of *Energy Efficiency: A New Agenda.* Recently, he has concentrated his analysis on technologies and policies to reduce transportation sector energy consumption.

James J. MacKenzie is a Senior Associate in the Climate, Energy and Pollution Program of the World Resources Institute. Previously, he was Senior Staff Member for Energy at the President's Council on Environmental Quality and co-chaired the Impacts Panel of the U.S. Domestic Policy Review. He was also Senior Staff Scientist at the Union of Concerned Scientists. He has published books and major policy reviews on the linkages among the problems of climate change, air pollution and energy security; the impacts of global motor vehicle use on climate change; and the effects of multiple air pollutants on U.S. forests and crops. His present research is concerned with energy and environmental strategies to foster the transition to a sustainable energy future.

Martin V. Melosi is professor of history and Director of the Institute for Public History at the University of Houston. His book *Coping with Abundance: Energy and Environment in Industrial America* is a highly regarded history of the interdependence of energy and American industrialization and its environmental consequences. His is also the author of *Garbage in the Cities: Refuse, Reform and the Environment, 1880-1980* and numerous articles on energy and environmental issues. Dr. Melosi has published extensively in the areas of history of technology, urban environmental history, public policy history, as well as the history of energy. He is currently working on a study of the impact of technical systems on urban growth and the environment.

Mohan Munasinghe is Division Chief for Environmental Policy at the World Bank and visiting professor of the Institute for Technology Policy in Development, State University of New York. He is also a member of the United Nations University, the Third World Academy of Sciences, and the National Academy of Sciences (U.S.A.). He has served as Senior Energy Advisor to the President of Sri Lanka, Chairman of the Computer and Information Technology Council of Sri Lanka and President of the Sri Lanka Energy Managers Association. Professor Munasinghe is the recipient of a number of international research honors and is the author of over thirty books on energy, environment, economics and information technology issues. His current work examines the energy and environmental issues and choices of developing countries.

Daniel Rich is Dean of the College of Urban Affairs and Public Policy and Senior Research Fellow in the Center for Energy and Urban Policy Research, University of Delaware. He holds a visiting faculty appointment at the University of Strathclyde (Scotland) and is a past Fellow of the Salzburg Seminar. He is co-author of *Strategic Alternatives for Energy Conservation*, and co-editor of *The Politics of Energy Research and Development* and *The Solar Energy Transition.* His research is in the areas of energy policy, political economy and the politics of urban development.

Marc Ross is professor of physics at the University of Michigan and Senior Scientist in the Energy and Environmental Systems Division of the Argonne National Laboratory. He co-directed the American Physical Society's 1974 study of efficient energy use and worked on the Mellon Institute's project on Industrial Energy Productivity and the Alliance to Save Energy's project on Industrial Investment in Energy Efficiency during the 1980s. Recently he has assisted the U.S. Office of Technology Assessment on issues of technology and energy demand. He is co-author of *Our Energy: Regaining Control* and numerous articles on energy and environmental policy. Professor Ross' current research is on the energy and environmental implications of transportation.